Best Hikes Near Reno and Lake Tahoe

HELP US KEEP THIS GUIDE UP TO DATE

Every effort has been made by the author and editors to make this guide as accurate and useful as possible. However, many things can change after a guide is published—trails are rerouted, regulations change, techniques evolve, facilities come under new management, and so on.

We would appreciate hearing from you concerning your experiences with this guide and how you feel it could be improved and kept up to date. While we may not be able to respond to all comments and suggestions, we'll take them to heart, and we'll also make certain to share them with the author. Please send your comments and suggestions to the following address:

GPP
Reader Response/Editorial Department
PO Box 480
Guilford, CT 06437

Or you may e-mail us at: editorial@globepequot.com

Thanks for your input, and happy trails!

Best Hikes Near Reno and Lake Tahoe

TRACY SALCEDO-CHOURRÉ

GUILFORD, CONNECTICUT
HELENA, MONTANA
AN IMPRINT OF GLOBE PEQUOT PRESS

This book is dedicated to the memory of Howard Friedman, who read my last Lake Tahoe hiking guide from cover to cover. Rest in peace.

FALCONGUIDES®

FalconGuides is an imprint of Globe Pequot Press.
Falcon, FalconGuides, and Outfit Your Mind are registered trademarks of Morris Book Publishing, LLC.

TOPO! Explorer software and SuperQuad source maps courtesy of National Geographic Maps. For information about TOPO! Explorer, TOPO!, and Nat Geo Maps products, go to www.topo.com or www.natgeomaps.com.

All photos by Tracy Salcedo-Chourré

Text design: Sheryl P. Kober
Layout artist: Maggie Peterson
Project editor: Ellen Urban

Maps by Alena Pearce © Morris Book Publishing, LLC

Library of Congress Cataloging-in-Publication Data is available on file.

ISBN 978-0-7627-8157-7

Printed in the United States of America

10 9 8 7 6 5 4 3 2 1

Contents

South Shore and Beyond

RENO

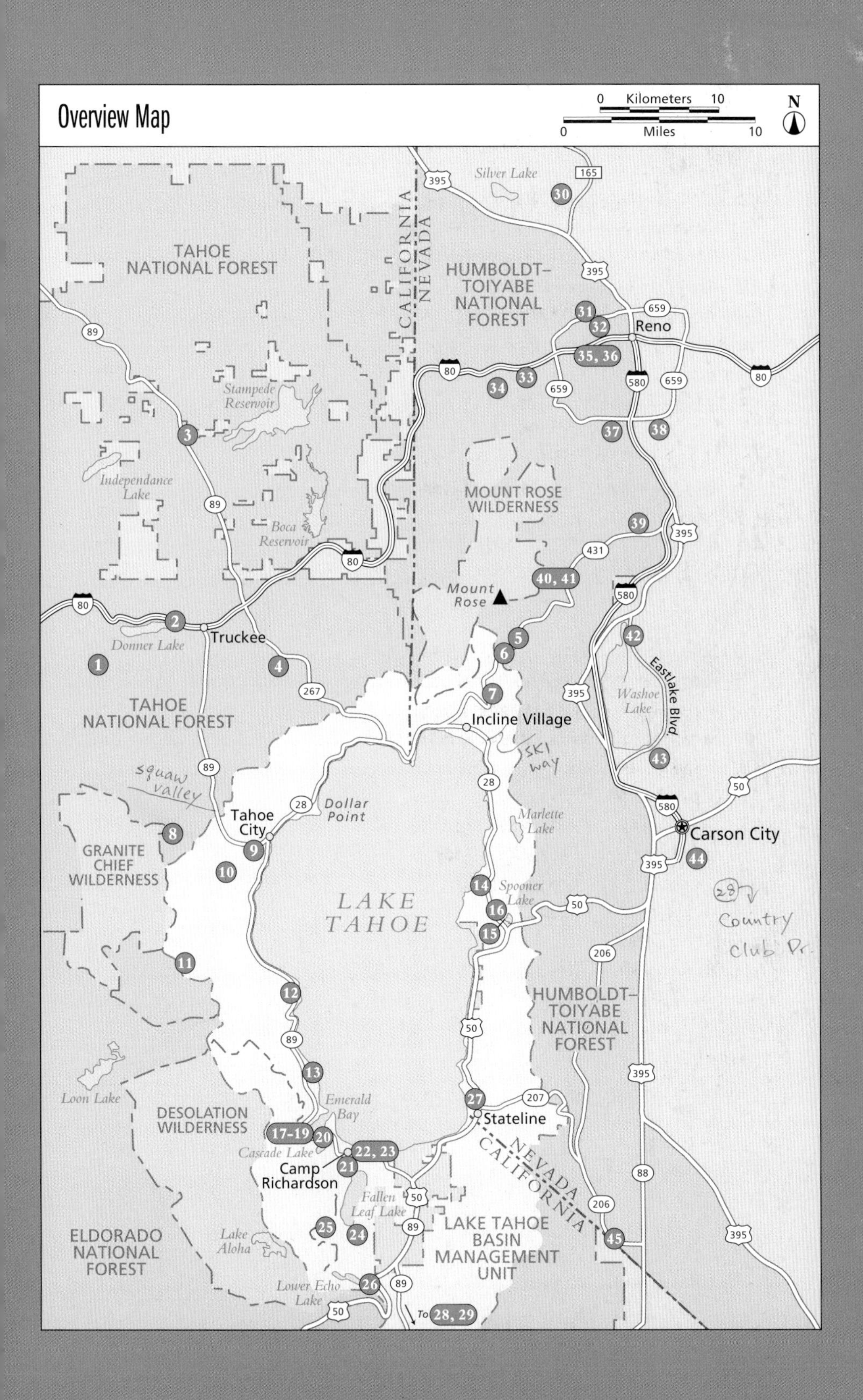
Overview Map
0 Kilometers 10
0 Miles 10
N
TAHOE NATIONAL FOREST
CALIFORNIA
NEVADA
HUMBOLDT–TOIYABE NATIONAL FOREST
Silver Lake
Reno
Stampede Reservoir
Independance Lake
Boca Reservoir
MOUNT ROSE WILDERNESS
Mount Rose
Donner Lake
Truckee
TAHOE NATIONAL FOREST
Incline Village
Washoe Lake
Eastlake Blvd.
Dollar Point
Tahoe City
Marlette Lake
Carson City
GRANITE CHIEF WILDERNESS
LAKE TAHOE
Spooner Lake
HUMBOLDT–TOIYABE NATIONAL FOREST
Loon Lake
DESOLATION WILDERNESS
Emerald Bay
Stateline
NEVADA
CALIFORNIA
Cascade Lake
Camp Richardson
Fallen Leaf Lake
LAKE TAHOE BASIN MANAGEMENT UNIT
ELDORADO NATIONAL FOREST
Lake Aloha
Lower Echo Lake
To 28, 29

Acknowledgments

My thanks for advice and help in the production of this guide and previous Reno and Lake Tahoe guides to Don Lane, Mike St. Michel, and Lindsay Gusses of the USDA Forest Service–Lake Tahoe Basin Management Unit; Mark Kimbrough of the Tahoe Rim Trail Association; Hal Paris and Pandora Bahlman of the Incline Village General Improvement District; Roger Adamson of the Tahoe City Public Utility District; Bill Houdyschell of the Tahoe Donner Association's forestry division; Bill Champion of Lake Tahoe–Nevada State Park; Dean Lutz, Jeff Wiley, and Susanne Jensen of the USFS Tahoe National Forest; Jacqui Zink, park ranger with the US Army Corps of Engineers at Martis Creek Lake; Dave Nettle; Gisela Steiner of Tahoe Trail Trekkers; Billy Sibley of the City of Reno Parks, Recreation and Community Services Department; Cheryl Surface of Washoe County's Department of Regional Parks & Open Space; Arthur Callen of the Bureau of Land Management's Carson City District; Donna Silver at Washoe Lake State Park; and Steve Hale of the Humboldt-Toiyabe National Forest, Carson City Ranger District.

Aspen turn golden along the trail to Marlette Lake.

Thanks to the editors and publishers whose efforts have made this (and my other guidebooks) the best they can be, including Bill Schneider, David Lee, Charlene Patterson, Erica Olsen, Julie Marsh, Scott Adams, and Jessica Haberman. A huge shout-out to former publishers George Meyers and Merrill Wilson, who helped get it all started.

Thanks to my hiking partners, trail advisors, and support staff, including Penn Chourré, Julianne Roth, Linda Madan, Deb Rodman, and Mitchell and Karen Friedman. Thanks also to Linda and Mike Madan for the advice on eateries in the Reno area.

Thanks to these folks for everything: Howard and Rita Friedman and the entire Friedman/Rodman clan; Jesse and Judy Salcedo; Chris Salcedo and Angela Jones; Nick and Nancy Salcedo; Sarah Chourré and Martin Chourré; Karen, Kelly, Sara, Julie, and Kerin; and my colleagues at Dunbar Elementary School and Streetwise Reports for their flexibility.

Finally, my gratitude always to my sons Jesse, Cruz, and Penn, who never complain when I take off for the hills without them—or when I drag them along.

Slabs of polished granite swoop up off the Velma Lakes Trail in the Desolation Wilderness.

Introduction

We all face challenges. In the grand scheme of things, the dilemma posed by having to select the best hikes in the Reno–Lake Tahoe area is relatively minor. But it has been a challenge nonetheless, given the grandeur of California's Range of Light and the boundless network of trails that weaves through it.

Then again, how could I go wrong?

The trick has been in the exploration. The Sierra Nevada have been in my soul and under my soles for decades now. I know what I like and I know where to find it. I could have stuck with my old favorites (and they are in this guide), but Sierran hikers are as varied as the terrain, so I broadened my scope. Routes in this guide range from super-short wheelchair-accessible interpretive trails to thigh-burning treks to high-altitude destinations. They ramble through scree fields above treeline, wind into thick yellow pine forests, and climb into desert scrublands. They lead to excellent viewpoints, verdant wildflower fields, calming beaches, historic sites, and awesome summits. They are informed by water, whether by Lake Tahoe itself, or the Truckee River, or smaller streams or lakes. The goal was not to be comprehensive. I hope I've selected a tasty sampling, like chocolates in a gift box. But a whole warehouse of deliciousness remains open to the adventurer.

Most trails around Lake Tahoe feature climbing—they are in the Sierra Nevada, after all. But none will bust a gut. You may encounter comparable steepness on tracks in Reno, but the lesser altitude eases the workload. Spectacular mountain backdrops and extremes of weather lend a wildland feel to even the more urban treks around the city.

Routes in this guide are intended to be day hikes, though many of the trails extend farther into the wilderness or link to other paths that reach into remoter regions. With a good map, a little planning, and the right gear, you can use many of these trails to launch weekend backpacking trips or treks lasting a month or more. Climb onto the Pacific Crest Trail and you can head north through the Cascades to Canada, or south to Yosemite, Mount Whitney, and the Mexican border.

Hands-down winner in the beauty contest is Lake Tahoe, vast and blue and rimmed with snowcapped peaks. A mecca for the outdoorsy, the lake boasts a healthy population of year-round residents that swells with visitors on weekends in summer and winter. Summer draws the boaters and hikers; winter brings the skiers and snowboarders. The influx from Sacramento and the San Francisco Bay Area is huge, and residents of Reno head upslope regularly as well. The good news for hikers is that, despite the popularity of Tahoe trails, if you hike in the off-season (especially fall), and during the week, you will miss the crowds.

Reno's setting is no slouch: The Biggest Little City's gambling heart is bounded on the west by the same Sierran peaks that embrace Lake Tahoe, and on the east by the stark, imposing high desert ranges of the Great Basin. While its downtown casinos draw tourists year-round, Reno is also a university town, with industry and agriculture fortifying its economic base. The population of more than 220,000 is diverse, but sharing a love of the outdoors is almost universal. Living in the shadow of the Sierra will inspire that, whether you like to hike, fish, hunt, or ride an all-terrain vehicle.

Trails have linked Reno and Tahoe for thousands of years. Washoe Indians abiding in the Truckee Meadows (where Reno would later be established) traveled up through the canyons to summer hunting grounds around Lake Tahoe. The Sierra were a formidable barrier to colonists, both Americans headed west and the Spaniards who established a mission and rancho system in what was then known as Alta California. For nearly a century after "discovery" the trails through the mountains were traversed almost exclusively by natives and by mountain men such as Jedediah Smith.

But the discovery of gold and silver in the mid-nineteenth century changed everything. Trails that had once been passable only in season became year-round travel routes for forty-niners and those who followed them. And new trails were blazed, to facilitate the booming timber and mining industries and to help move the massive quantities of water needed by both. Once the booms went bust wildland lovers moved in—renowned advocates such as John Muir, one of the founders of the Sierra Club—and the trails became paths for modern-day explorers, women and men seeking to rediscover the beauty of the Sierra and their inherent awe of the high country.

To walk in the wilderness is, I believe, to renew the soul. I hope that anyone who embarks on any trail near Reno or Lake Tahoe will find the same peace and sense of well-being that I feel there. Get out, take a hike, and let yourself be stunned, reverent, and healed.

The Nature of Reno and Lake Tahoe

Trails in the Reno-Tahoe region range from rugged and mountainous to flat and paved, and hikes in this guide cover the gamut. Regardless of the trail you choose, knowing a few details about the nature of the region will enhance your explorations.

Flora and Fauna

The Reno-Tahoe region encompasses several ecosystems, each with distinctive flora and fauna.

The high desert surrounding Reno is at the lowest elevation. The sagebrush scrub (or steppe) plant community thrives in the hot, dry climate, with big sagebrush, black sagebrush, and rabbitbrush dominating the landscape. Cactus and wildflowers bloom briefly in early spring, splashing color among the browns, grays, and greens of the landscape.

As you move up in altitude on the mountain slopes, the sage steppe becomes interspersed with junipers, piñon pines, and Jeffrey pines. Wildlife is abundant, including mule deer, coyote, jackrabbits, and cottontail rabbits; songbirds, grouse, and raptors; foxes; a variety of cats including mountain lions; lizards and snakes.

Moving higher, you enter the montane zone. This is a forested ecosystem, reaching from roughly 4,000 feet in elevation to 7,000 feet. The lower montane zone features a mixed evergreen forest composed of Jeffrey and ponderosa pines, white firs, and incense cedars; in the upper montane zone lodgepole pine and red fir are the dominant species. Songbirds thrive in the lower montane zone; wildlife also includes deer, rabbits, squirrels and chipmunks, and black bear. Populations thin in the higher altitudes, though the golden-mantled ground squirrel can often be seen scurrying across trails ahead of hikers. Lake Tahoe, at 6,224 feet, sits square in the montane zone.

Open yellow pine forest is typical of the lower montane zone outside Reno.

The subalpine zone begins near 8,000 feet and reaches to treeline. The forest here, composed of whitebark pine and mountain hemlock, is stunted by wind and snowfall. Wildlife is scarce. But low-growing wildflowers enliven the meadows of the zone.

Finally, at the summits of the peaks along the Sierra crest and the Carson Range, at about 10,000 feet and above treeline, you'll enter the alpine zone. Here the plants and animals must contend with harsh conditions year-round. Pikas, noisy little creatures, abide in rock fields and chirp warnings to each other. A variety of insects tolerate the extremes of the zone, including bees and crickets. Low-growing flowers and shrubs, including varieties of aster, buckwheat, sorrel, paintbrush, and clover, provide fodder for both bee and pika.

Weather

The hiking season around Lake Tahoe generally stretches from the first of May to the end of October, with trails at lower elevations melting off before those at higher elevations. When a particular trail opens is dependent on the amount of winter snowfall and the speed of the snowmelt. Snowshoe hikers and cross-country skiers can travel into areas traversed by these trails during winter, weather and backcountry skills permitting.

Deposited long ago, this glacial erratic rests on slabs on the trail leading from Glen Alpine to Gilmore Lake and Lake Aloha.

High temperatures in spring and fall range from the low 50s to the mid-70s. In July, August, and September, temperatures jump into the high 70s and 80s, with occasional hot spells. Overnight lows are in the 30s and 40s.

Afternoon thunderstorms are fairly common in the summer months and taper off by autumn. Regardless of the season hikers should be prepared for changeable weather—rain, cold, snow, or heat—by wearing layers and packing waterproof gear.

Reno's high desert climate is dominated in the hiking season by low humidity and lots of sunshine. Spring and fall, when high temperatures range from the 40s to the 70s, offer the best hiking weather, but with a few caveats, you can hike in Reno year-round.

Rainfall averages 7.5 inches annually, falling mostly in winter and during thunderstorms in spring. Snowfall averages 25 inches annually, mostly in small doses of 1 to 2 inches, and generally melts off quickly. Winter lows plunge into the 20s and 30s, while highs creep into the low 40s. Layers of clothing are a prerequisite for winter hiking.

Summertime temperatures are usually not oppressive, with averages in the high 80s and 90s. Heat waves can drive temps into the 100s. Temperature variations can be extreme, however, with nighttime lows dropping into the 40s and

Lake Tahoe forms the horizon on the descent from Eagle Lake.

50s. Hiking in the morning or evening is recommended. These times offer lovely light and a greater opportunity to see wildlife. Midday hiking may also be a poor choice because the combination of heat and low humidity can lead to rapid dehydration.

Etiquette for Animals

You'll encounter mostly benign creatures on trails in Reno and around Lake Tahoe, such as squirrels, rabbits, lizards, and a variety of birdlife. More rarely seen are coyotes, deer, and raccoons. Encounters with wildlife that poses a potential threat to hikers are even more rare but are definitely possible, so beware the black bear, mountain lion, and venomous snake.

Black bears are most commonly seen in the Lake Tahoe area, where they've learned that yummies can be found in cars, in unsecured garbage cans, and in the kitchens of weekend cabins. Encounters usually involve some kind of food. Bears have been known to remove windshields from automobiles to get at coolers and to stroll through the open doors of homes to rummage in refrigerators.

If you encounter a bear on the trail, do not run. Stand still and make noise, and the bear will most likely scram. Never come between a mama bear and her cubs; if you see cubs, leave the area immediately.

A fish ladder filters the stream leading into Marlette Lake in the Marlette-Hobart backcountry.

Nevada is home to five species of pit vipers, including the western diamondback and Great Basin rattlesnakes. Snakes generally only strike if they are threatened—you are too big to be dinner, so they typically avoid contact with humans. Keep your distance, and they will keep theirs. If you encounter a snake on the trail, back away slowly. Use caution when climbing over rocks or venturing into caves. Snakes are also known to seek shelter under cars in hot weather.

Mountain lions are most active at dawn and dusk. Like snakes they generally avoid contact with humans, but to further reduce the chances of an encounter, make noise while hiking. Don't jog or ride a bike in areas where a lion has been sighted, as those activities mimic prey behavior. If you come across a mountain lion, make yourself seem as big as possible and do not run. If you don't act like or look like prey, you stand a good chance of not being attacked. If the attack comes anyway, fight back.

Green Tips

Given the great beauty of the parks, trails, and wildlands in and around Reno and Lake Tahoe, and especially given the heavy use all receive, it's important that we do all we can to keep them clean, lovely, and healthy. The Green Tips scattered throughout this guide will help you do just that.

Getting Around

Pairing Reno and Lake Tahoe in a guidebook makes good sense, given their proximity. They are separated by 50 to 60 highway miles and a drive of less than two hours (depending on the route you choose). The granite escarpment—a little less than 2,000 feet high—that separates the city from the lake is the biggest impediment to travel, particularly when winter storms descend. But area residents and visitors easily ping-pong between the two destinations, depending on where they choose to play on any particular day.

All hikes in this guide are within an hour's drive from downtown Reno, or from one of the bigger little towns around Lake Tahoe.

Tahoe City, Incline Village, and South Lake Tahoe/Stateline serve as touchstones for directions to trailheads around the lake. A scenic highway, variously designated CA 89, CA 28, NV 28, and US 50, circumnavigates Tahoe. Most trailhead directions to hikes in the Lake Tahoe area are given from this road. Directions for trails in Donner and Truckee are given from I-80.

Most hikes in the Reno section are located in the Truckee Meadows and adjacent North and South Valleys, but some reach westward into the Sierra foothills and south into the Washoe and Carson River valleys. Two major highways intersect in Reno. I-80 runs east-west and links the city with Lake Tahoe in California. US 395 and I-580 run north-south and connect Reno to Carson City. Trailhead directions for Reno area hikes are given from these highways. McCarran

Boulevard circles the metropolitan area, offering easy alternative access to trails.

In addition to I-80, Reno and Tahoe are linked by the Mount Rose Highway (NV 431), which hitches Reno's southwestern suburbs to Incline Village. US 50 climbs from just south of Carson City over Spooner Summit onto Tahoe's East Shore. Farther south, the Kingsbury Grade (NV 207) runs between Mottsville and South Lake Tahoe.

Public Transportation

Tahoe Area Regional Transit (TART) provides public transportation for north Lake Tahoe. For information on routes and fares, call (530) 550-1212 or (800) 736-6365, or visit www.placer.ca.gov/departments/works/transit/TART.aspx.

The South Tahoe Area Transit Authority's BlueGO provides public transportation around Tahoe's South Shore. For more information call (530) 541-7149 or visit www.bluego.org.

Public transportation for Reno is provided by the Regional Transportation Commission (RTC), which operates a number of bus routes in the city and to outlying communities, including Carson City. Route information is available at rtc washoe.com. Call (775) 348-RIDE for more information.

Maps

The USGS quad is listed for every hike. If the hike is so short or well defined that no map is necessary, or if an adequate map is provided at the trailhead by the land manager, that is noted in the hike description.

There are several great regional maps available. They include:

- The US Forest Service's Lake Tahoe Basin Management Unit map, available at forest service visitor centers and from retail outlets around the region. The map is also online at www.fs.fed.us/r5/ltbmu/maps/index.shtml.
- The National Geographic/Trails Illustrated Lake Tahoe Basin Map (#803) covers most every trail in the region, in both California and Nevada. It is available at most outdoor retail outlets in the area, or at www.trails illustrated.com.
- The Tom Harrison Recreation Map of Lake Tahoe also includes most of the hikes in this guide. For more information call (415) 456-7940 or visit www .tomharrisonmaps.com.

How to Use This Guide

This guide is designed to be simple and easy to use. Each hike is described with a map and summary information that delivers the trail's vital statistics including length, difficulty, fees and permits, park hours, canine compatibility, and trail contacts. Directions to the trailhead are provided. Information about what you'll see along the trail, as well as about the route's natural and cultural history, is given in the hike description. A detailed route finder (Miles and Directions) sets forth mileages between significant landmarks along the trail.

How the Hikes Were Chosen

Hikes chosen for this guide range in difficulty from flat excursions along the Truckee River in downtown Reno to more challenging treks to mountaintops and highland lakes. I've selected hikes throughout the region, so regardless of your starting point you'll find a hike nearby.

While these trails are among the best, keep in mind that nearby trails may offer options better suited to your needs. Potential alternatives are suggested in the Options section at the end of hike descriptions and in the Honorable Mentions at the end of each chapter.

Floating Island Lake is a nice resting place along the trail to Cathedral Lake and Mount Tallac in the Desolation Wilderness.

Selecting a Hike

Terrain, altitude, weather, and your level of fitness should be taken into account when selecting a hike in the Reno-Tahoe region. I have rated these hikes (easy, moderate, strenuous) to give you an idea of what to expect, but these ratings are completely subjective.

Easy: The route involves minimal elevation changes, is easy to navigate, and can be completed by most hikers in less than two hours.

Moderate: The trail includes notable climbing and descending, may involve some route-finding, and can be completed in less than four hours.

Strenuous: The route includes significant elevation changes, may be narrow or exposed in sections, and takes longer than four hours to complete.

Factors other than fitness that play into hike selection include the adequacy of your gear (primarily shoes), the ratio of trail length to elevation change (gaining 200 feet in 1 mile is easy; gaining 1,000 feet in 1 mile is strenuous), and the trail's altitude (a lakeside hike at 6,000 feet above sea level is easier than climbing along the Tahoe rim at 10,000 feet).

In addition to listing hikes that might appeal to the hiker seeking a certain experience, the Trail Finder lists the trails by level of difficulty. If you are hiking with a group, select a hike that's appropriate for the least fit and prepared in your party.

Hiking times are based on the assumption that on flat ground, most walkers average 2 miles per hour. Adjust that rate by the steepness of the terrain and your level of fitness (subtract time if you're an aerobic animal and add time if you're hiking with kids), and you have a ballpark hiking duration. Be sure to add more time if you plan to picnic or take part in other activities like birding or photography.

Map Legend

580	Interstate Highway		Airport
395	US Highway		Boat Ramp
431	State Highway		Bridge
165 / FR1306	County/Forest Road		Building/Point of Interest
	Local Road		Campground
	Unpaved Road		Capital
	Railroad		Dam
	Featured Trail		Gate
	Trail		Lighthouse
	State Line	P	Parking
	Boardwalk/Steps		Pass/Gap
	Small River or Creek		Peak/Summit
	Intermediate Stream		Picnic Area
	Marsh/Swamp		Ranger Station
	Body of Water		Restrooms
	National Forest/Park/ Wilderness Area		Scenic View/Viewpoint
	State/County Park		Town
	Miscellaneous Area	1	Trailhead
		?	Visitor/Information Center
			Waterfall

Trail Finder

Hike No.	Hike Name	Best Hikes for Lake Lovers	Best Hikes for Great Views	Best Hikes for Rivers & Waterfalls	Best Hikes for Nature Lovers	Best Hikes for Children & Dogs	Best Hikes for History Lovers	Best Long Hikes	Best Urban Trails
1	Mount Judah		●					●	
2	Lakeside Interpretive Trail at Donner Lake				●				
3	Sagehen Creek	●							
4	Martis Creek Wildlife Area				●				
5	Mount Rose		●					●	
6	Tahoe Meadows Interpretive Trail				●	●			
7	The Incline Downhill		●						
8	Five Lakes Trail	●							
9	Truckee River Trail			●					●
10	Page Meadows				●				
11	Ellis Lake		●						
12	General Creek Loop at Sugar Pine Point						●		
13	The Lighthouse and Rubicon Point				●		●		
14	Skunk Harbor	●							
15	Spooner Lake Loop	●							

Trail Finder

Hike No.	Hike Name	Best Hikes for Lake Lovers	Best Hikes for Great Views	Best Hikes for Rivers & Waterfalls	Best Hikes for Nature Lovers	Best Hikes for Children & Dogs	Best Hikes for History Lovers	Best Long Hikes	Best Urban Trails
16	Marlette Lake	●						●	
17	Vikingsholm and Emerald Point	●	●				●		
18	Eagle Lake	●							
19	Velma Lakes	●	●		●			●	
20	Cascade Falls			●					
21	Cathedral Lake	●							
22	Rainbow Trail				●				
23	Lake of the Sky Trail and Tallac Historic Site						●		
24	Angora Lakes					●			
25	Gilmore Lake	●		●			●	●	
26	Pacific Crest Trail at Echo Lakes	●							
27	Lam Watah Nature Trail	●							
28	Tahoe Rim Trail at Big Meadows				●				
29	Winnemucca and Round Top Lake Loop	●	●						
30	South Side Interpretive Trail at Swan Lake				●				

Trail Finder

Hike No.	Hike Name	Best Hikes for Lake Lovers	Best Hikes for Great Views	Best Hikes for Rivers & Waterfalls	Best Hikes for Nature Lovers	Best Hikes for Children & Dogs	Best Hikes for History Lovers	Best Long Hikes	Best Urban Trails
31	Evans Canyon and Miner's Trail Loop				●				
32	May Arboretum and Herman Pond				●				
33	Steamboat Ditch and the Hole in the Wall		●			●			
34	Hunter Creek Falls			●					
35	Downtown River Walk			●		●			●
36	Oxbow Nature Study Area Loop			●	●				●
37	Bartley Ranch Regional Park Loop						●		
38	Lakeview Loop at Huffaker Hills		●						
39	Lower Whites Creek Trail								●
40	Jones-Whites Creek Loop		●			●			
41	Galena Creek Nature Trail					●			
42	Little Washoe Lake Trail				●				
43	Deadman's Overlook Trail		●						
44	Pasture River–Mexican Ditch Trail			●		●			
45	Fay-Luther Interpretive Loop		●						

TRUCKEE AND DONNER

Donner Lake sits below the east side of the Sierra crest.

From Donner Summit at the crest of the Sierra Nevada, miles of mountains stretch away in all directions. They hint at the treasures tucked in their folds, but you can't see them from here. Looking west, the long slide of I-80 becomes lost in the trees, but it reaches into Gold Country and California's Great Valley. To the south the mountains climb higher and become more inaccessible, the realm of long-distance hikers on the Pacific Crest Trail and the John Muir Trail. To the north, beyond Castle Peak, the Sierra are wooded and gentle, merging almost imperceptibly into the Cascade Range near Lassen Peak. Look east and . . . well, that's where Donner Lake and the high-country town of Truckee lie, with Lake Tahoe behind. The treasure may be out of sight, but Donner Summit is the gateway.

Donner Lake lies in a wooded oblong bowl east of the pass. Members of the ill-fated Donner Party met unfortunate ends near the shore of the lake in the winter of 1846-1847. The snow fell early and heavy that winter, trapping the travelers, and as they slowly succumbed to the cold and starvation, some were cannibalized. As gruesome and tragic as their story was, the party's name has been immortalized on the landscape.

Truckee's origins, like those of so many mountain towns, are linked to the gold rush and the Comstock Lode. It began as a way station for miners, a stop on the road leading from Sacramento over the summit and eventually into Virginia City, Nevada. The town boomed when the Central Pacific Railroad came through, serving as a staging area for lumber needed to complete the mighty transcontinental project. After the railroad was built, Truckee continued to thrive as a timber town, supplying lumber to growing cities such as Sacramento and Reno. These days the town's livelihood is tied to tourism; its quaint main street, hotels, and restaurants attract skiers and hikers instead of lumberjacks and miners.

Once you climb above treeline, as here on the Mount Rose Trail, the views are panoramic.

Mount Judah

Straddling the crest of the Sierra above Donner Lake, Mount Judah is an easy, accessible peak with summit views that stretch east over Donner Lake and west down the long wooded slopes toward California's Great Valley.

Start: At the Sugar Bowl Academy parking area on historic Donner Summit
Distance: 5.3-mile lollipop
Hiking time: 4–5 hours
Difficulty: Challenging
Trail surface: Dirt singletrack and ski area service roads
Best season: Summer
Other trail users: None
Trailhead amenities: Parking. If the lot is full, park carefully along the dirt road that leads to the trailhead and the Pacific Crest Trail.
Canine compatibility: Leashed dogs permitted
Fees and permits: None
Schedule: You can access the trail from sunrise to sunset daily in late spring, summer, and fall, when the Sugar Bowl Ski Area is not operating.
Maps: USGS Norden CA
Trail contact: Sugar Bowl Resort, 629 Sugar Bowl Rd., Norden, CA 95724; (530) 426-9000; www.sugarbowl.com

Finding the trailhead: From Tahoe City, follow CA 287 northwest to I-80. Head west on I-80 for 12 miles to the exit for Soda Springs and Norden. Head back east on Old Donner Pass Road to the summit of historic Donner Pass. Park in the lot for the Sugar Bowl Academy/Mount Judah. GPS: N39 18.097' / W120 19.570'

1

THE HIKE

Gone are the days when ski areas went lifeless after the snow melted in springtime. Now many Tahoe area ski resorts host a variety of summertime activities. Riding mountain bikes down trails that loop around ski runs is perhaps most popular, but other activities include taking gondolas to mountaintop restaurants and activity centers, including hiking trail systems. All this for a fee, of course.

There is no fee, however, to hike up the slopes of the Sugar Bowl ski area to the top of Mount Judah. That might be because this ski area lies farther afield, not on the rim of the Tahoe basin but on the Sierra crest near Donner Pass. Whatever the reason, climbing to the summit and enjoying the views is free to all.

The hike begins with a relatively steep climb up stony switchbacks. Fall color is vibrant along this stretch, and interesting views open at each switchback. This is the lollipop stick part of the route; it also follows a section of the Pacific Crest Trail (PCT).

By the half-mile mark you'll find yourself looking across the broad ski area bowl onto Lake Mary and west down the I-80 corridor (there is some road noise

The trail to the summit of Mount Judah begins amid foliage that changes color with the season.

here, but that fades as you climb away). The climb is a juxtaposition of ski area development and relatively untouched alpine woodland, with traverses through dense forest interspersed with crossings of ski slopes and side trails leading to ski lift stations.

Where the trail forks at 1.1 miles stay right, traveling the loop portion of the route in a counterclockwise direction. At the 2-mile mark reach a junction at a sharp switchback. Bear sharply left on the trail to Mount Judah; the PCT continues right, to Judah's neighbor Mount Lincoln and beyond.

A series of quick switchbacks and long traverses leads onto and then up along the shoulder of Mount Judah. The views are spectacular and panoramic. Plugs of rock line the trail, conglomerate masses of bulbs and nodes in black and pink that erupt from the slope. The trees grow more stunted, cowed by winter wind and snowfall.

Ski area boundary signs line the trail as you near the summit. The distinctive and aptly named Castle Peak dominates the northern skyline. Round the final switchbacks, passing a pimply rock outcrop, and arrive on the wide, flat, summit plateau, where you can look down upon Donner Lake and into the Martis Lake wildlife area to the east, south along the Sierra crest, and north over the I-80 corridor to Castle Peak and beyond.

Drop through a saddle; a side trail leads to the secondary, northern summit if you choose. To complete the loop, descend on the right-hand trail, dropping swiftly along the northeast-facing slopes of the mountain. If the summit was too windy to permit a lunch break, rock outcrops along the downhill stretch of trail offer perfect rest stops, with views of Donner Lake and Donner Peak.

At the junction with the trail to Donner Peak, continue on the Mount Judah Trail, which leads left. A short section follows an overgrown service road, then the singletrack resumes at an unsigned break to the right. The path drops into a flat, wooded area where you may have to do a bit of route-finding: Cross the water bar and look for a white triangle on a high stump to stay on track. Traverse the mountain's west-facing slope back to the junction with the PCT, where you'll close the loop. From there, retrace your steps to the trailhead.

MILES AND DIRECTIONS

0.0 Start by walking down the dirt road for about 0.1 mile to the signed trailhead on the left.

0.5 Reach the top of the first set of switchbacks.

0.8 Pass a ski area sign (with skull and crossbones) that urges you to ski back to the lift. Not an issue, of course, for hikers in the off-season.

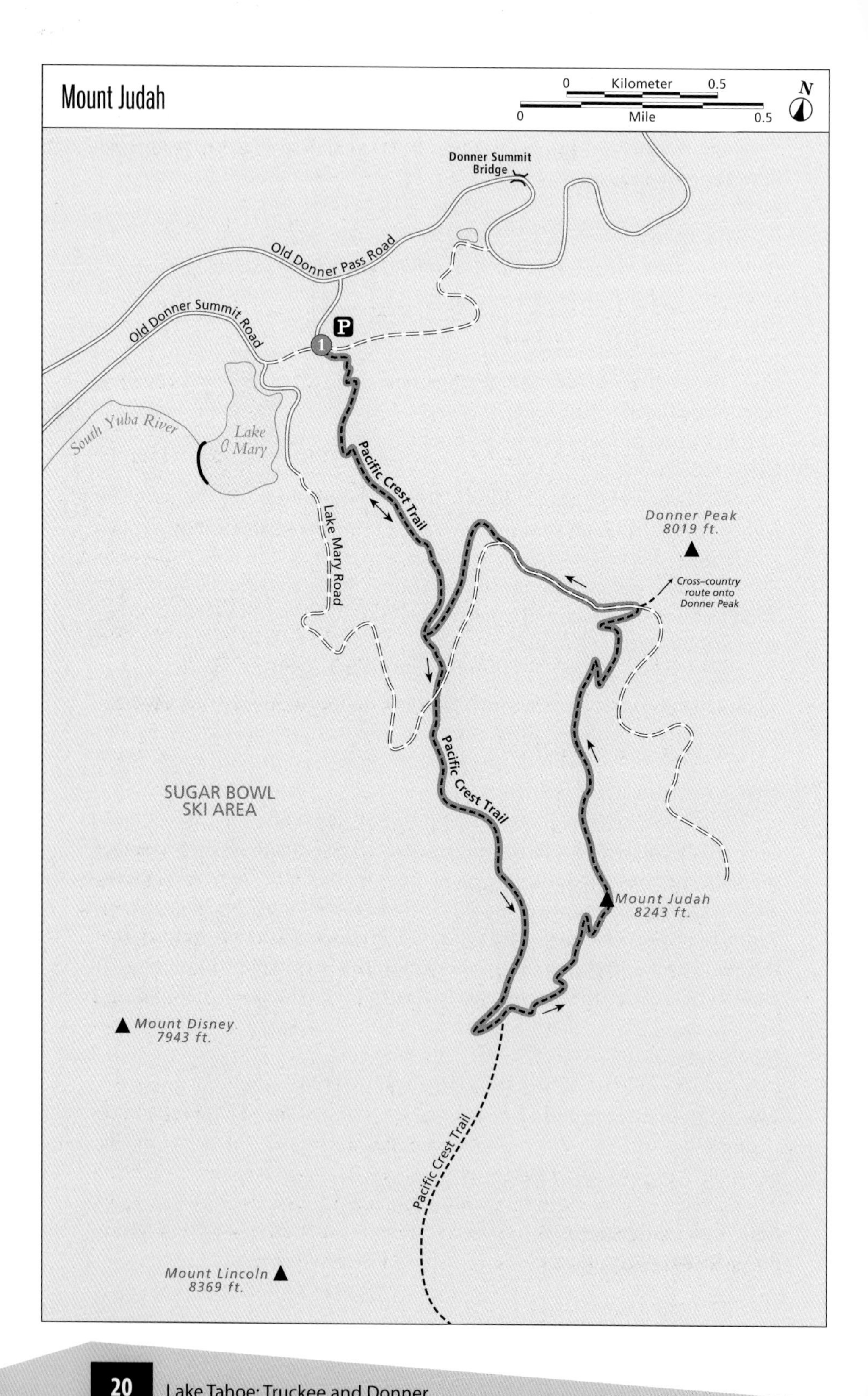
Mount Judah
0
Kilometer
0.5
0
Mile
0.5
N
Donner Summit
Bridge
Old Donner Pass Road
Old Donner Summit Road
P
1
South Yuba River
Lake
Mary
Lake Mary Road
Pacific Crest Trail
Donner Peak
8019 ft.
Cross-country
route onto
Donner Peak
Pacific Crest Trail
SUGAR BOWL
SKI AREA
Mount Judah
8243 ft.
Mount Disney
7943 ft.
Pacific Crest Trail
Mount Lincoln
8369 ft.

1.1 Cross a streamlet, then traverse a ski slope. At the trail junction stay right, remaining on the Pacific Crest Trail (PCT) to complete the loop section in a counterclockwise direction.

1.25 Cross a service road, picking up the obvious trail on the other side.

1.5 A side trail breaks off to a ski lift station. Stay left, continuing uphill.

2.0 At the trail junction, bear sharply left to continue on the Mount Judah Trail. The PCT continues to the right.

2.75 Arrive on the summit plateau. Begin the descent by heading north along the ridgeline.

2.9 At the north end of the saddle, the trail splits. The left path leads to the northern summit; go right to begin the descent.

3.5 At the junction with the trail to Donner Peak, go left on the Mount Judah Trail.

4.0 After a brief walk on an overgrown roadway, take the unsigned but obvious trail that breaks right. Drop into a flat, wooded area; stay left and cross the water bar. A white triangle on a high stump marks the route.

4.3 Reach the junction with the PCT to close the loop portion of the lollipop.

5.3 Arrive back at the trailhead.

HIKE INFORMATION

Local information: Soda Springs and Norden, while supporting a healthy winter recreational industry, are small and primarily residential in summer. Truckee is the nearest large town. The Truckee Donner Chamber of Commerce and California Welcome Center are at 10065 Donner Pass Rd., Truckee, CA 96161; call (530) 587-8808; www.truckee.com. The chamber website is www.truckeechamber.com.
Local events/attractions: Sugar Bowl Ski Resort hosts summer camps for kids. Contact the resort at (530) 426-9000 or visit www.sugarbowl.com for more information.
Camping: Donner Memorial State Park offers camping during the summer months. The park's 123 sites are equipped with metal bear boxes, where all food should be stored. Some sites are suitable for RVs, but they cannot exceed 28 feet in length. Campers have access to all park facilities. A fee is charged. For more information call (530) 582-7892. Online reservations can be made by visiting the Donner Memorial State Park page at www.parks.ca.gov; the link will take you to the park's ReserveAmerica (www.reserveamerica.com) page.

2

Lakeside Interpretive Trail at Donner Lake

Deep blue Donner Lake hosts a wonderful interpretive trail focused on both the lake's spectacular alpine setting and on the history of the infamous pass that shares its name.

Start: In the picnic area parking lot in Donner Memorial State Park
Distance: 2.4 miles out and back
Hiking time: 2 hours
Difficulty: Easy
Trail surface: Dirt singletrack
Best seasons: Late spring, summer, and fall
Other trail users: None
Trailhead amenities: Parking, restrooms, picnic facilities, trash-cans. Information, water, and campsites are available elsewhere in the park.
Canine compatibility: Leashed dogs permitted
Fees and permits: A day-use fee to enter the park. Free parking is available along Donner Pass Road outside the park. To reach the trail-head from the free parking area, follow the park road to the picnic area lot.
Schedule: Park hours vary with the season. Visitor center hours are 9 a.m. to 5 p.m. daily in summer; 9 a.m. to 4 p.m. after Labor Day.
Maps: USGS Truckee CA and Norden CA; park trail map available at the entrance station and on an information board at the entrance
Trail contact: Donner Memorial State Park, 12593 Donner Pass Rd., Truckee, CA 96161; (530) 582-7892; www.parks.ca.gov or www.donnermemorial.org
Other: Other park amenities include the Emigrant Trail Museum, the Pioneer Monument, and the Murphy family cabin site (a remnant of the Donner Party expedition).

Finding the trailhead: From Truckee, head west on I-80 to the Donner Pass Road exit (about 0.7 mile west of the CA 89 interchange). Go left (south) on Donner Pass Road to the well-signed park entrance on the left (south). Follow the park road past the entrance station and across the bridge, staying right at the gated campground road. GPS: N39 19.415' / W120 14.220'

THE HIKE

The story of the Donner Party is part of the lore of the West: Trapped by deep snow that buried the Sierra Nevada in the winter of 1846-1847, a wagon train of emigrants endured madness, despair, and cannibalism in their fight to survive. More than thirty souls perished in the scattering of cabins and camps established around Donner Lake in that long winter. Two of those cabin sites are within the boundaries of Donner Memorial State Park.

No worries of encountering similar hardships on this hike, however—it is barely arduous enough to bring on a hankering for a handful of trail mix. Interpretive signs along the trail satisfy any curiosity about how this rugged country was eventually tamed, with panels describing settlement and industry in the area and the construction of the railroad and highway that would make travel over the pass easy even in winter.

The interpretive part of the trail is located at the west end, and if you pay the entrance fee, you can park at the beach at China Cove and hike back toward the entrance station. It's described here beginning at the picnic area at the Donner Creek dam, with easy access from free parking on the road outside the park.

Donner Lake laps against the beach at China Cove.

The route begins at a small sign near the gauging station on Donner Creek, with the blue-green lake welling up alongside the dirt track. The trail roughly parallels the park road, offering access to lakeside beaches, picnic grounds, and restrooms along most of its length. Expect road noise from the nearby interstate and the park road—and the occasional rumble and whistle blow of a train on the tracks riding high on the mountainside to the south—but you'll also be able to hear birds chirping in the lakeside brambles and the wind whirring through the treetops.

Tile mosaics touting the benefits of recycling, healthy forests, and responsible development, created by local fifth-graders, line the trail starting at the 0.3-mile mark. The open forest allows glimpses of the gray granite heights of Donner Peak and Schallenberger Ridge to the south and west. Pass a chain of picnic areas, with a prime spot perched on a spit of sand that offers views across the water to lakeshore cabins on the north side.

The interpretive signs begin at the half-mile mark, focusing on the human and natural history of the area. Topics range from how fire helps maintain forest health to the geologic origins of the Sierra Nevada; from descriptions of the Native Americans that summered near Donner Lake to the lives of early European settlers; from construction of a wagon road over the pass in the 1850s to the completion of the interstate in the 1960s.

China Cove's crescent beach, with great views across the lake to the western peaks and ridges, is at trail's end. Picnic tables and restrooms make the cove a perfect place to eat lunch and relax. Return as you came (the most scenic route) or follow the park road back to the trailhead.

MILES AND DIRECTIONS

0.0 Start at the trail sign near the gauging station, heading southwest on the path.

0.3 Pass tile mosaics.

0.5 Pass a picnic site on a sand spit, then continue past a series of picnic sites on the left (south) side of the trail. Interpretive signs line the track.

1.2 Reach the beach at China Cove, take a break, then retrace your steps to the trailhead.

2.4 Arrive back at the trailhead.

HIKE INFORMATION

Local information: The Truckee Donner Chamber of Commerce maintains an online database of information about the mountain town, including where to eat, where to stay, and local events. Visit the site at www.truckee.com, or contact

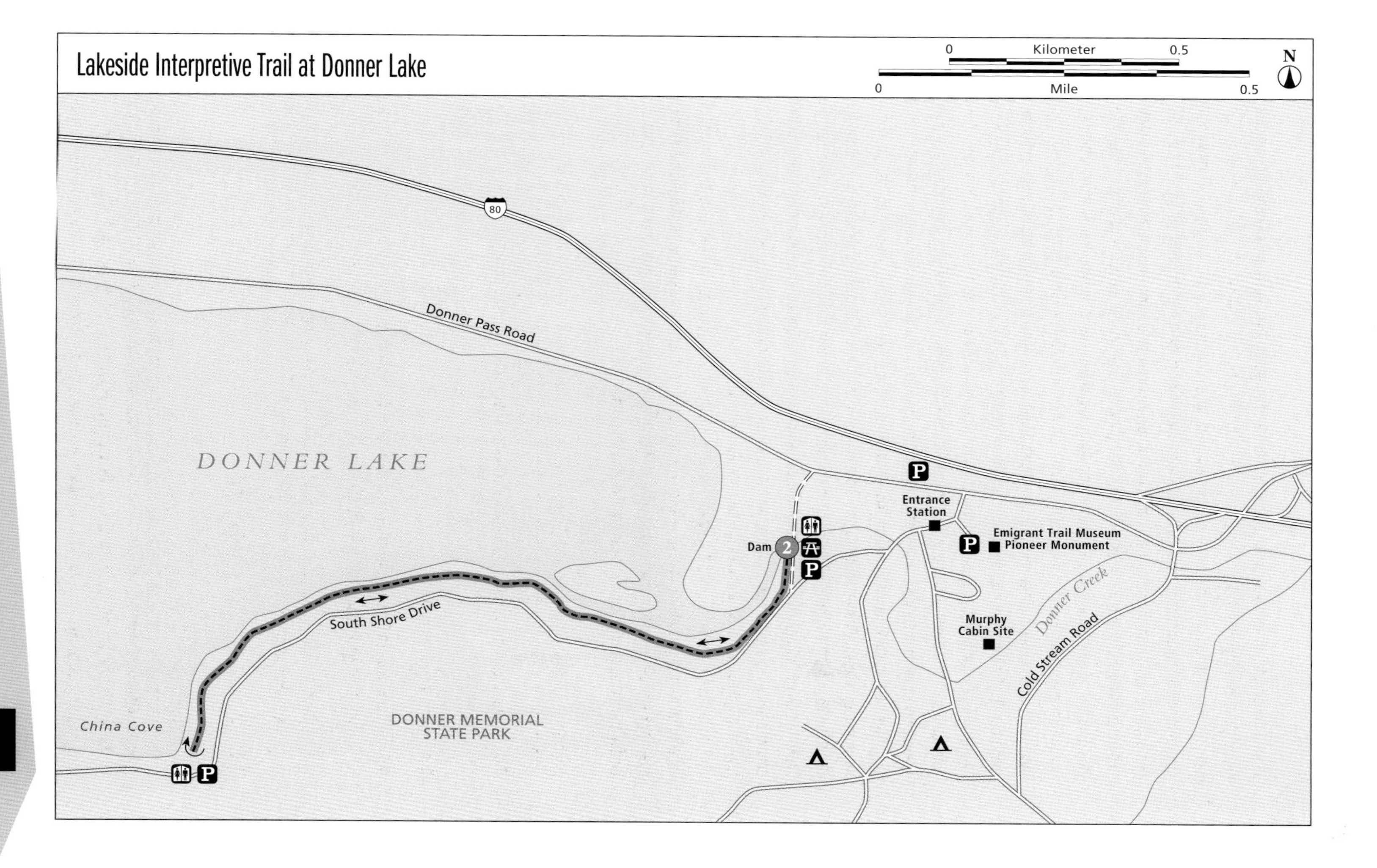
Lakeside Interpretive Trail at Donner Lake
0
Kilometer
0.5
0
Mile
0.5
N
80
Donner Pass Road
DONNER LAKE
P
Entrance Station
Emigrant Trail Museum
Pioneer Monument
Dam
2
Donner Creek
Murphy Cabin Site
Cold Stream Road
South Shore Drive
China Cove
DONNER MEMORIAL STATE PARK

the chamber by calling (530) 587-8808. The mailing address is 10065 Donner Pass Rd., Truckee, CA 96161.

Local events/attractions: Visitors to Donner Memorial State Park should take time to visit both the Emigrant Trail Museum (soon to be the High Sierra Crossing Museum), the Pioneer Monument, and the Murphy Cabin, where members of the Donner Party passed a long winter long ago. The museum documents the Donner Party, as well as other residents and travelers who left a legacy on the pass, including the native peoples and the builders of the western leg of the transcontinental railroad. It also has a gift shop. Museum hours are from 10 a.m. to 5 p.m. daily in the summer months. It is closed Thanksgiving, Christmas, and New Year's Day. It is also closed Tues and Wed from Sept to May.

Camping: Donner Memorial State Park offers camping during the summer months. The park's 123 sites are equipped with metal bear boxes, where all food should be stored. Some sites are suitable for RVs, but they cannot exceed 28 feet in length. Campers have access to all park facilities. A fee is charged. For more information call (530) 582-7892. Online reservations can be made by visiting the Donner Memorial State Park page at www.parks.ca.gov; the link will take you to the park's ReserveAmerica (www.reserveamerica.com) page.

Lodgepole pines grow with parklike perfection along the interpretive trail in Donner Memorial State Park.

Sagehen Creek

A lovely trail leads through wildflower-filled meadows and woodlands to the shoreline of an arm of Stampede Reservoir.

Start: An unsigned trailhead alongside CA 89 north of Truckee
Distance: 4.7 miles out and back
Hiking time: 2–3 hours
Difficulty: Easy
Trail surface: Dirt singletrack
Best seasons: Late spring, summer, fall
Other trail users: Mountain bikers, trail runners
Trailhead amenities: Parking for about 15 cars in a roadside pullout
Canine compatibility: Leashed dogs permitted
Fees and permits: None
Schedule: Sunrise to sunset daily
Maps: USGS Hobart Mills CA
Trail contact: Tahoe National Forest, Truckee Ranger District, 10811 Stockrest Springs Rd., Truckee, CA 96161; (530) 587-3558; www.fs.usda.gov/tahoe
Special considerations: The meadowlands and creek foster a healthy population of insects in spring. To be able to enjoy the wildflower display without losing pints of blood, use bug juice and dress appropriately.

Finding the trailhead: From the junction of CA 267/CA 89 and I-80 in Truckee, head north on CA 89 toward Sierraville and Graeagle. The unsigned parking area for the trailhead is 7.3 miles north of the junction with the interstate. GPS: N39 26.040' / W120 12.297'

THE HIKE

This gentle ramble leads through meadowlands alongside Sagehen Creek to a remote stretch of Stampede Reservoir shoreline. The trail is flat and straightforward, with plenty of wildflowers in season and wonderful views across the reservoir arm year-round.

Begin with a creekside ramble, with side paths leading to the right, down to the stream. Willows and small aspen crowd the path. Bend to the northeast and the creek drainage widens, skunk cabbage growing amid grasses in the shallow stream valley.

At about the 1-mile mark, as the trail traverses above Sagehen Creek, you can look down onto a shallow pond. Young pines have begun to colonize the grasslands, though the evergreens grow relatively thick on higher ground, including on the steeper slope to the left of the trail.

The path widens into a doubletrack as it heads across a broadening meadow, with views of Stampede Reservoir ahead. Pass through the wildflowers and into parklike stands of evergreens. Timbers form a bridge over a side stream; continue through the grasses to a second bridge, this one constructed of planks, that spans the main channel of Sagehen Creek.

The turnaround point is a bench that offers great views of the quiet waters of Stampede Reservoir. An overgrown trail continues south through the marshy grasslands, which you can explore if you desire. Otherwise, return as you came.

MILES AND DIRECTIONS

0.0 Start by heading down the trail alongside Sagehen Creek.

1.0 Pass a small, shallow pond.

1.7 The trail separates into a doubletrack and enters a broad meadow.

2.25 Cross a bridge made of hewn timber.

2.35 Cross the main channel of Sagehen Creek. Enjoy views of Stampede Reservoir from a bench, then return as you came.

4.7 Arrive back at the trailhead.

The Sagehen Creek Experimental Forest, a research collaboration between the University of California–Berkeley and the USDA Forest Service, harbors a variety of mountain evergreen species, including the lodgepole pine, the mountain hemlock, and the red fir. Ecological and meteorological data have been collected on the site for more than fifty years.

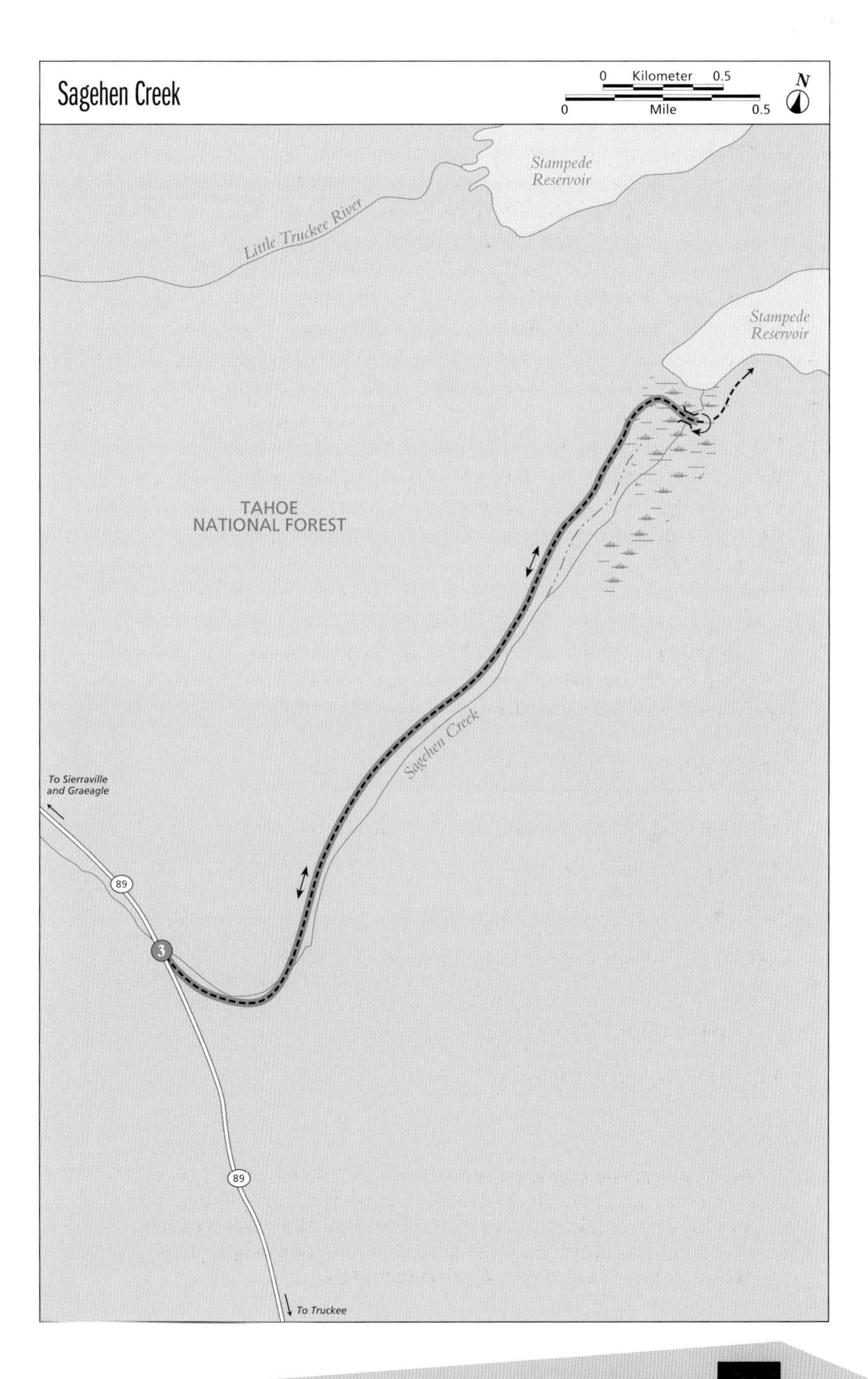
Sagehen Creek
0 Kilometer 0.5
0 Mile 0.5
N
Stampede Reservoir
Little Truckee River
Stampede Reservoir
TAHOE NATIONAL FOREST
Sagehen Creek
To Sierraville and Graeagle
89
3
89
To Truckee

3

HIKE INFORMATION

Local information: The Truckee Donner Chamber of Commerce maintains an online database of information about the mountain town, including where to eat, where to stay, and local events. Visit the site at www.truckee.com, or contact the chamber by calling (530) 587-8808. The mailing address is 10065 Donner Pass Rd., Truckee, CA 96161.

Restaurants: Wagon Trail Coffee Shop, PO Box 609, Truckee, CA 96160; (530) 587-8401; www.wagontraincoffeeshop.com. I've never eaten a meal in the Wagon Train, but it's where I stop to treat myself to an angel chocolate chip cookie after hiking. The cookies are buttery, flaky, light, and delicious. OK, maybe I don't stop for just one . . .

Camping: Rustic campsites are available at the forest service's Sagehen Creek Campground. To reach the campground, follow CA 89 north from Truckee for approximately 8 miles. Turn left onto FR 11 at the sign for Sagehen Creek. Follow the dirt road approximately 2 miles to the Sagehen Creek campground.

Colorful meadowland surrounds the trail that follows Sagehen Creek down to Stampede Reservoir.

Martis Creek Wildlife Area

The Martis Valley holds the biggest expanse of meadow and marshland in the Tahoe area. Birds flourish on the landscape, chirping, flitting, and soaring over winding Martis Creek. Whether you like birds or not, this exploration of the enormous grassland is enlivening.

Start: At the Martis Creek trailhead off CA 267 between Truckee and the base of Brockway summit
Distance: 4.2-mile loop
Hiking time: 2–3 hours
Difficulty: Moderate
Trail surface: Dirt singletrack, boardwalk
Best seasons: Late spring, summer, fall
Other trail users: Trail runners, mountain bikers on the Tomkins Memorial Trail (not permitted on the Martis Creek Trail)
Trailhead amenities: Parking, restrooms, picnic facilities, informational signboards
Canine compatibility: Leashed dogs permitted on the Tomkins Memorial Trail. Please pick up after your pet; bags are provided at the trailhead. Do not leave bags along the trail.
Fees and permits: None
Schedule: Sunrise to sunset daily
Maps: USGS Martis Peak CA and Truckee CA; maps are also posted at the trailhead and along the route.
Trail contact: US Army Corps of Engineers, PO Box 2344, Truckee, CA 96161; (530) 587-8113; corpslakes.usace.army.mil/visitors/martiscreek
Special considerations: The fragile Martis Creek Trail has been damaged by overuse; tread lightly or avoid it by remaining on the Tomkins Memorial Trail. The Martis Creek route passes through an important heritage area for the Washoe Indians. Removal of artifacts or damaging historic or prehistoric sites is prohibited by law.

Finding the trailhead: From the signalized junction of CA 28 and CA 267 in Kings Beach, follow CA 267 for 8.3 miles, over Brockway summit, to the signed Martis Creek Wildlife Area turnoff on the left (south). Follow the gravel access road for 0.1 mile to the trailhead. From I-80 in Truckee, take exit 188B and head south for 3 miles, past the main entrance for Martis Creek Lake, to the trailhead access road on the right. Parking is limited; if spaces are full, park along the access road or visit another day. GPS: N39 18.096' / W120 07.840'

4

THE HIKE

Martis Creek wanders through acres and acres of wetland meadow, cutting deeply into the turf, bending in sharp oxbows, watering a springtime bloom of wildflowers, and providing sustenance for a variety of creatures.

The birds are most prominent, their songs loud enough to be heard over the purr of cars passing on the nearby highway. Songbirds flit from willow to rose to sedge in flashes of brown, black, red, yellow, and sometimes vivid blue. Watch for raptors stilling in the clear mountain air and swallows shooting in and out of the shelter of the highway underpass. Fish, amphibians, and mammals, from ground squirrels to foxes to black bear, also visit or call the wildlife area home.

The Tomkins Memorial Trail arcs through the sanctuary in a long loop that first immerses hikers in the meadow ecosystem. It then leads into the evergreen forest that cloaks the slopes of the Lookout Peak, Northstar's ski mountain. The meadowland has known human habitation for 10,000 years or more and is presently hemmed in by the ski resort community, so you'll never be far from signs of civilization, be it the golf course, private homes, or the occasional airplane approaching or leaving the regional airport.

Dedicated bridges span meandering Martis Creek.

The Tomkins Memorial Trail loop is described clockwise. The trail parallels the highway at the outset, following a broad track easily shared with other trail users. At one of many named bridges spanning the wandering creek and its tributaries, the trail breaks south toward the Northstar resort, traversing sometimes soggy meadow via boardwalks and singletrack.

The metal roofs of private homes glint through the trees as you approach the base of the ski mountain. The trail curves west along the edge of the golf course, then through the forest at the bottom of the ski area. A brief foray into the woodland ends back in the meadow, where the Tomkins Memorial Trail links to the Martis Creek Trail.

According to its caretakers, the track along Martis Creek, a one-time cattle path, has been loved to near oblivion. Though it is possible to follow the trail along the meandering creek back to the trailhead, you will do the meadow good by finishing your tour via the Tomkins Trail, using a boardwalk and well-maintained path to circle back to the starting point. A bench along this final stretch offers hikers a chance to rest and enjoy views across the creek and valley. The Tomkins Trail meets the Martis Creek path below the parking area; a short easy climb leads out of the bottomlands and back to the trailhead.

MILES AND DIRECTIONS

0.0 Start on the signed Tomkins Memorial Trail, following the broad path that parallels the highway.

0.5 Cross Frank's Fish Bridge, the first of many named spans.

0.8 Reach Gumba's Crossing. Cross the bridge, then head southeast across the boardwalk.

1.0 Cross the Green Team's Bridge, then the Broken Bridge.

1.4 Pass under power lines and curl north as the trail runs along the fenced boundary between the wildlife area and the golf course.

1.6 At a break in the fence, marked by a trail sign, go right (north) to continue the loop. The left-hand path leads up into the neighborhood.

Green Tip:

Avoid sensitive ecological areas. Hike, rest, and camp at least 200 feet from streams, lakes, and rivers.

1.9 Pass a picnic table shaded by massive twin Jeffrey pines, then cross Michael Cousin's Bridge.

2.2 Now in the woodland, pass several junctions with social trails leading back into the neighborhood. Stay right (southwest) at the junctions on the obvious Tomkins Memorial Trail.

2.6 A picnic table and trail map at the edge of a small meadow mark a sharp turn in the trail.

2.9 Reach a bench at the interface between meadow and woodland.

3.1 Pass through scrubland to another trail sign. Ignore side trails, staying straight (west) on the broad main track.

3.3 Arrive at Pappe's Bridge, with a picnic table and a trail sign. The Tomkins Memorial Trail continues straight (west) via a boardwalk; continue on this track. The signed Martis Creek Trail breaks to the right (north).

4.1 Meet the Martis Creek Trail below the trailhead and climb toward the parking area.

4.2 Arrive back at the trailhead.

HIKE INFORMATION

Local information: The Truckee Donner Chamber of Commerce maintains an online database of information about the mountain town, including where to eat, where to stay, and local events. Visit the site at www.truckee.com, or contact the chamber by calling (530) 587-8808. The mailing address is 10065 Donner Pass Rd., Truckee, CA 96161.

Local events/attractions: Martis Creek Lake, run by the US Army Corps of Engineers and located across the road from the Martis Creek trailhead, offers a variety of outdoor activities, including boating, fishing, camping, picnicking, and cross-country skiing and snowshoeing in winter. Call (530) 587-8113 (Apr–Nov) or (530) 432-6427 (Dec–Mar), or visit www.spk.usace.army.mil/Locations/SacramentoDistrictParks/MartisCreekLake.aspx.

Camping: The Army Corps of Engineers maintains a campground across (north of) CA 267 from the wildlife area. Twenty-five campsites at the Alpine Meadows Campground are available on a first-come, first-served basis. Campsites are outfitted with tables, fire rings, grills, water, and restrooms. Two campsites are handicapped accessible and available by reservation; call the park ranger at (530) 587-8113. The campground is open from approximately May 15 to Oct 15, weather permitting.

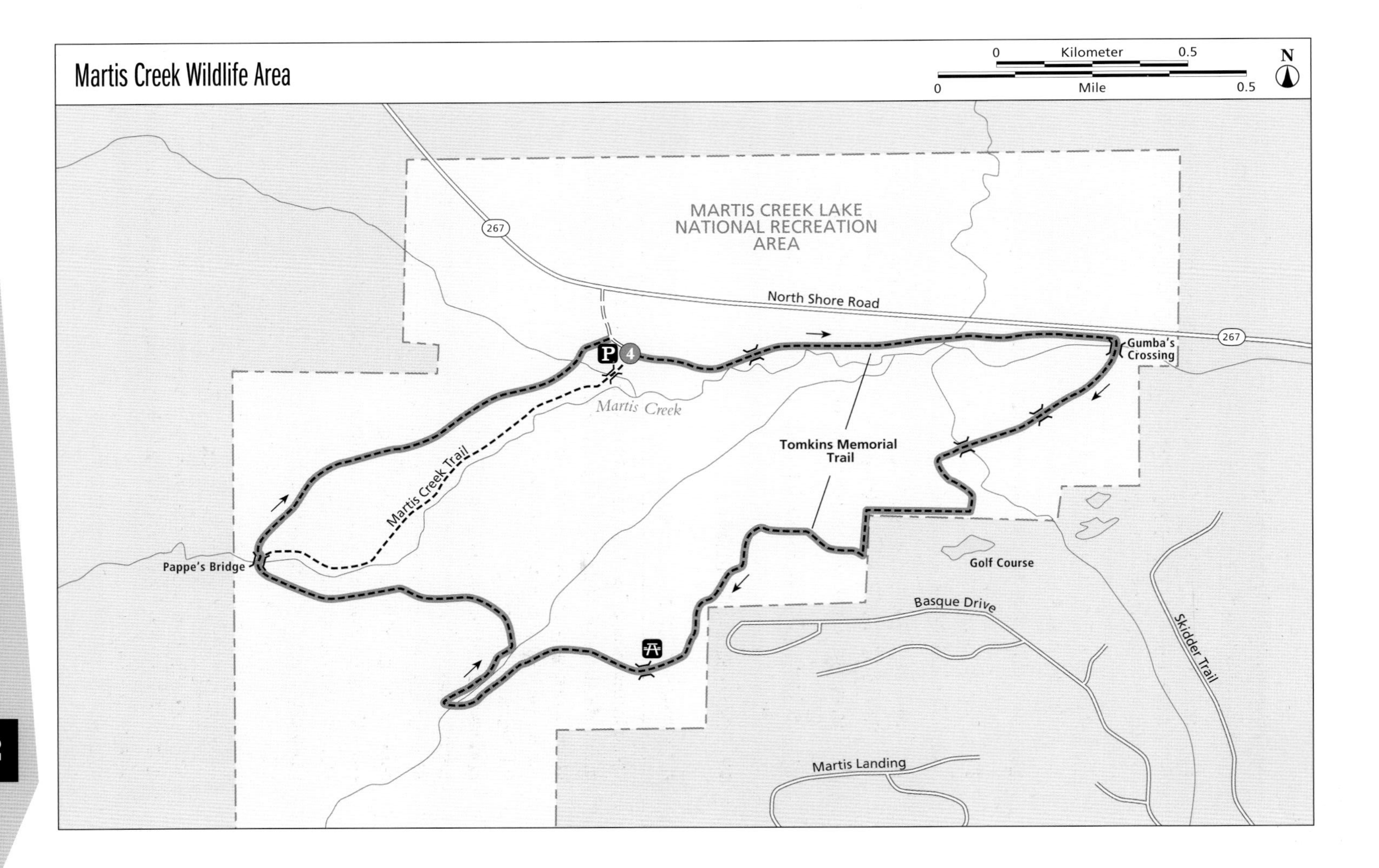

Martis Creek Wildlife Area
0
Kilometer
0.5
0
Mile
0.5
N
MARTIS CREEK LAKE NATIONAL RECREATION AREA
267
North Shore Road
267
Gumba's Crossing
P
4
Martis Creek
Martis Creek Trail
Tomkins Memorial Trail
Pappe's Bridge
Golf Course
Basque Drive
Skidder Trail
Martis Landing

Honorable Mention

Northwoods Nature Trail at Tahoe Donner

The meadows and woodlands surrounding Trout Creek in the Tahoe Donner subdivision north of Truckee provide a peaceful setting for this 2.1-mile-long nature loop. The boardwalk section is particularly inviting, with wildflowers flourishing in late spring and summer. The path is lined with interpretive signs describing the flora and fauna of the area.

The nature trail is part of a network of multiuse trails offering a variety of opportunities for exploration in the western reaches of Tahoe Donner. Many follow fire roads and offer great views of Donner Lake and the Truckee River valley. A trail map created by the Tahoe Donner Association is available at the trailhead; both a nature trail interpretive guide and the trail map can be found at www.tahoedonner.com.

To reach the trailhead from Truckee, head west on I-80 to the Donner Pass Road exit. Go right (east) on Donner Pass Road for 0.4 mile to Northwoods Boulevard. Turn left (north) onto Northwoods Boulevard and go 1.4 miles to the Northwoods Clubhouse and parking lot on the right (east). The signed trailhead is in the northwest corner of the clubhouse parking lot. Restrooms and information are available at the clubhouse.

The ski slopes of Northstar form a snowy backdrop to the trail along Martis Creek.

NORTH SHORE

Galena Falls spills onto the verge of the trail that leads to the summit of Mount Rose.

Mount Rose and Slide Mountain dominate the skyline of Lake Tahoe's north rim, with a plethora of trails converging in and around the peaks. Scenic NV 431, the Mount Rose Highway, features spectacular views of the lake and provides access to Tahoe Meadows, a sprawling complex of marsh and grassland. Ophir Creek and Galena Creek are part of the Mount Rose watershed, each splashing down scenic drainages into the Washoe Valley. The Tahoe Rim Trail passes through the area, and the summit of Mount Rose is a valuable prize for any hiker.

A strip of towns lines the north shore, including Kings Beach, anchored at the junction of CA 28 and CA 267, Brockway and Crystal Bay (at the California-Nevada border), and Incline Village, a year-round resort town with all the amenities. Beyond Incline Village development is limited. Lake Tahoe–Nevada State Park protects large swaths of the mountain landscape, stretching from just south of Incline down the east shore.

5

Mount Rose

Panoramic views from the summit of Mount Rose reach north and east across Truckee Meadows into the basin and range of Nevada, and south and west across Lake Tahoe into the highlands of Sierra Nevada. It's a climb, but every step is worth it.

Start: The trailhead at the summit of the Mount Rose Highway (NV 431)
Distance: 9.6 miles out and back
Hiking time: 6–7 hours
Difficulty: Strenuous
Trail surface: Dirt singletrack
Best seasons: Summer, early fall
Other trail users: None
Trailhead amenities: Parking, restrooms, picnic facilities, trash-cans, informational signboards
Canine compatibility: Leashed dogs are permitted on the lower sections of trail; dogs must be on leash within 1 mile of the trail-head. Dogs are permitted in the Mount Rose Wilderness; owners must keep them under control and clean up their waste.
Fees and permits: None
Schedule: Sunrise to sunset daily
Maps: USGS Mount Rose NV
Trail contact: US Forest Service, Lake Tahoe Basin Management Unit, Forest Supervisor's Office, 35 College Dr., South Lake Tahoe, CA 96150; (530) 543-2600; www.fs.fed.us/r5/ltbmu. Humboldt-Toiyabe National Forest, Carson Ranger District, 1536 S. Carson St., Carson City, NV 89701; (775) 883-2766; www.fs.usda.gov/htnf
Special considerations: The summit of Mount Rose is at 10,776 feet. If you experience any symptoms of altitude sickness, descend immediately. Pay close attention to the weather: If thunderstorms are predicted, choose another day to hike. If storms threaten, retreat to the safety of your vehicle.
Other: The parking lot can be crowded and/or full on busy summer days. If you must, park carefully alongside the highway. An alpine start (early departure) is recommended, both to secure safe parking and to avoid the possibility of inclement weather.

Finding the trailhead: From the junction of NV 28 and NV 431 (the Mount Rose Highway) in Incline Village (at the roundabout), go north on NV 431. Travel the scenic highway for 8 miles to the summit parking area. The trail-head is located behind the restrooms and informational signboards. GPS: N39 18.790' / W119 53.859'

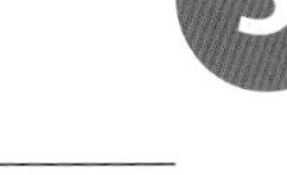

THE HIKE

Whether your base is in Reno or Tahoe, bagging the summit of Mount Rose is a necessary and relatively easy peak experience. It is among the highest ramparts of the Carson Range and with its neighbor, Slide Mountain, is an iconic element of Reno's mountain backdrop.

Strong legs, lungs, and willpower are prerequisites for this hike, which ascends nearly 2,000 feet from trailhead to apex. The summit is at more than 10,000 feet, so acclimation to altitude is also a prerequisite. If you bring a filter, you can get water at Galena Creek, but you should carry all you need.

Aside from a feeling of accomplishment, the summit of Mount Rose offers as reward a 360-degree viewscape that reaches into the Great Basin of Nevada, scans the rolling forested summits of the northern Sierra, and stretches across the expanse of Lake Tahoe, with the silvery peaks of the high Sierra shimmering on the southern horizon. You could call it breathtaking, but your breath will already have been lost on the final approach, sucked away by wind and altitude.

The hike begins with an easy, relatively flat traverse on a section of the Tahoe Rim Trail (TRT), skimming the flanks of Tamarack Peak. Views sprawl south across marshy Tahoe Meadows and down to the lake. Highway noise drifts up to the route, but once you top a knoll and begin to hike along northeast-facing slopes through the woods, you won't be able to discern the hum of engines from the wind ruffling the treetops. Openings in the woods allow great views down steep ravines into the Truckee Meadows.

The trail has a distinctly wild feel by the time you reach the junction of the TRT to Relay Peak and the trail to the summit of Mount Rose. Galena Falls spill down a steep rock face along willowy Galena Creek, and the meadow widening to the northeast blooms with wildflowers in spring and summer. This is an excellent turnaround spot for those not interested in attempting the peak.

Though the genesis might be different, the distinctively pinkish hue of this extinct volcano's slopes makes Mount Rose an apt name. Another apt name: The Bloody Rose, which is the moniker of an annual mountain bike event featuring more than 12 miles of climbing on dirt roads and singletrack.

To continue, bear right on the Mount Rose Trail, crossing the creek and beginning the climb up the pale pink slopes. Set your pace and plow on; there are no trail junctions from here to the top. Taking breathers is not a problem, given that nearly every stopping point boasts a great view. A saddle, where you'll cross into the Mount Rose Wilderness, offers a brief respite of relatively flat ground. Then the trail trends eastward and uphill along a ridge crest, with views alternating down into the high desert and out across the high Sierra to the south.

By the 4.5-mile mark you are above treeline. The views are panoramic, with the lake basin sparkling to the south. Push up the naked, often wickedly windy final stretch of trail to the rocky summit, where blocks of granite offer places to shelter for a quick bite and to pose for pictures with Tahoe in the background.

Return as you came. You'll find this a different trail on the return, with different views and different challenges. Take your time and enjoy.

MILES AND DIRECTIONS

0.0 Start at the Mount Rose trailhead at the summit parking area on NV 431, following the Tahoe Rim Trail and the signed trail to Mount Rose.

0.1 At the trail Y (the junction of the Tahoe Rim Trail heading south into Tahoe Meadows), go right (up the stairs) on the Mount Rose Trail.

0.5 Top a knoll and check out the views south across Lake Tahoe and northeast into the Truckee Meadows and Washoe Valley.

1.4 Round a knob with views of a lumpy wooded ridge.

2.4 Reach the junction of the TRT to Relay Peak and the trail to Mount Rose. Galena Falls is also at this juncture. Go right on the signed trail to the Mount Rose summit.

2.7 After crossing a scree field, reach a second junction with the TRT to Relay Peak. Remain on the summit trail.

3.3 Cross a tributary stream; the climb continues in the drainage.

3.75 Reach a saddle/pass and pass the signs denoting the Mount Rose Wilderness and Toiyabe National Forest boundaries. The trail continues to the right and is signed for the Mount Rose Summit.

4.5 Just below treeline, a small cluster of krummholz crowds the trail.

4.8 Reach the summit. Enjoy the views, then return as you came.

7.6 Return to the junction with the TRT to Relay Peak at Galena Falls.

9.6 Arrive back at the trailhead.

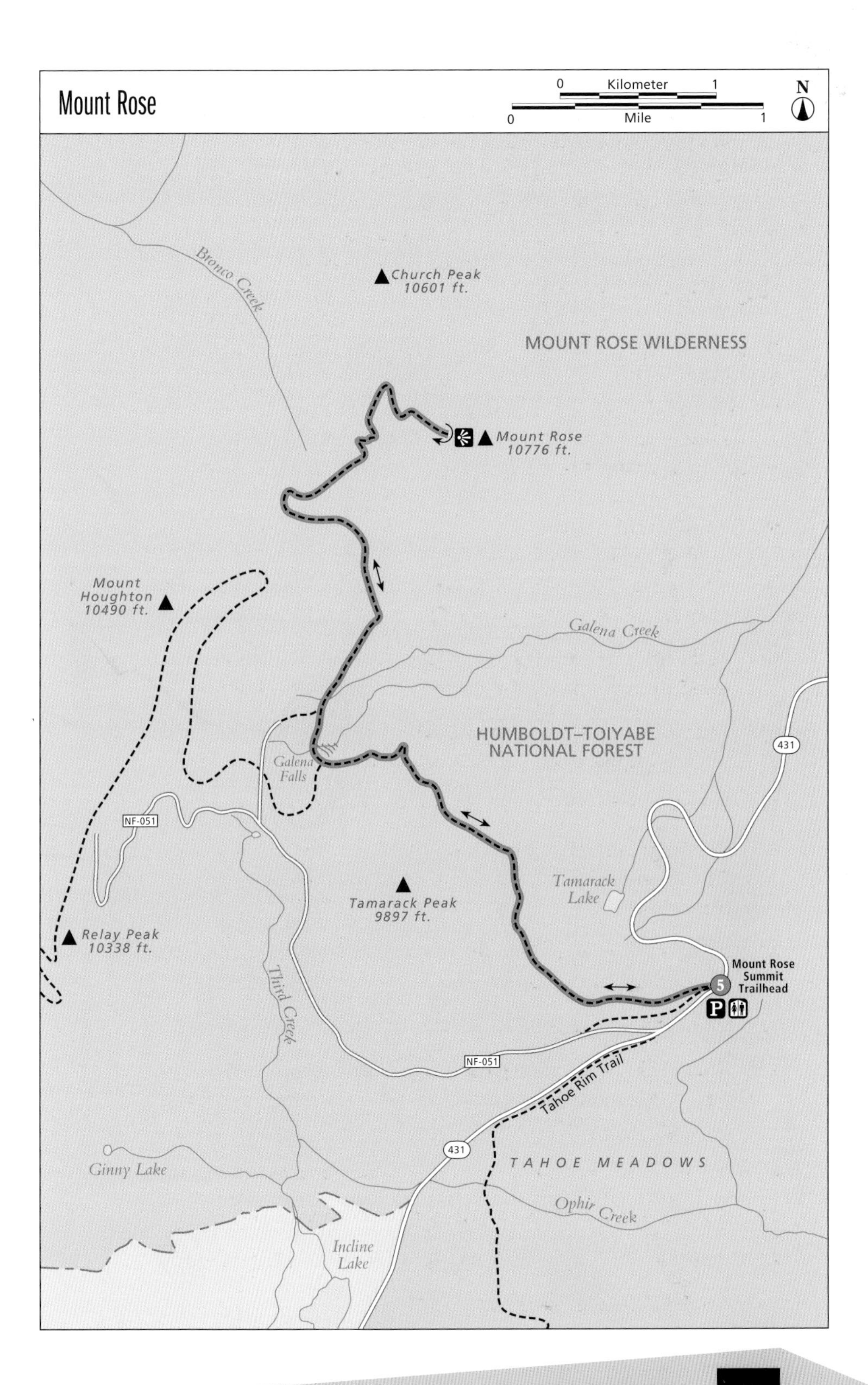
Mount Rose
0
Kilometer
1
0
Mile
1
N
Bronco Creek
Church Peak
10601 ft.
MOUNT ROSE WILDERNESS
Mount Rose
10776 ft.
Mount Houghton
10490 ft.
Galena Creek
HUMBOLDT–TOIYABE
NATIONAL FOREST
Galena Falls
431
NF-051
Tamarack Peak
9897 ft.
Tamarack Lake
Relay Peak
10338 ft.
Third Creek
Mount Rose Summit Trailhead
5
NF-051
Tahoe Rim Trail
431
TAHOE MEADOWS
Ginny Lake
Ophir Creek
Incline Lake

5

HIKE INFORMATION

Local information: Information about businesses, restaurants, and activities in North Lake Tahoe, including Incline Village and Crystal Bay, can be found at www.gotahoenorth.com. The Incline Village General Improvement District is another good resource. The IVGID administrative office is at 893 Southwood Blvd., Incline Village, NV 89451; call (775) 832-1100 or visit ivgid.org.

Local events/attractions: The Mount Rose Ski Area, which is on the Reno side of the pass and actually located on Slide Mountain, offers lift-served chutes, groomers, and a snow park for winter fun. The address is 22222 Mount Rose Hwy. (NV 431), Reno, NV 89511. Call (775) 849-0704 (in Nevada) or (800) SKI-ROSE (outside Nevada); www.skirose.com.

The views northeast from the summit of Mount Rose stretch across the Truckee Meadows into Nevada's basin and range.

6

Tahoe Meadows Interpretive Trail

Meandering through a lovely meadow beneath the summits of Slide Mountain and Mount Rose, this flat, friendly interpretive route is perfect for families, wildflower enthusiasts, and view seekers.

Start: At the signed trailhead in the parking lot on the east side of the Mount Rose Highway (NV 431)
Distance: 1.3-mile lollipop
Hiking time: 1 hour
Difficulty: Easy
Trail surface: Dirt singletrack
Best seasons: Summer and fall
Other trail users: None
Trailhead amenities: Parking, restrooms, information signboards. If no parking is available in the good-size lot, park in the pullouts/on the shoulder of NV 431.
Canine compatibility: Leashed dogs permitted
Fees and permits: None
Schedule: Sunrise to sunset daily
Maps: USGS Mount Rose NV
Trail contact: US Forest Service, Lake Tahoe Basin Management Unit, Forest Supervisor's Office, 35 College Dr., South Lake Tahoe, CA 96150; (530) 543-2600; www.fs.fed.us/r5/ltbmu. Tahoe Rim Trail Association, 948 Incline Way, Incline Village, NV 89451; (775) 298-0233; www.tahoerimtrail.org. Humboldt-Toiyabe National Forest, Carson Ranger District, 1536 S. Carson St., Carson City, NV 89701; (775) 883-2766; www.fs.usda.gov/htnf
Other: This was formerly known as the Tahoe Meadows Whole Access Trail. The route is wheelchair and stroller accessible for the first 0.5 mile.

Finding the trailhead: From the roundabout in Incline Village at the junction of NV 28 and NV 431 (the Mount Rose Highway), go right (northeast) onto NV 431 for 7.3 miles to the signed trailhead on the right (east). GPS: N39 18.433' / W119 54.436'

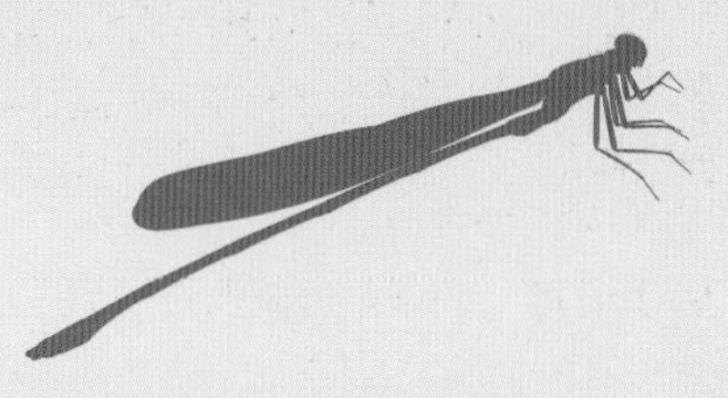

THE HIKE

Easy and scenic, the Tahoe Meadows Interpretive Trail explores stands of stately evergreens and a verdant meadow filled with wildflowers in season. The trail is at nearly 8,700 feet and features vistas of high ridges stretching south to Lake Tahoe, as well as up-close views of the stony summits of Slide Mountain and Mount Rose to the east.

The first part of the trail is accessible to hardy wheelchair users. Families with small children, whether in a stroller, a backpack, or toddling, can manage the entire loop. While paved trails on the shores of Lake Tahoe provide miles of opportunity for the wheelchair-bound to enjoy the great outdoors, this interpretive trail is the best "off-road" option. Though the Mount Rose Highway, a lovely and popular drive, is never distant, the scenery more than qualifies this as an alpine experience. And because of the altitude and depending on the winter's snowfall, the trail may hold snow into midsummer.

A trail sign behind the restroom marks the hike's start. Follow the well-groomed dirt track into the meadow; at an interpretive sign and boardwalk/bridge, the trail splits, forming a loop. Stay left (north), as the signs indicate, traveling the loop in a clockwise direction.

Boardwalks enable trail users in Tahoe Meadows to avoid the mush of the marshes surrounding Ophir Creek and its tributaries.

Though this section of the Tahoe Rim Trail gently climbs, the pitch is not strenuous. The path merges onto a patch of pavement, then reverts to natural surface as it traces the edge of the meadow. A pocket of altitude-stunted evergreens briefly blocks the meadow views, then the route traces the interface of forest and grassland as it approaches the head of the meadow.

Diverge from the Tahoe Rim Trail, which continues north and west toward Mount Rose, at a trail sign. Stay right (east) on the nature trail, curving south toward the Lake Tahoe basin and winding through a mature upper montane woodland. Interpretive signs along this stretch describe frogs and fish, butterflies and birds, human habitation and hibernation. Bridges span the meandering stream, and tiny fish that somehow survive and thrive at these heights dart through the dark, clear water.

The trail leaves the forest and proceeds across small bridges and boardwalks in the moist, sometimes buggy meadow. Views open into a blue void to the south: nothing but a bowl of sky, with the vast lake 2,000 feet below and out of sight.

Close the loop at the bridge and trail sign, then retrace your steps back to the trailhead.

Green Tip:

Carry a reusable water container that you fill at the tap. Bottled water is expensive, lots of petroleum is used to make the plastic bottles, and they're a disposal nightmare.

Snow Plant

A surprising parasite erupts every spring from the mulching duff of the forest floor. As the snow melts in late spring and early summer, the striking red snow plant appears. You can't miss it—the conical "flower" stalks quite literally glow like crimson lightbulbs when caught in the sun, and once you spot one, you'll see them everywhere.

Snow plant is relatively common in the lower montane forests surrounding the lake and on the eastern slope of the Sierra above Reno. The red color indicates the plants have no chlorophyll, instead gleaning nutrition from rotting plants on the forest floor and from a parasitic relationship with a fungus in the root systems of pines. Its scientific name, according to the US Forest Service's Rangeland Management Botany Program website, translates to "the bloody flesh-like thing." An accurate, if gory, description.

MILES AND DIRECTIONS

0.0 Start at the information sign.

0.1 The trail splits at an interpretive sign and bridge; take the left leg as directed by the trail sign, traveling in a clockwise direction.

0.5 Reach the intersection with the Tahoe Rim Trail, which continues north and west toward Mount Rose. Go right (east) on the interpretive trail.

0.8 Pass a trail marker and cross a bridge over the stream.

1.2 Close the loop at the trail junction.

1.3 Arrive back at the trailhead.

HIKE INFORMATION

Local information: Information about businesses, restaurants, and activities in North Lake Tahoe, including Incline Village and Crystal Bay, can be found at www.gotahoenorth.com. The Incline Village General Improvement District is another good resource. The IVGID administrative office is at 893 Southwood Blvd., Incline Village, NV 89451; call (775) 832-1100 or visit ivgid.org.

The Mount Rose Wilderness forms the backdrop for the easy interpretive trail through Tahoe Meadows.

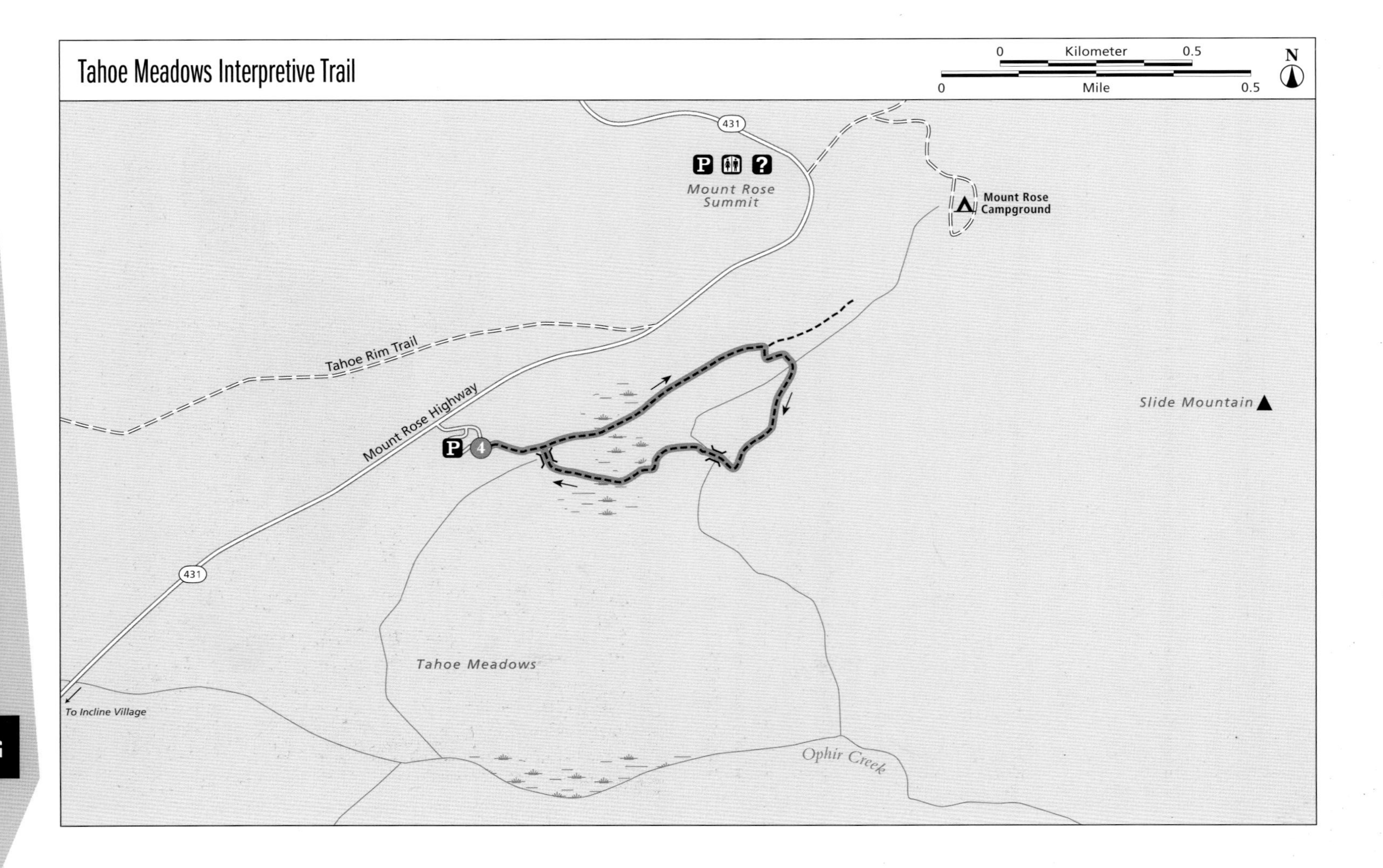
Tahoe Meadows Interpretive Trail
0
Kilometer
0.5
0
Mile
0.5
N
431
Mount Rose Summit
Mount Rose Campground
Tahoe Rim Trail
Mount Rose Highway
Slide Mountain
431
Tahoe Meadows
To Incline Village
Ophir Creek

7

The Incline Downhill

The Incline Downhill is popular with hikers and mountain bikers, offering access to lovely views, a rollicking stream, and a thigh-pumping descent and ascent.

Start: From the gated trailhead along the Mount Rose Highway (NV 431)
Distance: 2.75-mile shuttle; 5.5 miles out and back
Hiking time: 1–2 hours one way; 2–3 hours out and back
Difficulty: Moderate
Trail surface: Dirt singletrack
Best seasons: Summer, fall
Other trail users: Mountain bikers, trail runners
Trailhead amenities: Limited parking at the trailhead; more parking available across the Mount Rose Highway in a large, paved, roadside pullout
Canine compatibility: Dogs are permitted
Fees and permits: None
Schedule: 24 hours a day, 7 days a week, year-round
Maps: USGS Mount Rose NV and Marlette Lake NV
Trail contact: US Forest Service, Lake Tahoe Basin Management Unit, Forest Supervisor's Office, 35 College Dr., South Lake Tahoe, CA 96150; (530) 543-2600; www.fs.fed.us/r5/ltbmu

Finding the trailhead: From the junction of NV 28 and NV 431 in Incline Village, follow the roundabout onto NV 431 and head up toward the Mount Rose summit. The trailhead is on the right at the 3.9-mile mark, just above the scenic overlook. GPS: N39 16.115' / W119 55.835'

THE HIKE

Views of Lake Tahoe are framed by pines and firs at the top of the Incline Downhill. On the lower section it's a different picture: The path is wedged between a canyon wall and Incline Creek, which sprints toward the lake through a shady riparian zone.

This hike is described upside down, starting with the descent and ending with the ascent. It can be traveled in the other direction if you have access to parking on Tirol Drive or don't mind walking to the trailhead from the Diamond Peak Ski Resort parking lot. Starting on the verge of NV 431 eliminates the short stretch of street and virtually guarantees parking. Doing the hike as a shuttle is an option as well.

Starting from the Mount Rose Highway trailhead, the route begins with a traverse along a section of trail that follows the historic Incline Flume. The grade

Green Tip:
Car shuttles on point-to-point hikes add to the carbon load; loop hikes just take foot power.

Views of Lake Tahoe appear through breaks in the trees at the top of the Incline Downhill.

is gentle and the path meandering, with views of the lake at nearly every turn. As you drop toward the Incline Creek draw, the trail splits several times; at the first Y take the high track to the left, and at the second and third junctions stay right, crossing a stream that waters a lovely little meadow via a small plank bridge. Where trails merge just beyond the bridge stay straight and enjoy the views as you begin the snaking descent.

Round a sharp curve (a side trail breaks left to an overlook rock), and the trail enters the Incline Creek drainage. The pitch is relatively steep and the trail surface a bit rocky as you trace the creek downhill. Riparian growth—dogwood, willow, and alder—provide ample shade, with evergreens towering above. In early season look for distinctive red snow plant on the forest floor.

By the 2.5-mile mark you've completed the downhill. Cross the stream and follow the track, which widens to road width, as it continues behind neighborhood homes. A beaver pond is trailside a bit farther along, outfitted with a beaver deceiver (a beaver-friendly device that helps control flooding near beaver ponds). This makes a lovely spot for a break before the climb back to NV 431.

The trail formally ends at a chain blocking access from Tirol Drive. If you've left a shuttle car in the Diamond Peak Ski Area parking lot, follow Tirol Drive downhill to the resort. Otherwise, return as you came.

MILES AND DIRECTIONS

0.0 Start by walking down the broad dirt track. After about 300 feet stay left and begin the traverse.

0.7 At the unsigned trail junction stay left, on the high track, with a meadow below on the right.

0.9 At the Y, go right and down on the unsigned trail.

1.0 Cross a stream, then stay right at the trail split. Cross the stream again on a little bridge.

1.1 Where unsigned trails merge, stay straight (left). The downhill begins.

2.0 The trail parallels Incline Creek as it descends.

2.5 Cross the creek and enter the neighborhood.

2.6 Pass the beaver dam.

2.75 Reach trail's end at the chain and Tirol Drive. Follow Tirol Drive down to shuttle parking at Diamond Peak Ski Resort, or retrace your steps.

5.5 Arrive back at the trailhead.

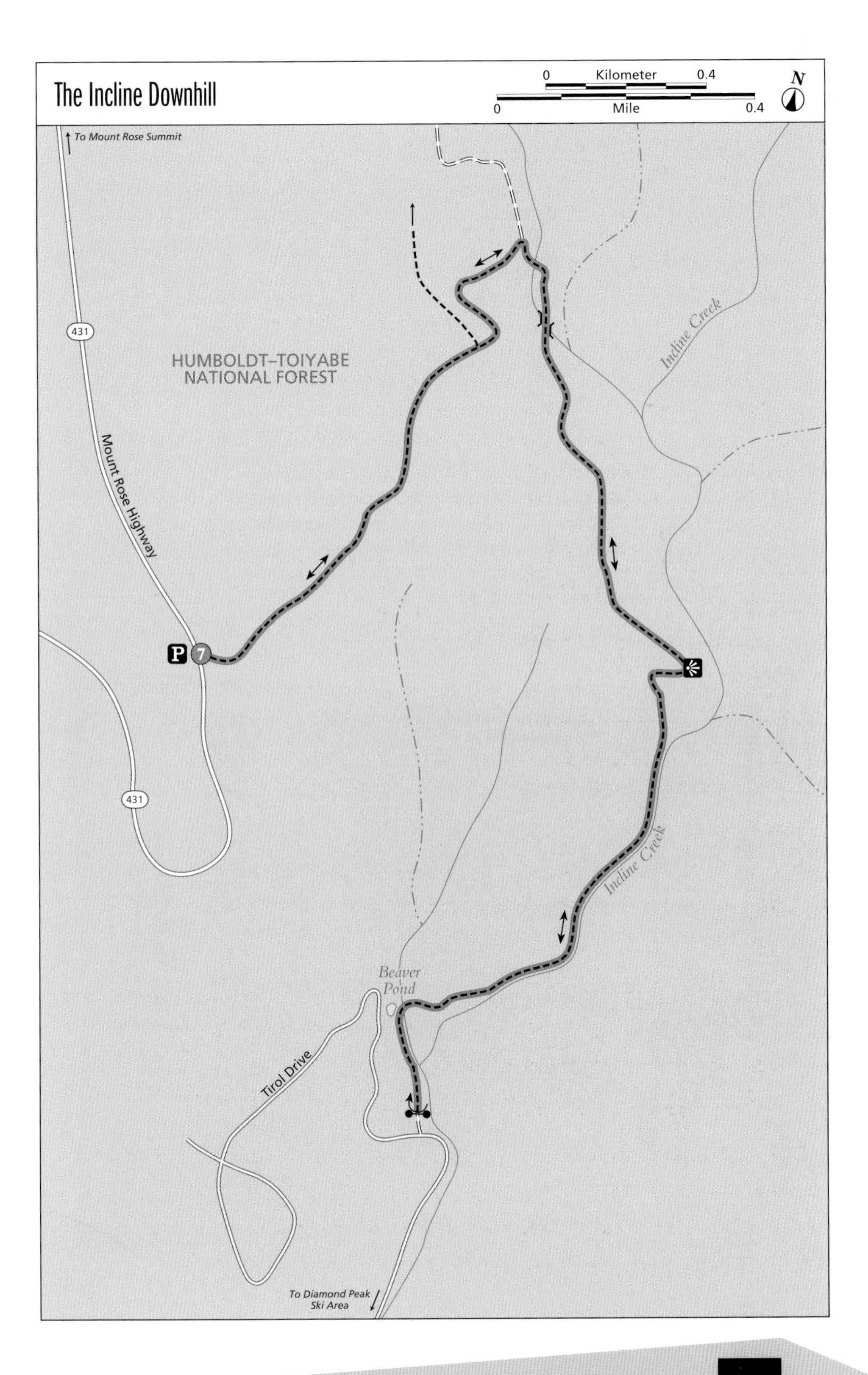
The Incline Downhill
0 Kilometer 0.4
0 Mile 0.4
N
To Mount Rose Summit
431
HUMBOLDT–TOIYABE NATIONAL FOREST
Mount Rose Highway
Incline Creek
P
7
431
Incline Creek
Beaver Pond
Tirol Drive
To Diamond Peak Ski Area

HIKE INFORMATION

Local information: Information about businesses, restaurants, and activities in North Lake Tahoe, including Incline Village and Crystal Bay, can be found at www.gotahoenorth.com. The Incline Village General Improvement District is another good resource. The IVGID administrative office is at 893 Southwood Blvd., Incline Village, NV 89451; call (775) 832-1100 or visit ivgid.org.

Restaurants: For a sophisticated meal on the shore of Lake Tahoe in Incline Village, try the Lakeside Beach Bar and Grill at the Hyatt Regency. Fresh seafood and creative salads are on the menu. The grill is at the junction of Country Club Drive and Lakeshore Boulevard; call (775) 832-1234 for more information.

Tahoe's famous Flume Trail, a must-do for many mountain bikers, lies farther south on the lake's East Shore. Mountain bikers have access to the section of the Tahoe Rim Trail between the Flume Trail at Marlette Lake and the Mount Rose summit on even calendar days.

A hiker enjoys the views from the Incline Downhill—as well as the ease of the descent.

Honorable Mentions

Incline Village Exercise Loop

The 1.1-mile-long Incline Village Exercise Loop features a trickling stream as its centerpiece. It is as urban a hike as you'll find on the North Shore, meandering through woods just off the beach and close to shopping and lodging. Frequented by dog walkers, trail runners, and families, the exercise stations seem an afterthought—except for those looking to firm up as well as mellow out. This is another spot where snow plant thrives once the snow melts.

A network of walking trails follows Lakeshore Drive and winds through the neighborhoods of Incline Village. Mostly paved, these paths connect businesses, schools, and recreation sites throughout the village.

To find the trailhead from the signalized junction of Village Boulevard and NV 28 in Incline Village, follow Village Boulevard toward the lake for 0.6 mile to Lakeshore Boulevard. Go left (east) on Lakeshore Boulevard for 0.1 mile to the Aspen Grove parking lot. The signed trailhead is just inside the parking lot entrance on the left.

Tahoe Rim Trail at Brockway Summit

The Tahoe Rim Trail crosses Brockway Summit, which straddles the high ground between Kings Beach and Truckee. Head south from the summit to Watson Lake; the trail heading north leads to the Martis Peak Lookout and beyond. The trip to Watson Lake is about 6.8 miles one way, making for an über-long day hike or a pleasant overnight trip. The trail to Martis Peak and the Martis Peak Lookout is about 4.5 miles one way, a nice distance for a long day hike.

To reach the trailhead, follow CA 267 west from the traffic light in Kings Beach for about 3 miles. Trailheads are marked on both sides of the highway, with parking available (though this can be tricky on summer weekends).

WEST SHORE

Heavy snowpack has sculpted these aspens near Page Meadows, bending their trunks but not stifling their will to survive.

A series of little communities—Carnelian Bay, Tahoe City, Homewood, Meeks Bay—line the west shore of Lake Tahoe. The towns offer places to stay and access to activities on the water, as well as touchstones for trails that lead into the high country.

Sugar Pine Point State Park is the outdoor enthusiast's basecamp on this side of the lake. Unless, of course, that outdoor enthusiast has access to one of the numerous private residences (or vacation rentals) that line the highway. Access to trails in the backcountry is primarily via Blackwood Canyon or through the state park, with other opportunities located off CA 89 as it winds west along the Truckee River outside of Tahoe City.

In terms of culture, Tahoe City is the West Shore's hub. Most modern amenities can be found in this strip of a town—restaurants, grocery stores, sporting goods, souvenirs, hardware, coffee shops, raft rentals (for those with a hankering to float the Truckee River), gas stations, etc. Paved trails parallel the main drag, offering walkers and cyclists safe passage from Dollar Point all the way to Homewood and beyond.

A former hunting ground for native peoples, established as a mining town for operations out of Squaw Valley, and once the end of the road for the Lake Tahoe Railway and Transportation Company, Tahoe City now thrives on tourism. The town bustles in summer, when the hikers and boaters converge, but the little burg is arguably even busier in winter, when the skiers descend. Surrounded by ski areas, including Squaw Valley, Alpine Meadows, Granlibakken, and Homewood, Tahoe City is a year-round destination.

Walkways and railings form barriers along exposed sections of the Rubicon Trail.

8

Five Lakes Trail

In the summertime, the bare rock underpinnings of ski slopes are revealed—and become hikeable. The climb to Five Lakes offers access (not lift-served) to the slopes near Alpine Meadows, and then mellows in the wilderness surrounding secluded Five Lakes.

Start: At the signed trailhead on right side of Alpine Meadows Road below the Alpine Meadows Ski Area
Distance: 4.2 miles out and back
Hiking time: 2 hours
Difficulty: Strenuous due to 1,000-foot elevation gain
Trail surface: Dirt singletrack
Best seasons: Late spring, summer mornings, fall
Other trail users: None
Trailhead amenities: Parking
Canine compatibility: Dogs permitted except where posted in the Granite Chief Wilderness
Fees and permits: None
Schedule: Sunrise to sunset daily
Maps: USGS Tahoe City CA and Granite Chief CA
Trail contact: US Forest Service Tahoe National Forest, 9646 Donner Pass Rd., Truckee, CA 96161; (530) 587-3558; www.fs.fed.us/r5/tahoe. US Forest Service Lake Tahoe Basin Management Unit, Forest Supervisor's Office, 35 College Dr., South Lake Tahoe, CA 96150; (530) 543-2600; www.fs.fed.us/r5/ltbmu
Special considerations: Given the elevation gain and exposure to the elements, do not attempt the hike if you have heart, respiratory, or knee problems. The trail is mostly shadeless and can be hot in the middle of a sunny summer day.

Finding the trailhead: From the intersection of CA 89 and CA 28 in Tahoe City, follow CA 89 northwest (toward Truckee) for 3.6 miles. Turn left (west) onto Alpine Meadows Road and go 2.2 miles to the trailhead, which is across from the second intersection with Deer Park Drive. Limited parking is available along Alpine Meadows Road; no other amenities are available. GPS: N39 10.749' / W120 13.790'

THE HIKE

The most arduous part of the trek to Five Lakes is at the outset, where switchbacks climb through an exposed thicket of manzanita, mule ear, and snowberry. Once you attain the high ground on the slopes of the Alpine Meadows Ski Area, with ski lift towers punched into colorful granite slabs, you'll be treated to lessening pitches and views across the Bear Creek valley. An exposed traverse of a granite-walled canyon ends in a thick fir forest that obscures the views and hides all but one of the Five Lakes for which the trail is named.

The hike begins on the switchbacks ascending the hillside north of Bear Creek. Switchback, then switchback, then switchback again—up through the scrub and onto granite slabs. Very alpine in feel, from the rocky section of trail among the slabs you can look down-canyon toward the Truckee River valley and up-canyon onto the slopes of the Alpine Meadows Ski Area.

Traverse to yet another switchback, then climb under ski lift towers into a saddle, where the trail enters a narrowing side canyon with black-streaked walls. Two switchbacks are built like giant stair steps into orange rock; beyond, the trail traverses to more switchbacks. At the outskirts of the fir forest, a sign denotes the boundary of the Granite Chief Wilderness.

A trail sign points the way as you climb into the heights toward Five Lakes.

Several trails meet in the woods. At the signed junction with the Pacific Crest Trail (PCT), go left (south) to the shoreline of one of the small lakes, where social trails lead to inviting rest spots on the water. You'll have to bushwhack and do some clever off-trail navigating to find the other, nearby lakes. Visit for a time, then return as you came.

MILES AND DIRECTIONS

0.0 Start at the GRANITE CHIEF WILDERNESS trail sign. It's all uphill from here, with switchbacks and granite steps aiding the climb. Set a comfortable pace and enjoy the views.

1.1 Pass under several ski area lift towers (you may wish there was a chair running by this point!).

1.25 Cross a small saddle and curve into a side canyon, passing a trail marker and a PRIVATE PROPERTY sign.

1.4 Negotiate switchbacks carved into orange rock.

1.7 Pass the GRANITE CHIEF WILDERNESS sign.

2.0 At the signed junction of the Five Lakes Trail and the PCT to Whiskey Creek Camp, stay left.

2.1 Reach the shoreline of one of the Five Lakes. The others can't be seen. This is the turnaround point.

4.2 Arrive back at the trailhead.

Options: The trail continues through a meadow and on to a second junction with the PCT at 2.5 miles. From there you can hike or backpack to Whiskey Creek Camp and other destinations in the Granite Chief Wilderness.

HIKE INFORMATION

Local information: Information about businesses, restaurants, and activities in north Lake Tahoe, including Tahoe City, Kings Beach, Brockway, Homewood, and other North and West Shore towns, can be found at www.gotahoenorth.com. The phone number for the clearinghouse is (888) 434-1262. The Tahoe City Visitors Information Center is at 380 North Lake Blvd., Tahoe City, CA 96145; (530) 581-6900.

Another source of information for town residents and visitors is the Tahoe City Downtown Association. Call (530) 583-3348 for more information; www.visittahoecity.org.

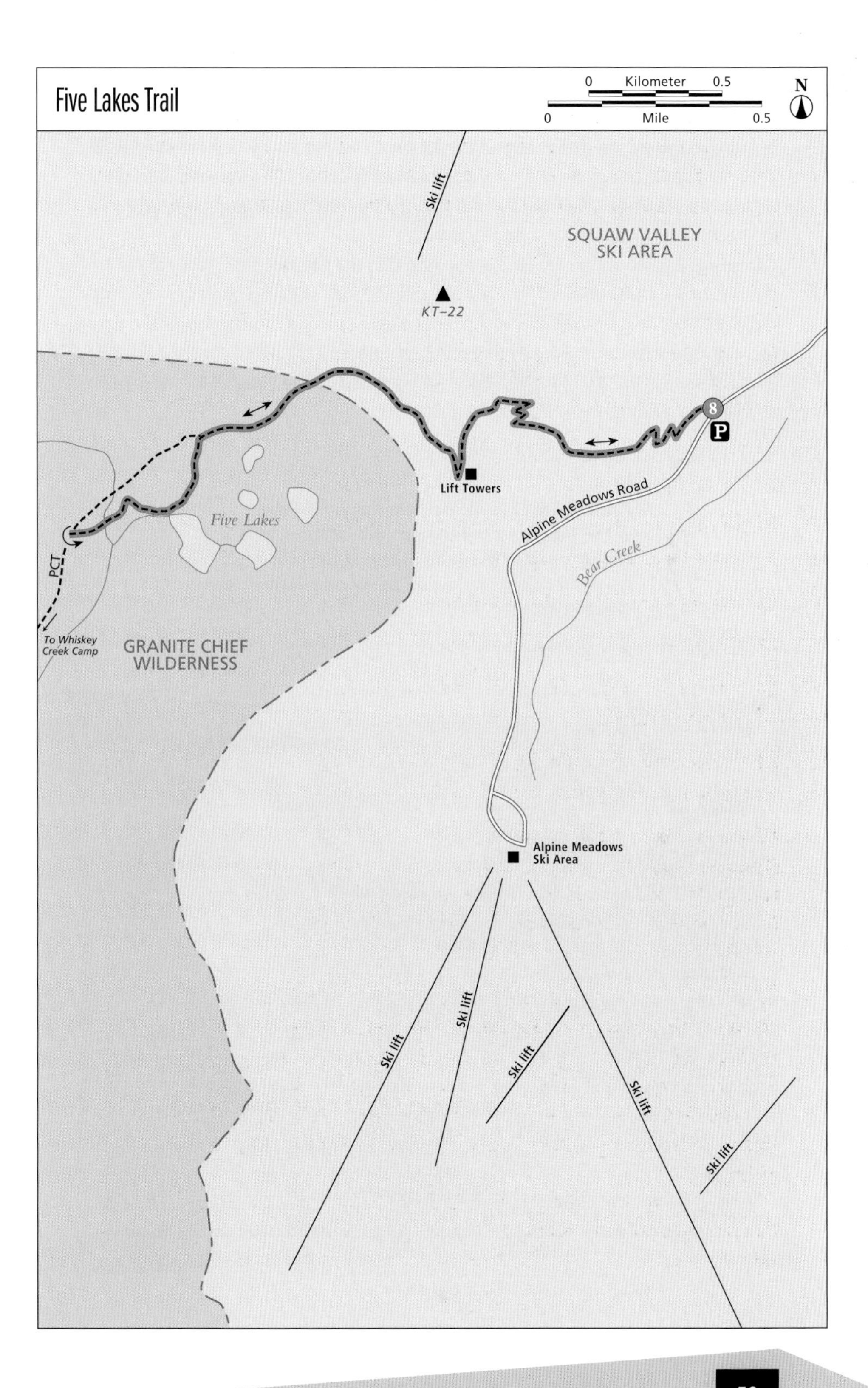
Five Lakes Trail
0 Kilometer 0.5
0 Mile 0.5
N
Ski lift
SQUAW VALLEY
SKI AREA
KT-22
8
P
Lift Towers
Alpine Meadows Road
Five Lakes
Bear Creek
PCT
To Whiskey
Creek Camp
GRANITE CHIEF
WILDERNESS
Alpine Meadows
Ski Area
Ski lift
Ski lift
Ski lift
Ski lift
Ski lift

Local events/attractions: Alpine Meadows ski area is sleepy in summer, but in winter the mountain comes alive. With its back door in Squaw Valley's backyard, the area shares a legacy of world-class winter sporting. The ski area is at 2600 Alpine Meadows Rd., Tahoe City, CA 96145; call (800) 403-0206; visit www.ski alpine.com.

Camping: Backcountry camping is permitted in the Granite Chief Wilderness. No permits or fees are required. No camping, campfires, or camp stoves are permitted within 600 feet of the lakes in the Five Lakes basin. For more information contact the Tahoe National Forest, Truckee Ranger District, 10811 Stockrest Springs Rd., Truckee, CA 96161; (530) 587-3558, or visit the Granite Chief Wilderness page at www.fs.usda.gov/main/ltbmu/home.

The Granite Chief Wilderness was established in 1984 and encompasses 25,079 acres of high country west of the Tahoe basin. It can also be accessed via Blackwood Canyon and Ward Creek Road.

Only one of the Five Lakes is easily accessible from the trail.

Truckee River Trail

One of the easiest and most popular trails in north Lake Tahoe, this well-maintained paved route traces the Truckee River from Tahoe City to Alpine Meadows Road and beyond. Enjoy views of the sparkling river, the lush riparian habitat that thrives on the riverbanks, the evergreen forest that blankets the valley walls, and the crowds that float the river and enjoy the trail with you.

Start: At the signed trailhead in 64 Acre Park near the junction of CA 89 and CA 28 in Tahoe City
Distance: 7.2 miles out and back
Hiking time: 4 hours
Difficulty: Moderate due only to length
Trail surface: Paved bike path
Best seasons: Spring, summer, and fall
Other trail users: Cyclists, in-line skaters, runners
Trailhead amenities: Parking, restrooms, interpretive signs. Portable restrooms are available along the trail. If you do a shuttle hike, parking is also available at River Ranch. The trail is wheelchair accessible.
Canine compatibility: Leashed dogs permitted
Fees and permits: None
Schedule: Sunrise to sunset daily
Maps: USGS Tahoe City CA; maps available at the Tahoe City Public Utility District office. No map is necessary.
Trail contact: Tahoe City Public Utility District, Parks and Recreation Department, PO Box 5249, Tahoe City, CA 96145; (530) 583-3440 ext. 10; www.tcpud.org

Finding the trailhead: From the signalized intersection of CA 89 and CA 28 in Tahoe City, go 0.2 mile south on CA 89 to a signed right turn into the large trailhead parking area at 64 Acre Park. GPS: N39 9.877' / W120 8.840'

THE HIKE

On hot summer days, the Truckee River is blanketed with river rafters. The clear water, reflecting the browns and grays of its rocky bottom, is topped by the neon blues, oranges, and yellows of the rafts occupied by boaters in equally colorful swimwear and varying states of repose. This riotous rainbow spills onto the Truckee River Trail, where the bright Lycra of cyclists, runners, and in-line skaters mingles with the pastels worn by babies in strollers and the muted greens, blues, and grays favored by hikers.

It is virtually impossible to get lost on the Truckee River Trail; if you wander into the water or find you are sharing pavement with automobiles, you've strayed. Mile markers line the paved path. A broken yellow line down the center of the path separates downstream traffic from those headed upstream. Proximity to the highway precludes any illusion of this being a wilderness hike, but the trail provides the perfect venue for an entertaining family outing.

The hike begins by crossing the arcing bridge to the north shore of the river, where the trail bears left (west) and occupies a narrow strip of greenbelt between the river and CA 89. At the outset you will pass businesses and cross several driveways on the border of Tahoe City. Then the trail drops waterside,

Fishing is just one of the pastimes that visitors to the Truckee River Trail can enjoy.

where dense willow sometimes hides the meandering river. The only intersections along the trail for a good long stretch are with the driveways and private bridges of lucky souls whose homes are perched on the riverbanks.

Sandbars in the river offer respite for the rafters; for hikers and other trail users, narrow social paths lead to small rocky or sandy beaches that serve as wonderful viewpoints, picnic sites, or rest and turnaround spots.

You can hike as far as you'd like, but if you have the time and energy, follow the trail all the way to Alpine Meadows Road and the River Ranch resort. The roughest part of this stretch of the river run occurs just above the restaurant at Bells Landing. Rafting the Truckee is far from radical, but the little bit of fast water before the river pools below the restaurant's outdoor seating area provides a quick thrill for the river rafters, and entertainment for both hikers and diners. Return as you came.

Brook trout were introduced to the Lake Tahoe watershed in 1877, part of an effort to eradicate shrimp that were clogging water pipes in the boomtown of Virginia City.

Bikers, hikers, skaters, rafters, anglers, swimmers: They all enjoy the long paved stretch of trail that offers easy access to a friendly stretch of the Truckee River.

MILES AND DIRECTIONS

0.0 Start by crossing the bridge in 64 Acre Park. Turn left (west) onto the paved path.

0.2 Cross the access drive for Tahoe City Lumber.

1.0 Pass a mile marker.

2.0 Pass another mile marker and a CONGESTED AREA sign.

3.0 Pass a third mile marker and a private driveway.

3.4 Climb the only hill along the route (it's short) to the rafters' staging area.

3.6 Reach Bells Landing and the inn at River Ranch. Have a cool drink on the patio, then retrace your steps to the trailhead.

7.2 Arrive back at the trailhead.

Options: From River Run you can continue west on the Truckee River Trail to Squaw Valley Road. The total round-trip is 10 miles.

The Truckee River trailhead in Tahoe City also serves as the junction with lakeshore bike paths that head north to Dollar Point and south to Sugar Pine Point State Park.

HIKE INFORMATION

Local information: Information about businesses, restaurants, and activities in north Lake Tahoe, including Tahoe City, Kings Beach, Brockway, Homewood, and other North and West Shore towns, can be found at www.gotahoenorth.com. The phone number for the clearinghouse is (888) 434-1262. The Tahoe City Visitors Information Center is at 380 North Lake Blvd., Tahoe City, CA 96145; (530) 581-6900.

Another source of information for town residents and visitors is the Tahoe City Downtown Association. Call (530) 583-3348 for more information; www.visittahoecity.org.

In Addition

Reflections on the Truckee River

The Truckee River hitches the high country to the high desert. It begins in Lake Tahoe, spills through the dam at Fanny Bridge in Tahoe City, rambles briefly westward past the Alpine Meadows and Squaw Valley ski areas, then curls east at Truckee and slithers down the dry eastern face of the escarpment into Truckee Meadows, where Reno lies. From there, the river runs northeast to its terminus in Pyramid Lake. Like the bass drum in a musical ensemble, the 105-mile-long

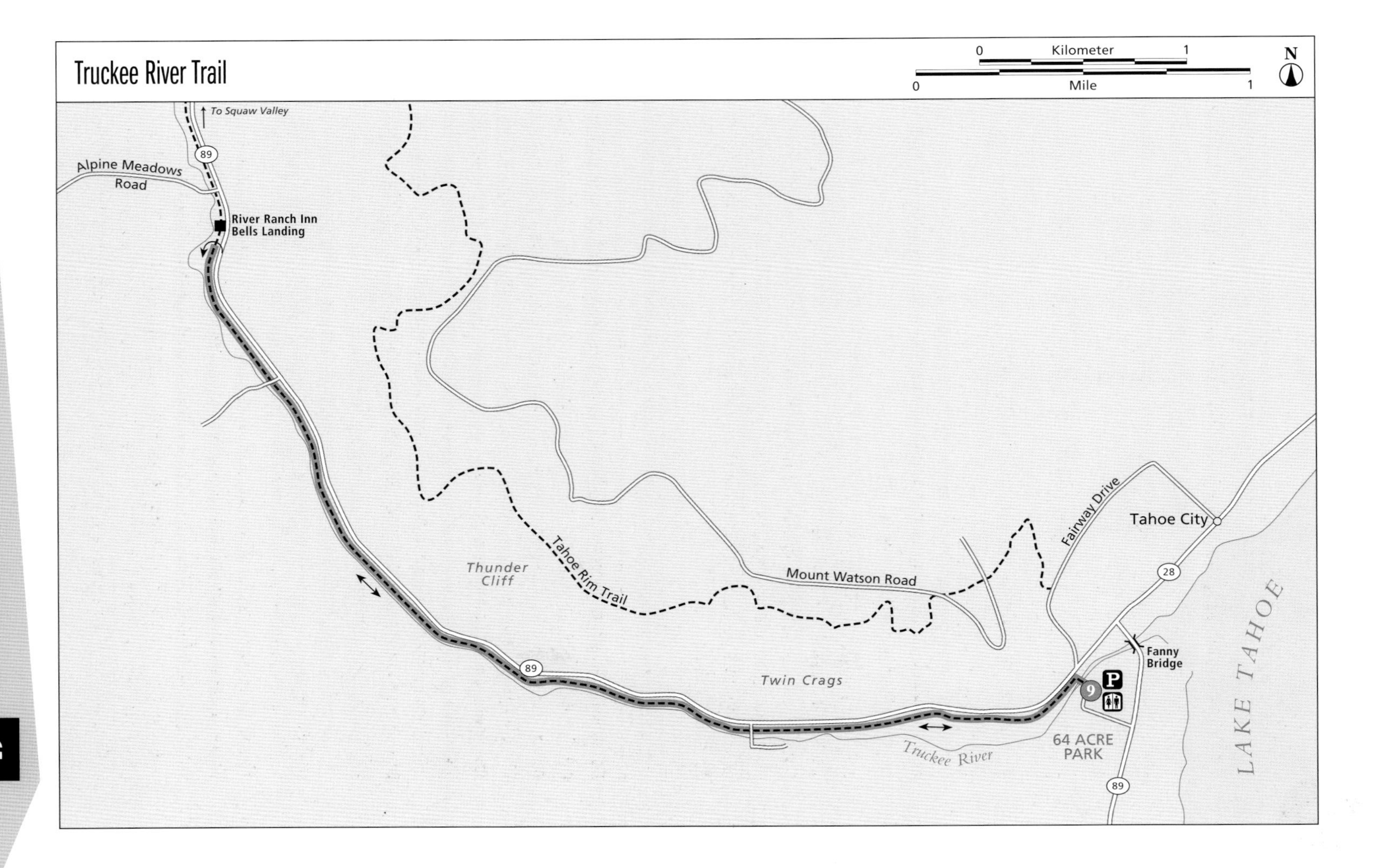
Truckee River Trail
0 Kilometer 1
0 Mile 1
N
To Squaw Valley
89
Alpine Meadows Road
River Ranch Inn
Bells Landing
Thunder Cliff
Tahoe Rim Trail
Mount Watson Road
Fairway Drive
Tahoe City
28
89
Twin Crags
Fanny Bridge
9
64 ACRE PARK
Truckee River
89
LAKE TAHOE

Truckee is the steady backbeat in the exotic composition of this section of the Sierra Nevada.

The Truckee's origins date back to the origins of Lake Tahoe, itself the product of faulting and glaciation. In that long-ago era the river fell out of Tahoe into the massive Lake Lahontan, which covered vast expanses of northeastern Nevada. Remnants of the ancient lake include Pyramid Lake and Lake Winnemucca, which dried up in the 1930s.

The river, reportedly, was named for an Indian guide called Truckee, or Chief Truckee, who led grateful emigrants through the Sierra via the river canyon in the 1840s. That Truckee River route was briefly abandoned after the disastrous Donner expedition, was later revived, and its preeminence was cemented when tracks for the Central Pacific Railroad were laid in the river canyon. The canyon now harbors a section of I-80, the main highway through the northern Sierra Nevada.

As you would expect, the river was essential to the mining legacy of the Reno-Tahoe area. Water from the Truckee was used to facilitate mining operations on the Comstock Lode in the 1850s and 1860s. Timber harvested from the slopes around Tahoe floated down to the Comstock mines in flumes that ran with water diverted from the lake and river. Water levels were adversely affected by mining activity, the watershed degraded by lumbering, and accumulations of sawdust clogged both natural and man-made waterworks. The Truckee was also diverted into irrigation ditches, which watered ranchland in the Washoe and Carson Valleys, and was dammed to supply power to burgeoning towns and cities.

The river did fight back, flooding the Truckee Meadows on a number of occasions. Swollen by rainfall and/or snowmelt, it breached its banks and inundated portions of the Reno-Sparks metropolitan area repeatedly. Dams and reservoirs throughout the watershed were constructed in the twentieth century (Prosser, Stampede, and Martis among them), sequestering water for agriculture and hydroelectric power, and also helping with flood control. In the late 1950s and early 1960s, the river was subject to a major flood mitigation project that included construction of channels to control flows through Reno and neighboring Sparks. Still, the Truckee would not be contained.

Growing awareness of the environmental damage being caused by interruptions in the Truckee's flow, along with the implementation of the Clean Water Act, the Endangered Species Act, and other environmental protections in the late 1970s, led to restoration efforts that are ongoing. These days the Truckee flows with relative freedom, with the health of the lakes at either terminus benefitting, as well as wildlife, ecosystems, and tourism along the river's length.

Page Meadows

Page Meadows hosts one of the best wildflower blooms in the basin. It greens up by late May, glows with color by late June, and remains a restful, scenic destination through the rest of the hiking season. A steady climb on the Tahoe Rim Trail leads to the meadows.

Start: At the signed trailhead on Ward Creek Boulevard
Distance: 3.3 miles out and back
Hiking time: 2 hours
Difficulty: Moderate
Trail surface: Singletrack and logging road
Best seasons: Late spring and early summer for the wildflower bloom
Other trail users: Mountain bikers, equestrians, off-road vehicles on adjacent trails
Trailhead amenities: Parking alongside Ward Canyon Boulevard, an informational signboard with maps
Canine compatibility: Dogs permitted
Fees and permits: None
Schedule: Dawn to dusk daily
Maps: USGS Tahoe City CA; Tahoe Rim Trail map for the Barker Pass to Tahoe City section available at the trailhead and online
Trail contact: US Forest Service Lake Tahoe Basin Management Unit, Forest Supervisor's Office, 35 College Dr., South Lake Tahoe, CA 96150; (530) 543-2600; www.fs.fed.us/r5/ltbmu. Tahoe Rim Trail Association, 948 Incline Way, Incline Village, NV 89451; (775) 298-0233; www.tahoerimtrail.org

Finding the trailhead: From Tahoe City follow CA 89 south toward Homewood to Pineland Drive (with large PINELAND signs). Turn right (west) onto Pineland Drive and go 0.3 mile to Twin Peaks Drive, where a sign points you toward Ward Valley. Go left (south) onto Twin Peaks, then quickly right (west) onto Ward Creek Boulevard. Follow Ward Creek Boulevard for 1.5 miles to the signed Tahoe Rim Trail trailhead. Park carefully on the roadside. GPS: N39 08.435' / W120 11.522'

THE HIKE

High country wildflower displays are understated, flowers blooming modestly in patches that mingle with meadow grasses. Some varieties, like mule ears with their bright yellow sunflower-like flowers and the tall white umbrellas of cow parsnip, border on flamboyance, but most flourish low to the ground, their subtle beauty best appreciated upon close inspection.

Page Meadows, situated above the Ward Valley at about 7,000 feet, is the perfect destination for the wildflower or mountain meadow lover. Rimmed by a thick evergreen forest with a lacy edge of aspens that have been sculpted into a tangle by winter snows, the meadow blushes in season with red Indian paintbrush, purple shooting star, pink pussy paws, white yarrow, and purple and yellow asters (among others).

The section of the Tahoe Rim Trail (TRT) that leads to the meadow begins steeply, with the sound of Ward Creek a pleasant accompaniment. The climb mellows by the 0.5-mile mark. The craggy headwall of Ward Valley, where the architecture of the ridgetops is defined by snow well into June and early July, rises to the west and is visible where the trees permit.

The section of Tahoe Rim Trail that leads to Page Meadows offers fleeting views of the peaks at the head of Ward Creek.

Once on the ridgetop the trail is intersected by a number of access and OHV roads, and the forest floor is littered with slash, but the route is clearly marked with distinctive TRT trail markers, as well as other signage. Follow the winding trail through the woods until the meadow opens before you.

A narrow path cuts through the thick turf of the meadow, which can remain snowy early in the season. Portions of the route may lie underwater—in shallow vernal pools—into early summer. Cement landscaping tiles delineate the TRT and protect the fragile ecosystem (they also help keep hikers' boots dry), and side trails branch off to explore the meadow. The bugs can be voracious, so wear long sleeves or douse yourself in repellent—otherwise, you may not be able to linger long enough to enjoy the display.

The TRT bridges the main meadow and a smaller meadow through a narrow band of trees, then reenters the forest and rises to a sign noting the distances to Ward Creek Road and Tahoe City. This is the turnaround point. Return as you came to the trailhead.

Raised walkways help protect the fragile wildflowers that thrive in Page Meadows.

MILES AND DIRECTIONS

0.0 Start on the north side of Ward Creek, where signs mark the TRT and describe camping regulations.

0.1 At the signed junction with a steep dirt roadway, go left (west) and uphill through the woods.

0.5 The climb mellows at a bend in the road with views west to the head of Ward Valley.

0.7 Climb to a junction marked with an OHV sign. Trail markers for the TRT are about 25 yards ahead, as well as a sign for Page Meadows. Stay left (southwest) on the marked route, crossing two streamlets that may be dry in late season. The route narrows to singletrack.

1.1 Reach another trail junction and stay right (northwest) on the signed TRT, passing low posts that prevent motor vehicle access.

1.2 Arrive at the first (main) meadow.

1.5 Pass through a narrow band of trees to a second, smaller meadow.

1.65 Reach the trail junction with a sign noting distances to Ward Creek Road and Tahoe City. Turn around here and retrace your steps.

3.3 Arrive back at the trailhead.

HIKE INFORMATION

Local information: Information about businesses, restaurants, and activities in north Lake Tahoe, including Tahoe City, Kings Beach, Brockway, Homewood, and other North and West Shore towns, can be found at www.gotahoenorth.com. The phone number for the clearinghouse is (888) 434-1262. The Tahoe City Visitors Information Center is at 380 North Lake Blvd., Tahoe City, CA 96145; (530) 581-6900.

Restaurants: Gar Woods, 5000 North Lake Blvd., Carnelian Bay, CA 96140; (530) 546-3366; (775) 833-1234; (800) BY-TAHOE (298-2463); www.garwoods.com/index.html. Ah, the Wet Woody. A classic wooden-hulled boat skimming the blue surface of Lake Tahoe or . . . a rum drink that is a party in a glass. You'll find both at Gar Woods, along with a menu of appetizers and entrees that perfectly complement a day on the trail.

Camping: Ed Z'berg Sugar Pine Point State Park offers camping during the summer months. The park's 123 sites are equipped with metal bear boxes, where all food should be stored. Some sites are suitable for RVs, but they cannot exceed

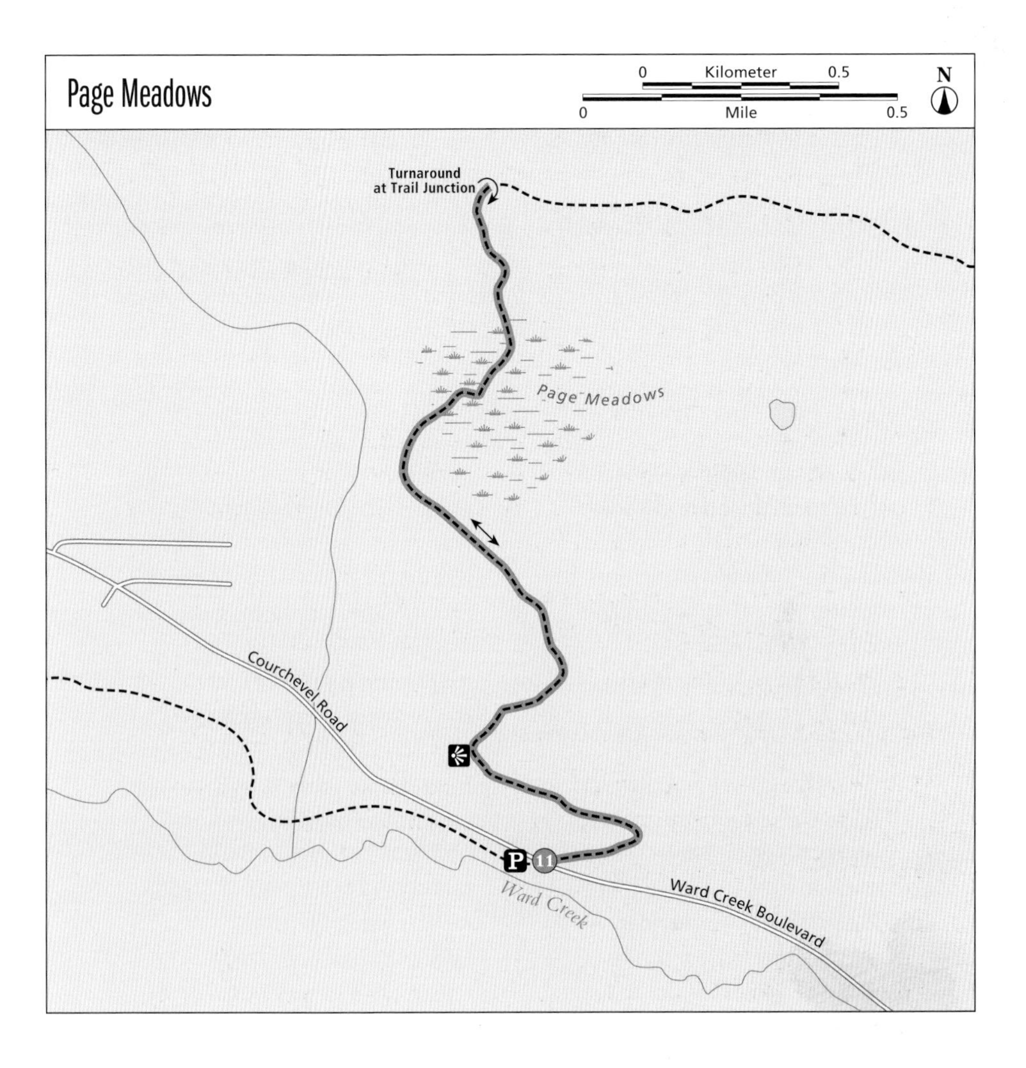

32 feet in length. Campers have access to all park facilities. A fee is charged. For more information call (530) 525-7982 in the summer; (530) 525-3345 year-round. You can make online reservations through the Sugar Pine Point State Park website at www.parks.ca.gov; the link will take you to the park's ReserveAmerica (www.reserveamerica.com) page.

Green Tip:
Consider citronella as an effective natural mosquito repellent.

11

Ellis Lake

All the work you'll do climbing onto the ridge above Blackwood Canyon is more than rewarded by the views from the top, where you'll look down onto Lake Tahoe in one direction and onto the polished granite domes and aprons of the Desolation Wilderness in the other. The goal is peaceful Ellis Lake, a rewarding destination for those with thighs of steel.

Start: At the signed trailhead in the dirt parking lot atop Barker Pass
Distance: 2 miles out and back to ridgetop views; 5 miles out and back to Ellis Lake
Hiking time: 1.5 hours to the ridgetop; 3 hours to Ellis Lake
Difficulty: Strenuous
Trail surface: Rocky singletrack
Best seasons: Summer, fall
Other trail users: The occasional mountain biker; the even more occasional motorcycle rider
Trailhead amenities: Limited parking in a small dirt lot at the trailhead; additional parking in pullouts along Barker Pass Road
Canine compatibility: Leashed dogs permitted
Fees and permits: None
Schedule: Sunrise to sunset daily
Maps: USGS Homewood CA
Trail contact: For the trail, contact US Forest Service Tahoe National Forest, 9646 Donner Pass Rd., Truckee, CA 96161; (530) 587-3558; www.fs.fed.us/r5/tahoe. For trailhead access via Barker Pass Road contact the US Forest Service Lake Tahoe Basin Management Unit, Forest Supervisor's Office, 35 College Dr., South Lake Tahoe, CA 96150; (530) 543-2600; www.fs.fed.us/r5/ltbmu.
Special considerations: Do not attempt this steep climb if you have heart, respiratory, or knee problems. Barker Pass Road to the summit receives heavy winter snow and typically does not open until mid-June.

Finding the trailhead: From Tahoe City take CA 89 south for 4.1 miles to the turnoff marked for Kaspian and Blackwood Canyon. Turn right (west) onto Barker Pass Road. Stay left (south) where the road splits, crossing Blackwood Creek, and go about 7 miles to the signed trailhead on the left (west) side of the road just before the end of the pavement. GPS: N39 04.309' / W120 13.868'

THE HIKE

The splendor of the northern Sierra is showcased atop the rocky ridge crested by the Ellis Peak Trail. Cliffs drop sharply into the wooded greenery of Blackwood Canyon, with Lake Tahoe an inky stain on the gray and green landscape. The forbidding gunmetal ramparts of the Desolation Wilderness, an impressive expanse of flowing granite, lingering snowfields, and small, iridescent lakes, lie to the west.

Beyond this aerie, the Sierra shows yet another aspect of its makeup. As the trail drops off the ridge on approach to Ellis Lake, towering firs create a shady canopy, and the dense pack of fallen needles on the forest floor muffles the footfalls of hikers. Thunderhead-dark, the battlements of Ellis Peak rise above peaceful Ellis Lake, a pretty tarn in a classic alpine setting of evergreens and talus.

This hike begins with a relatively brutal climb up steep switchbacks. The views begin as you traverse a ridgetop field dense with broad-leafed mule ear and wildflowers that hunker close to the ground. Tortured evergreens turn barren backsides to the prevailing west wind, forming a spindly windbreak as the route passes precipitous rock outcrops that hover over Blackwood Canyon.

The trail to Ellis Lake leads along a high ridge with views of Lake Tahoe and the Desolation Wilderness.

Uninterrupted sunlight and tundra grasses blanket the hike's highest points. Wind-lashed trees hook over the trail; look for a side trail leading left (east) onto a lovely rock perch where 360-degree views can be enjoyed. This is a great turnaround point for those who may not be able or willing to go all the way to Ellis Lake.

Beyond the overlook rocks, the trail descends into forest. The drop begins gradually but grows steeper before the pitch moderates amid thick, lichen-coated firs. Skirt a meadow on the right (west) side of the trail, then begin a gentle climb. The trail curls through a stand of old firs to a marked trail junction. Go left (east) on the gravel roadway, passing a shallow pond that lies in a depression on the left (north).

The final stretch skirts a talus field that spills from the cliffs of Ellis Peak. A mixed pine-fir forest circles three-quarters of the bottle-green lake, with a steep spill of talus pouring into the water on the south shore. Alpine scrub hugs the slope above the rockfall. Once you've enjoyed the lake's amenities—take a swim if the weather permits and the water doesn't numb your feet before you submerge—return as you came.

MILES AND DIRECTIONS

0.0 Start by passing the trail sign and climbing steep switchbacks into the woods.

0.4 The climb mellows as you reach a saddle with views of Lake Tahoe to the east, Loon Lake to the west, and the Desolation Wilderness to the southwest.

1.0 Follow the ridgeback up to where it mellows and offers viewpoints from overlook rocks. This is a nice turnaround point for those without the time or wherewithal to continue to Ellis Lake. To reach the lake, follow the obvious route heading south, which drops into the woods.

2.2 Reach the marked junction where the trail intersects a gravel road. Go left (north) on the roadway toward Ellis Lake. The singletrack that rises straight ahead (east) climbs to Ellis Peak. The road leading right (south) drops to the McKinney Rubicon Trail.

2.5 Arrive at Ellis Lake. Enjoy the scene, then retrace your steps.

5.0 Arrive back at the trailhead.

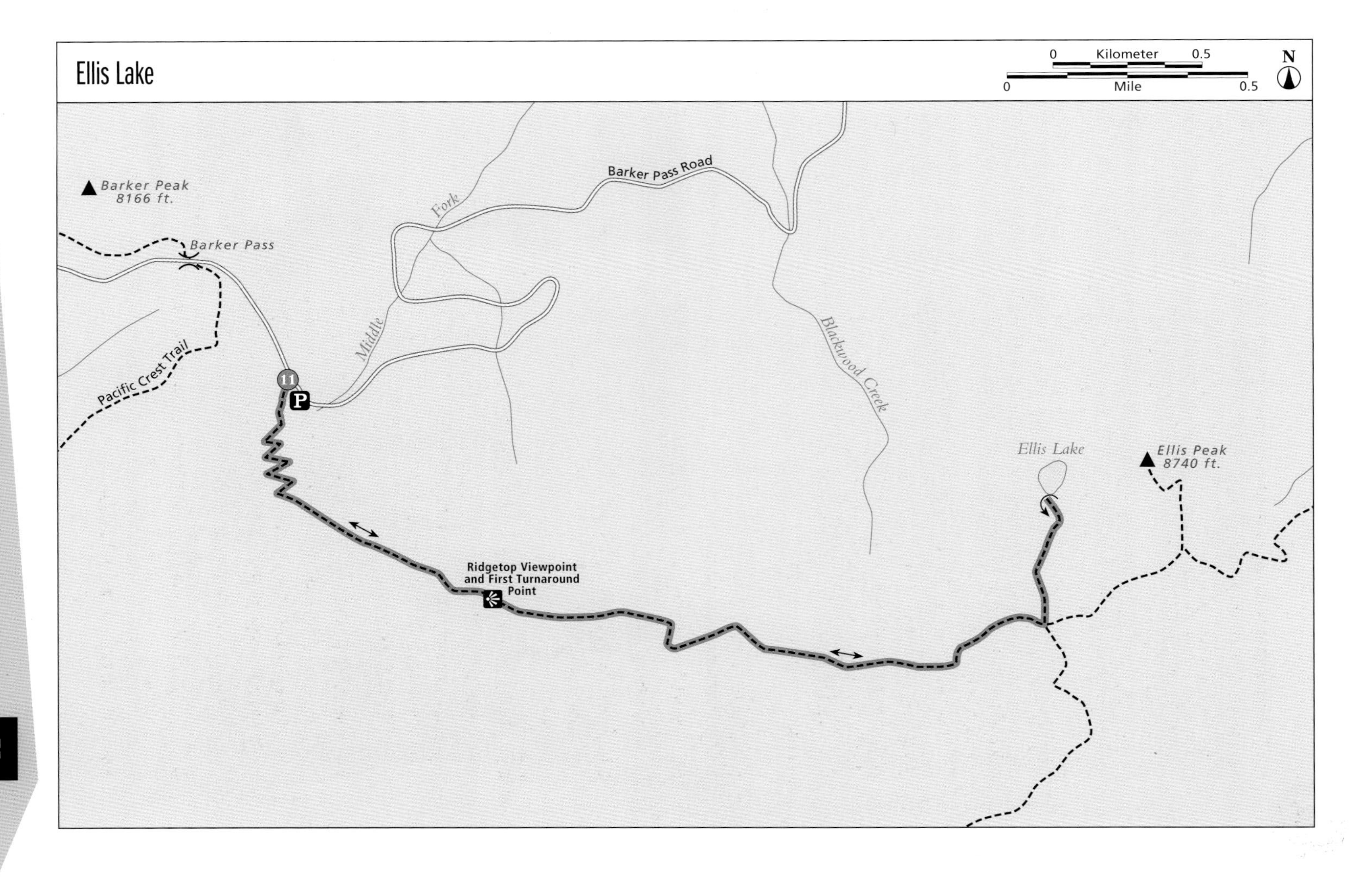
Ellis Lake
0
Kilometer
0.5
0
Mile
0.5
N
Barker Peak
8166 ft.
Barker Pass
Pacific Crest Trail
11
P
Middle
Fork
Barker Pass Road
Blackwood Creek
Ridgetop Viewpoint
and First Turnaround
Point
Ellis Lake
Ellis Peak
8740 ft.

HIKE INFORMATION

Local information: Information about businesses, restaurants, and activities in north Lake Tahoe, including Tahoe City, Kings Beach, Brockway, Homewood, and other North and West Shore towns, can be found at www.gotahoenorth.com. The phone number for the clearinghouse is (888) 434-1262. The Tahoe City Visitors Information Center is at 380 North Lake Blvd., Tahoe City, CA 96145; (530) 581-6900.

Camping: Ed Z'berg Sugar Pine Point State Park offers camping during the summer months. The park's 123 sites are equipped with metal bear boxes, where all food should be stored. Some sites are suitable for RVs, but they cannot exceed 32 feet in length. Campers have access to all park facilities. A fee is charged. For more information call (530) 525-7982 in the summer; (530) 525-3345 year-round. You can make online reservations through the Sugar Pine Point State Park website at www.parks.ca.gov; the link will take you to the park's ReserveAmerica (www.reserveamerica.com) page.

Weather-battered white pines cling to the high ground along the trail to Ellis Lake.

General Creek Loop at Sugar Pine Point

Walk in the footsteps (or ski tracks) of Olympic biathletes as you follow peaceful General Creek into Sugar Pine Point State Park's wooded backcountry.

Start: At the day-use trailhead in the campground amphitheater parking lot
Distance: 4.7-mile lollipop
Hiking time: 3 hours
Difficulty: Moderate
Trail surface: Dirt forest roads; paved road
Best seasons: Spring, summer, fall
Other trail users: Mountain bikers, trail runners
Trailhead amenities: Parking at the trailhead. Restrooms, information, and water are available in the campground.
Canine compatibility: Leashed dogs permitted
Fees and permits: A day-use fee is charged.
Schedule: The Sugar Pine Point State Park trail system is open year-round from sunrise to sunset daily. Entrance station hours vary; in summer it is open from about 8 a.m. until 8 p.m.
Maps: USGS Homewood CA and Meeks Bay CA; map in the Sugar Pine Point State Park brochure available at the campground entrance station and online
Trail contact: Ed Z'berg Sugar Pine Point State Park, PO Box 266, Tahoma, CA 96142-0266; (530) 525-7982; www.parks.ca.gov

Finding the trailhead: From the Y junction of US 50 and CA 89 in South Lake Tahoe, follow CA 89 north for 17.5 miles to the signed entrance for Sugar Pine Point State Park. From the Y junction of CA 89 and CA 28 in Tahoe City, follow CA 89 south for 9.2 miles to the campground entrance on the right (west). Go left (south), behind the entrance station, to parking for the campground amphitheater. This is the day-use trailhead; the trailhead can also be accessed from the campground. GPS: N39 03.38' / W120 07.287'

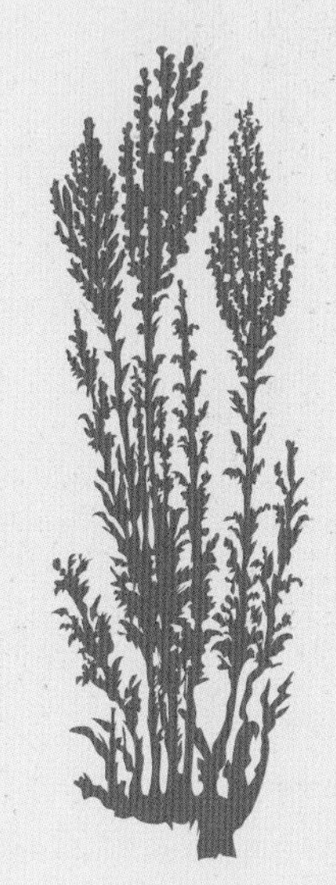

THE HIKE

The biathlon has to be one of the most challenging—and bizarre—sporting events ever conceived. Cross-country skiing (an exhausting sport even when you are not racing) is paired with marksmanship; top speed on skis and greatest accuracy with a rifle determine the winner.

The General Creek Loop follows part of the route biathletes used in the 1960 Squaw Valley Olympic Games, offering hikers a chance to gain a new appreciation (or sense of astonishment) for the sport. Interpretive signs near the trailhead describe the Nordic trail system established for the games. But the sign near the second bridge crossing General Creek, more than 2 miles into the woods, is a real eye-opener. The pictures say it all: Skiers sprawled belly-down in the snow with the rifles they've carried on their backs aimed at targets across the white meadow. Stand where they lay and imagine . . .

The hike begins with a tour of the Sugar Pine Point campground. The most direct route to the trailhead proper is to follow the main campground road to the westernmost campground loop; the signed trail begins between campsites 76 and 125. Other trails, including a nature trail, are shown on the campground map. Some loop through the woods and eventually intersect the trail up General Creek.

The dirt road that serves as the General Creek trail leads away from the campground through an open woodland. Pass a side trail that breaks left (south)

A verdant undergrowth thrives below the pines along General Creek.

back into the campground, following the roadway to the start of the loop. At the junction, go left (south) to the first General Creek crossing. A bridge spans the waterway; on the south side go right (west) on the gently climbing track.

Follow the creek westward for a meditative mile through the quiet forest, passing a burned area where the undergrowth has come back thick and lush. Bend north past the biathlon sign ("a contest of contrast") to the second General Creek crossing. On the north side of the bridge, the singletrack Lily Pond Trail heads left (west). Stay right on the broad General Creek Loop, which follows the north side of the creek back toward the campground. The route again passes through an old burn, where wildflowers, thimbleberries, and ferns flourish in spring and early summer.

Pass an unmarked junction with a dirt road on the descent to the end of the loop portion of the lollipop, staying right (east). The route drops to the junction near the creek crossing; from this point retrace your steps to the campground trailhead, then through the camp to the day-use parking lot and trail's end.

The Bounty of Sugar Pine Point State Park

While Ed Z'berg Sugar Pine Point State Park encompasses the cabin of one of the first settlers ("General" William Phipps) on the west shore of Lake Tahoe, the Hellman-Ehrman Mansion is the park's most famous unnatural attraction. Built by a businessman from San Francisco, the impressive 11,000-square-foot residence, known by the rather humble name of Pine Lodge, accommodated the guests of I. W. Hellman and his daughter, Florence Hellman Ehrman, throughout the early part of the twentieth century. Tours of the house are offered daily from Memorial Day weekend through Sept 30. Hours are from 10 a.m. to 3 p.m., from mid-June through Labor Day, with a reduced tour schedule in early June and in Sept. Call (530) 525-7232 for tour times.

The park covers about 2,000 acres, stretches more than 3 miles west from Lake Tahoe's shoreline into the Desolation Wilderness, and boasts 7,000 feet of lakefront beach. Swimming, fishing, boating, camping, and in winter, cross-country skiing, are all available. Aside from the General Creek route, hikers can also explore the Lakefront Interpretive Trail, the Ron Beaudry Trail, the Dolder Nature Trail, and the trail to Lily Pond. A few of the trails wind through the Edwin L. Z'berg National Preserve, named for the California state assemblyman who championed preservation and restoration efforts, and whose name was added to the park in 2003.

The park's brochure, along with a brochure describing the Olympic biathlon course that led into the General Creek drainage, is available on the Sugar Pine Point web page at www.parks.ca.gov.

MILES AND DIRECTIONS

0.0 Start in the amphitheater parking lot, passing behind the closed gate on the paved roadway. Ski trail and nature trail signs mark a convergence of paved paths. Stay right on the paved trail to the main camp road, then go left (west) on the camp road.

0.9 Arrive at the signed General Creek trailhead, between campsites 76 and 125. Head down the wide graded dirt road into the woods.

1.0 Pass a trail that leads left (south) into the campground. Stay straight on the main trail.

1.4 At the trail junction (the start of the loop) go left (south). Cross the bridge over the creek. At the trail intersection on the south bank, turn right (west).

2.4 Pass the biathlon sign and cross the creek via the bridge. The Lily Pond Trail heads left (west) on the north side of the bridge; stay right (east) on the General Creek trail.

3.1 At the unsigned junction with a dirt road, stay right (east).

3.4 Close the loop. Retrace your steps to the campground trailhead.

4.7 Arrive back at the amphitheater parking area.

HIKE INFORMATION

Local information: Information about businesses, restaurants, and activities in north Lake Tahoe, including Tahoe City, Kings Beach, Brockway, Homewood, and other North and West Shore towns, can be found at www.gotahoenorth.com. The phone number for the clearinghouse is (888) 434-1262. The Tahoe City Visitors Information Center is at 380 North Lake Blvd., Tahoe City, CA 96145; (530) 581-6900.

For the scoop on lodging, restaurants, and activities in South Lake Tahoe, look to the Lake Tahoe South Shore Chamber of Commerce. The chamber is located at 169 US 50, 3rd Floor, Stateline, NV 89449; call (775) 588-1728; visit www.tahoechamber.org.

Sugar pines, among the most massive of the pines, produce the enormous cones that litter the woodland floor. The cones can be more than a foot long.

General Creek Loop at Sugar Pine Point

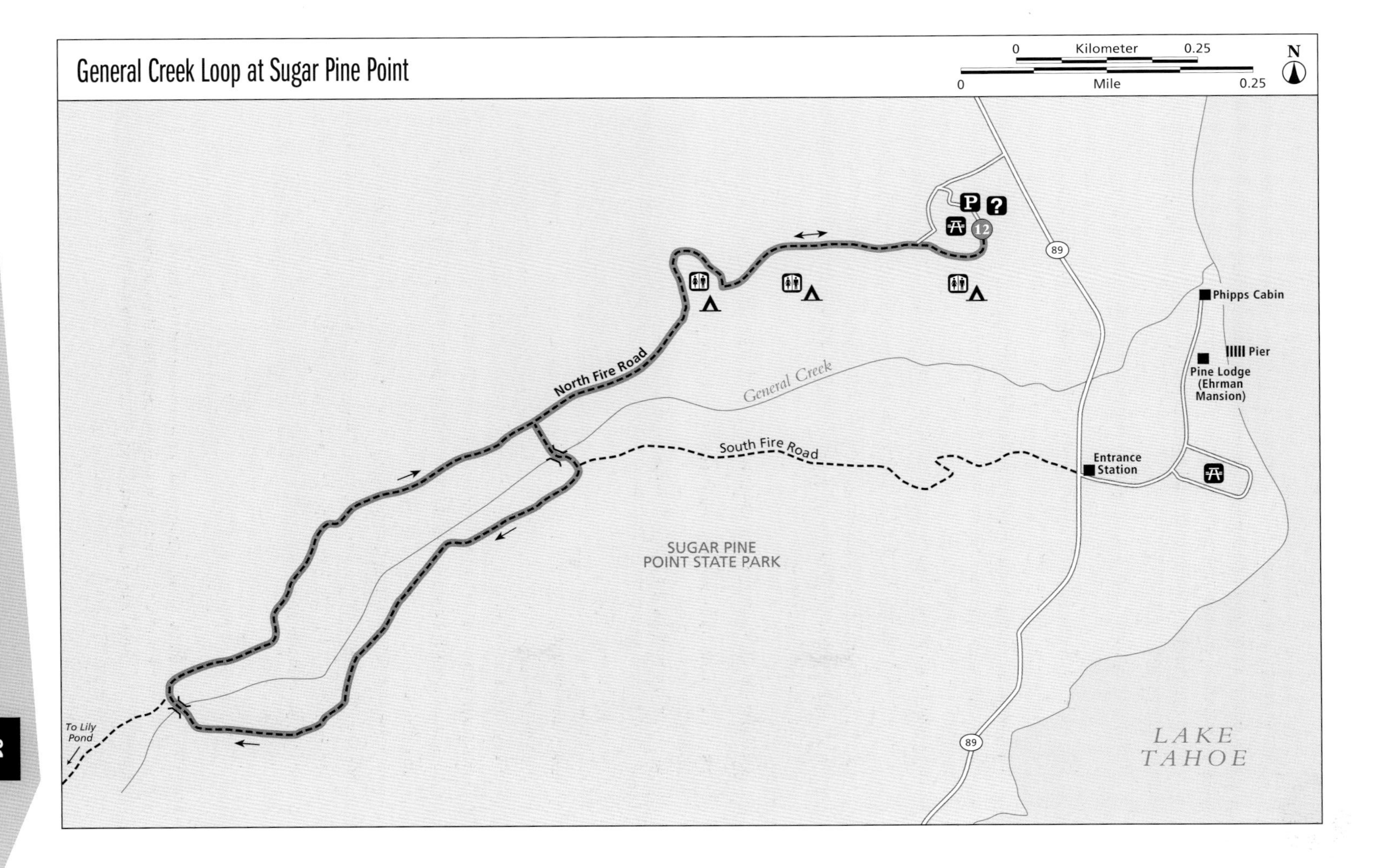

Local events/attractions: Cross-country skiing is popular at the park in winter, with about 20 miles of groomed trails winding through Sugar Pine Point Park's backcountry. Contact the park for more information by calling (530) 525-7982. A map is available at www.parks.ca.gov/pages/510/files/EdZSugarPinePtSkiTrail MapWinter2011.pdf.

Restaurants: Jake's on the Lake, 780 North Lake Blvd., Tahoe City, CA 96145; (530) 583-0188; www.jakestahoe.com. This lakeside restaurant and bar features delicious fresh entrees and appetizers, including ahi tuna poke rolls and excellent burgers.

Camping: Ed Z'berg Sugar Pine Point State Park offers camping during the summer months. The park's 123 sites are equipped with metal bear boxes, where all food should be stored. Some sites are suitable for RVs, but they cannot exceed 32 feet in length. Campers have access to all park facilities. A fee is charged. For more information call (530) 525-7982 in the summer; (530) 525-3345 year-round. You can make online reservations through the Sugar Pine Point State Park website at www.parks.ca.gov; the link will take you to the park's ReserveAmerica (www.reserveamerica.com) page.

General Creek was the site of the Olympic biathlon in 1960.

The Lighthouse and Rubicon Point

The historic lighthouse on Rubicon Point is at the high point of this loop, which also encompasses panoramic views of Lake Tahoe and a stretch of trail that skims a rocky cliff above the lake.

Start: At the trailhead parking area located about 1 mile down the park road
Distance: 2.5-mile loop
Hiking time: 2 hours
Difficulty: Moderate
Trail surface: Singletrack; rock staircases
Best seasons: Late spring, summer, fall
Other trail users: None
Trailhead amenities: Parking at the trailhead proper. Restrooms, information, and picnic facilities are available elsewhere in the park.
Canine compatibility: Leashed dogs permitted in the park; no dogs permitted on the trails
Fees and permits: A day-use fee is charged.
Schedule: The trail may be hiked from sunrise to sunset daily; visitor center hours are from 10 a.m. to 4 p.m. daily.
Maps: USGS Emerald Bay CA; map provided in the D. L. Bliss State Park brochure
Trail contact: D. L. Bliss State Park, PO Box 266, Tahoma, CA 96142; (530) 525-7277; www.parks.ca.gov

Finding the trailhead: From the intersection of US 50 and CA 89 in South Lake Tahoe, head north on CA 89 for 12.5 miles to the signed turnoff for D. L. Bliss State Park on the right (east). From Tahoe City, take CA 89 south for 15.8 miles to the park entrance. Follow the park road 1 mile east to the trailhead, which is on the left (west) side of the road. A limited number of visitors are admitted into the park; if you arrive after 10 a.m., check at the visitor center for availability. GPS: N39 59.353' / W120 05.915'

13

THE HIKE

The lighthouse that once warned sailors of submerged dangers off Rubicon Point is small and unassuming. It most resembles, of all the unfortunate possibilities, a wooden outhouse. But in the early days of the twentieth century, the humble structure housed a brilliant acetylene light that was integral to navigation on the lake. The light no longer guides boaters, but the structure, rebuilt in 2001, is a highlight along this loop through D. L. Bliss State Park.

The lighthouse isn't the only example of innovative high country construction along the trail. Climbing away from Calawee Cove, the path tightropes across the face of a steep cliff high above the lake. Views from this aerie are superlative and the exposure is thrilling. A word of caution: Though protected by a railing, this stretch is not for those afraid of heights, and children should be watched carefully.

The Lighthouse Trail begins by climbing through a fire-scarred woodland. It flattens atop a ridge amid evergreens and boulders, then drops through more hauntingly beautiful burned forest. Drop to a trail junction with great views. The granite staircase leading to the lighthouse is to the left and descends steeply to the small wooden structure, which is perched on a rocky shelf overlooking the lake.

The lighthouse on Rubicon Point no longer guides boats on the lake, but it makes a fine destination for a hike.

Climb back to the trail crossing and go right (north) on the Lighthouse Trail, which follows long, shaded switchbacks down to the paved parking area at Calawee Cove. The cove's little beach, though crowded in summer, is a nice place for a break or lunch. The signed junction with the Rubicon Trail is in the parking lot. Pick up that footpath and head up and south around Rubicon Point.

The trail is spectacularly exposed for a stretch, with a rail guarding against the abrupt drop, boardwalks spanning clefts, and head-thumping overhangs looming over the walkway. It's so invigorating you might forget you are climbing . . . until you reach the granite staircase heading up and past a side trail to the lighthouse. Stay left (south) on the Rubicon Trail, enjoying heavenly views as the trail flattens.

As you near the end of the loop, the trail curves away from the lake into dense forest. At the signed trail junction in a clearing, take the side trail to the right (northwest); the left-hand trail, the Rubicon, leads south to Emerald Bay and Vikingsholm. The dark, needle-carpeted path leads to the park road and the Lighthouse trailhead.

Tahoe Tessie

She may be a freshwater eel, she may be a massive Macinaw trout, she may be a sturgeon, she may be an ichthyosaur . . . and she may be a figment of the imagination. Regardless, she's part of the lore of Lake Tahoe. She's Tahoe Tessie, and she's been a mystery since the time of the Washoe.

According to online sources there have been numerous Tessie sightings over the last seventy years or so. But none has been substantiated, and Tessie's true identity, not to mention her very existence, remains entirely speculative.

Still, I'd bet there isn't a swimmer who has dived into Tahoe's deep blue waters, especially in the middle of the lake, that hasn't peered past her toes into the deep blue and wondered . . .

If you have a chance to boat on the lake, head over to the base of the cliffs at Rubicon Point. You'll find an impressive 30-foot rock below the lighthouse with a rope slung down its backside. If you are a thrill-seeker, you can use the rope to climb to the top and jump off. Or you can do what the sane people do, enjoying the daredevil show from the comfort of your vessel.

MILES AND DIRECTIONS

0.0 Start at the signed Lighthouse trailhead, crossing a small bridge and climbing into a burned woodland.

0.75 Drop to a trail intersection. Go left (north) for about 10 feet to an interpretive sign and the top of the stone staircase leading down to the lighthouse.

0.8 Arrive at the lighthouse. Check it out, then climb back to the Lighthouse Trail and turn right (north).

1.4 Descend to the parking lot and restrooms at Calawee Cove. Pick up the signed Rubicon Trail and head right (south).

1.6 Reach the exposed part of the trail, with the wire rail, boardwalk, rock faces, and great views.

1.8 Climb the granite staircase up to and past the trail to the lighthouse, staying left (south) on the Rubicon Trail.

2.1 Pass a trailside overlook.

2.4 Reach the clearing and trail junction. Go right (west) to the park road and trailhead.

2.5 Arrive back at the trailhead.

HIKE INFORMATION

Local information: Information about businesses, restaurants, and activities in north Lake Tahoe, including Tahoe City, Kings Beach, Brockway, Homewood, and other North and West Shore towns, can be found at www.gotahoenorth.com. The phone number for the clearinghouse is (888) 434-1262. The Tahoe City Visitors Information Center is at 380 North Lake Blvd., Tahoe City, CA 96145; (530) 581-6900.

For the scoop on lodging, restaurants, and activities in South Lake Tahoe, look to the Lake Tahoe South Shore Chamber of Commerce. The chamber is located at 169 US 50, 3rd Floor, Stateline, NV 89449; call (775) 588-1728; visit www.tahoechamber.org.

Camping: D. L. Bliss State Park offers camping during the summer months (the park is closed in winter). There are 138 sites, all equipped with metal bear boxes, where all food should be stored. Some sites are suitable for RVs, but they cannot exceed 18 feet in length. Campers are free to use all park facilities. A fee is charged. For more information call (530) 525-7277 or (530) 525-3345 (in summer). Online reservations can be made by visiting the D. L. Bliss State Park page at www.parks.ca.gov; the link will take you to the park's ReserveAmerica (www.reserveamerica.com) page.

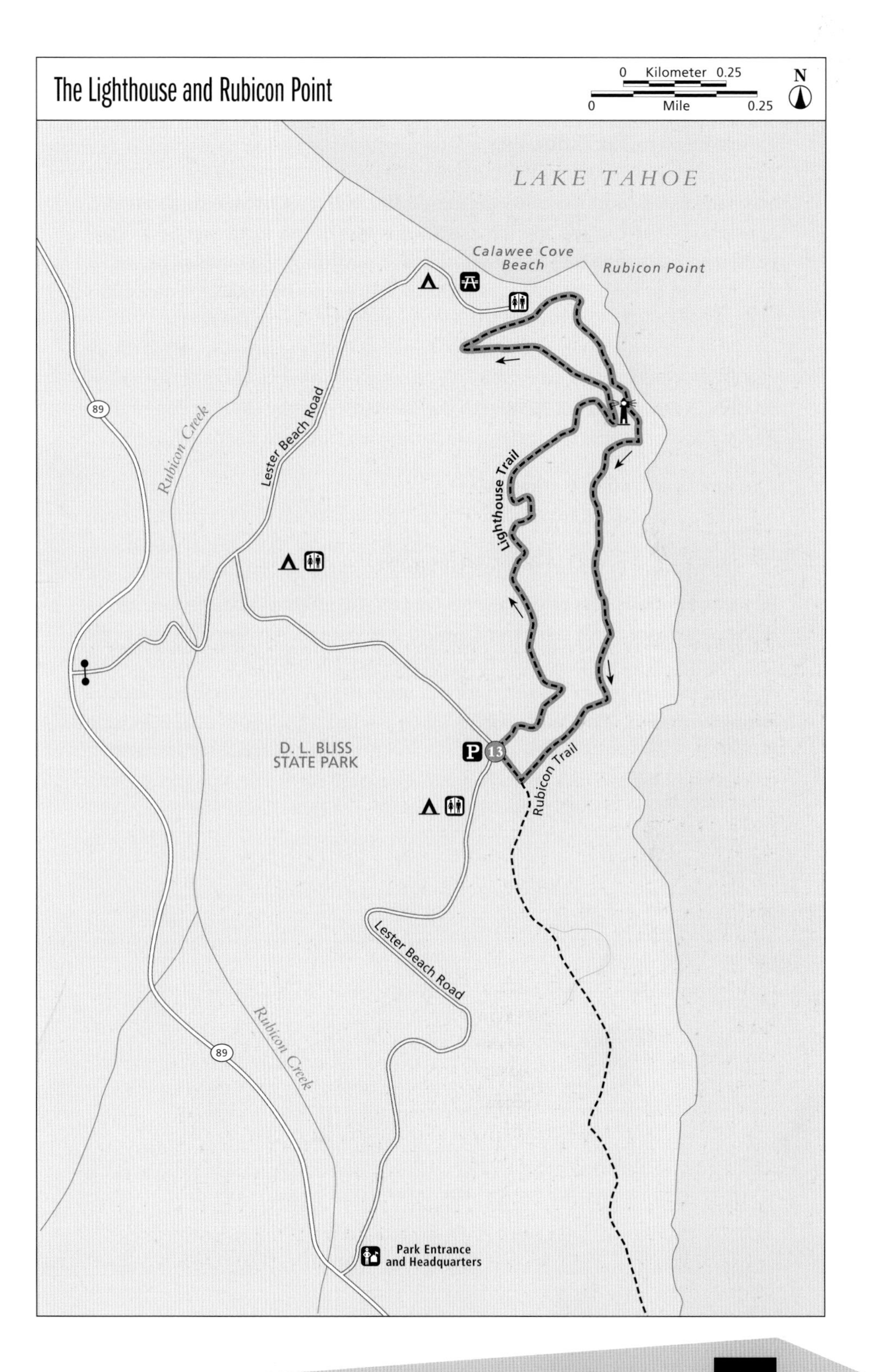
The Lighthouse and Rubicon Point
0 Kilometer 0.25
0 Mile 0.25
N
LAKE TAHOE
Calawee Cove Beach
Rubicon Point
89
Rubicon Creek
Lester Beach Road
Lighthouse Trail
D. L. BLISS STATE PARK
P
13
Rubicon Trail
Lester Beach Road
Rubicon Creek
89
Park Entrance and Headquarters

Honorable Mentions

Tahoe Rim Trail at Tahoe City

You can follow a section of the Tahoe Rim Trail out of Tahoe City for a nice out-and-back trek of about 4 miles (or more). The first recognizable turnaround is a vista point overlooking the Truckee River valley; to get there and back again you'll gain more than 800 feet in altitude and pass through stands of big cedar and patches of fern. The trail is marked by Tahoe Rim Trail placards and offers glimpses of Lake Tahoe through the lichen-covered trunks of the trees.

To reach this stretch of the Tahoe Rim Trail from the intersection of CA 89 and CA 28 in Tahoe City, take CA 89 west toward Truckee for 0.1 mile. Turn right on Fairway Drive, and go 0.2 mile to the parking lot at the Fairway Community Center. The trailhead is on the left side of the road, opposite the parking lot.

Pacific Crest Trail at Barker Pass

A 3-mile out-and-back hike heading north on the Pacific Crest Trail (PCT) from Barker Pass offers a sampling of the rigors and beauty of the national scenic trail. Rugged but well maintained, user-friendly but not overcrowded, the singletrack offers wonderful views of Blackwood Canyon, Lake Tahoe, and the Desolation Wilderness. It traverses a stark and exposed landscape, mellowed by the puffy pink blooms of pussy paws that cling to the inhospitable soils in season. Stands of lichen-dressed firs, a meadow thick with mule ear, and a spectacular avalanche slide path littered with deadwood lie along the first 1.5 miles of trail. Traverse a final stretch of open, barren slope to a saddle, and use a social trail to reach a plug of dark volcanic rock jutting from rose-colored earth. The plug (don't climb as the rock is not stable) presents a grand view of Lake Tahoe and serves as a turnaround point for a half-day hike, though you can follow the PCT all the way to Washington State.

To reach the trailhead from Tahoe City, take CA 89 for 4.4 miles south to the turnoff marked for Kaspian and Blackwood Canyon. Turn right on Blackwood Canyon Road, and go 7.7 miles to the trailhead, which is on the right (east) side of the road beyond both the summit of Barker Pass and the end of the pavement.

EAST SHORE

The deep blue of Lake Tahoe from Sand Harbor.

Lake Tahoe–Nevada State Park protects much of the landscape between Incline Village in the north and the junction of US 50 and NV 28 at Spooner Summit. The park presents two recreational faces: The Marlette-Hobart Backcountry, dedicated to primitive, nonmotorized uses such as hiking, backpacking, and mountain biking, and what I'll call the park's front country, including the beach and facilities at Sand Harbor on the lakeshore and the developed picnic and staging areas at the park's entrance near Spooner Lake.

While hiking in Lake Tahoe–Nevada State Park is concentrated in the 13,000-acre backcountry, a land of lakes and flumes that provided water for the Comstock Lode and Virginia City, Sand Harbor is a great destination. Its half-moon yellow sand beach buzzes with activity during the summer months, colorful with swimmers and picnickers. A short interpretive nature trail winds around a small point of land, with a second trail following the rocky shoreline north to Memorial Point, a scenic overlook outfitted with interpretive signs. A visitor/information center operates throughout the summer months, and the Lake Tahoe Shakespeare Festival takes place at the harbor each August. Other activities include scuba diving among the interesting rock formations along Sand Harbor's shoreline.

South of US 50 the East Shore becomes more developed. Pass through Tunnel Rock and into Zephyr Cove, a residential community and recreational hub with lakeshore access, boating facilities, restaurants, and other amenities. Pass the intersection with Kingsbury Grade and you'll be on the outskirts of Stateline, twin city to South Lake Tahoe and all the fun offered by those shoreline communities.

The Newhall House sits on the shoreline at Skunk Harbor, offering visitors a verandah to picnic on.

Skunk Harbor

A broad, steep track leads down to Skunk Harbor, a secluded bay where the clear water of Lake Tahoe washes in a rainbow arc onto the stone-strewn beach, melting from indigo to turquoise to gold as it approaches the shore. An "upside down" hike, with the climb on the return trip, you can prepare for the ascent by enjoying lunch and resting in the front yard of the old Newhall House.

Start: At the green gate on NV 28 that marks the unsigned trailhead
Distance: 3 miles out and back
Hiking time: About 2 hours
Difficulty: Moderate due to an elevation change of more than 600 feet
Trail surface: Dirt roadway
Best seasons: Late spring, summer, fall
Other trail users: Mountain bikers
Trailhead amenities: Limited roadside parking for about five cars at the trailhead near the gate. Parking for ten to twelve cars is located in the pullout alongside NV 28 about 100 yards above (north of) the trailhead.
Canine compatibility: Leashed dogs permitted
Fees and permits: None
Schedule: Sunrise to sunset daily
Maps: USGS Marlette Lake NV
Trail contact: US Forest Service Lake Tahoe Basin Management Unit, Forest Supervisor's Office, 35 College Dr., South Lake Tahoe, CA 96150; (530) 543-2600; www.fs.fed.us/r5/ltbmu

Finding the trailhead: From the junction of NV 28 and Village Boulevard in Incline Village, follow NV 28 south along the east shore for 9.3 miles to the unsigned trailhead on the right (west/lakeside). From the intersection of US 50 and CA 89 in South Lake Tahoe, drive 17.9 miles north on US 50 to its intersection with NV 28 near Spooner Summit. Turn left (north) onto NV 28 and go about 2.4 miles to the trailhead, which is on the left side of the highway. GPS: N39 07.717' / W119 55.888'

THE HIKE

As if the sandy beach, sculpted rocks, and clear water weren't enough to draw hikers down to Skunk Harbor, the secluded inlet is also the site of the historic Newhall House, built in 1923 as a wedding gift from George Newhall to his wife, Caroline. A plaque explains the origin and preservation of the house, now a shell ornamented with rustic stonework, flagstone patios, peaked roofs, and heavy wooden window frames. Peek through the bars and glass to check out the gloomy, empty interior; the shade of sheltering pines makes it difficult to see much. But you can spread a picnic on one of the verandas and enjoy the same wonderful views that greeted Newhall's bride.

Swimming and picnicking are practically requisite for hikers who venture down the steep road to the harbor, which derives its name from the odiferous, white-striped mammals that once frequented the area. Powerboats sometimes drop anchor in the cove, their occupants dipping into the lake and relaxing on the beach. But even with some coming by land and others by water, the destination is seldom crowded.

The remnants of a dock stretch into Skunk Harbor, but no dock is needed to enjoy the sun and beauty of this hideaway on the east shore.

To begin, pass the gate and head downhill on the paved roadway, which quickly becomes dirt. The route flattens and circles through a drainage, then traverses the wooded slope. From the traverse you can catch views of Slaughterhouse Canyon and the lake beyond.

When you reach the unsigned junction with the trail/road into Slaughterhouse Canyon, stay right (straight) on the broad track heading down to Skunk Harbor. The route steepens in pitch, rounds a switchback, and passes through a clearing. Another switchback loops through a riparian woodland, then the trail narrows and passes through a swampy patch watered by an ephemeral stream.

The trail splits just beyond the stream. Go left (west), and meander through lush undergrowth, crossing a streamlet, to the Newhall House. Footpaths lead around to the lakefront side of the house and onto the Skunk Harbor beach proper, with a ruined dock stretching into the water. Explore the house and enjoy the beach, then return as you came, keeping in mind that it's all uphill from the cove. It takes a bit longer to climb out than it does to descend.

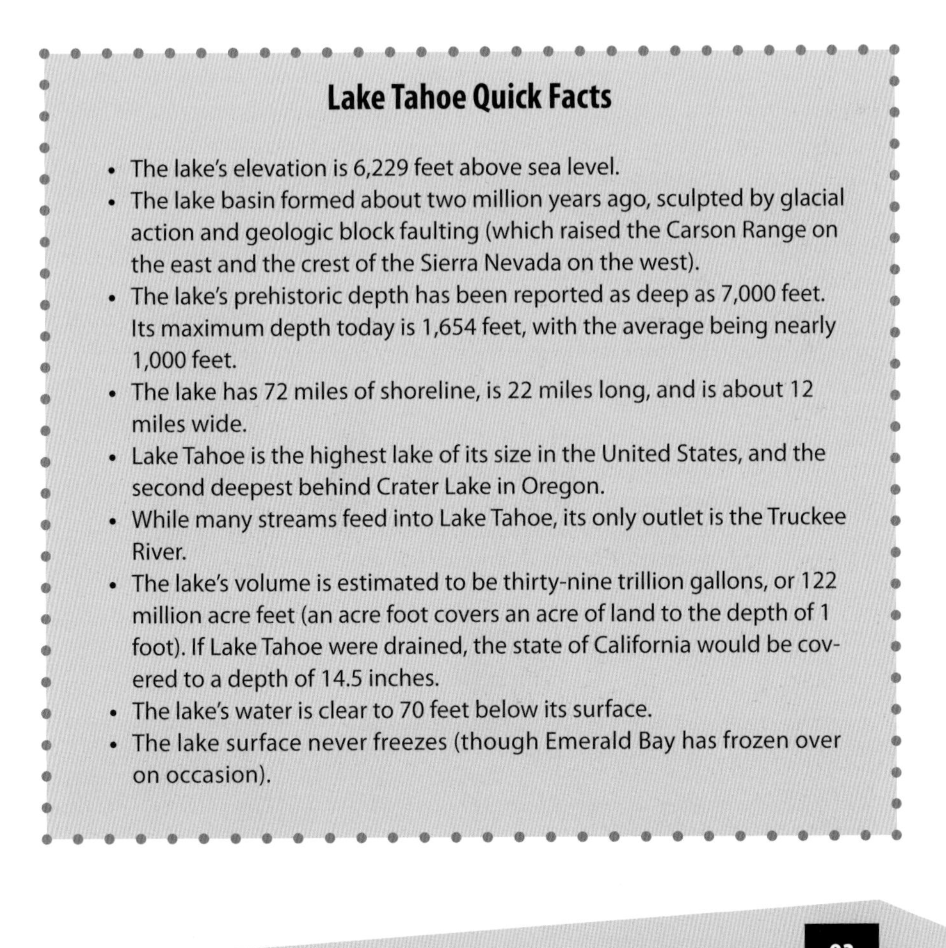

Lake Tahoe Quick Facts

- The lake's elevation is 6,229 feet above sea level.
- The lake basin formed about two million years ago, sculpted by glacial action and geologic block faulting (which raised the Carson Range on the east and the crest of the Sierra Nevada on the west).
- The lake's prehistoric depth has been reported as deep as 7,000 feet. Its maximum depth today is 1,654 feet, with the average being nearly 1,000 feet.
- The lake has 72 miles of shoreline, is 22 miles long, and is about 12 miles wide.
- Lake Tahoe is the highest lake of its size in the United States, and the second deepest behind Crater Lake in Oregon.
- While many streams feed into Lake Tahoe, its only outlet is the Truckee River.
- The lake's volume is estimated to be thirty-nine trillion gallons, or 122 million acre feet (an acre foot covers an acre of land to the depth of 1 foot). If Lake Tahoe were drained, the state of California would be covered to a depth of 14.5 inches.
- The lake's water is clear to 70 feet below its surface.
- The lake surface never freezes (though Emerald Bay has frozen over on occasion).

MILES AND DIRECTIONS

0.0 Start by passing the green gate and heading down the broad access road.

0.4 Pass the junction with the trail that leads left (down and south) to Slaughterhouse Canyon. Stay right (down and west) on the Skunk Harbor road.

1.0 Round a switchback.

1.4 Reach the T junction above the harbor. Beach access trails are to the right (north); the house is to the left.

1.5 Arrive at the house and beach. Rest and relax at the waterside, then retrace your steps.

3.0 Arrive back at the trailhead.

HIKE INFORMATION

Local information: Incline Village Crystal Bay Visitors Bureau provides information about lodging, recreation, and dining for the Nevada side of north Lake Tahoe. Contact the visitors bureau by calling (775) 832-1606 or (800) GoTahoe, or visit www.gotahoenorth.com. For information on lodging, restaurants, and activities in South Lake Tahoe, look to the Lake Tahoe South Shore Chamber of Commerce. The chamber is located at 169 US 50, 3rd Floor, Stateline, NV 89449; call (775) 588-1728; visit www.tahoechamber.org.
Camping: Lake Tahoe–Nevada State Park maintains three primitive walk-in camps in the Marlette-Hobart backcountry, with a 14-day camping limit within a 30-day period. Contact the park at (775) 831-0494 for more information or visit parks.nv.gov/parks/marlette-hobart-backcountry.

***The lodgepole pine, an indicator species of the upper montane zone, derives its common name from its utilitarian use as lodge poles in the tepees of Native Americans. The scientific name is* Pinus contorta.**

Green Tip:
Use phosphate-free detergent—it's less harmful to the environment.

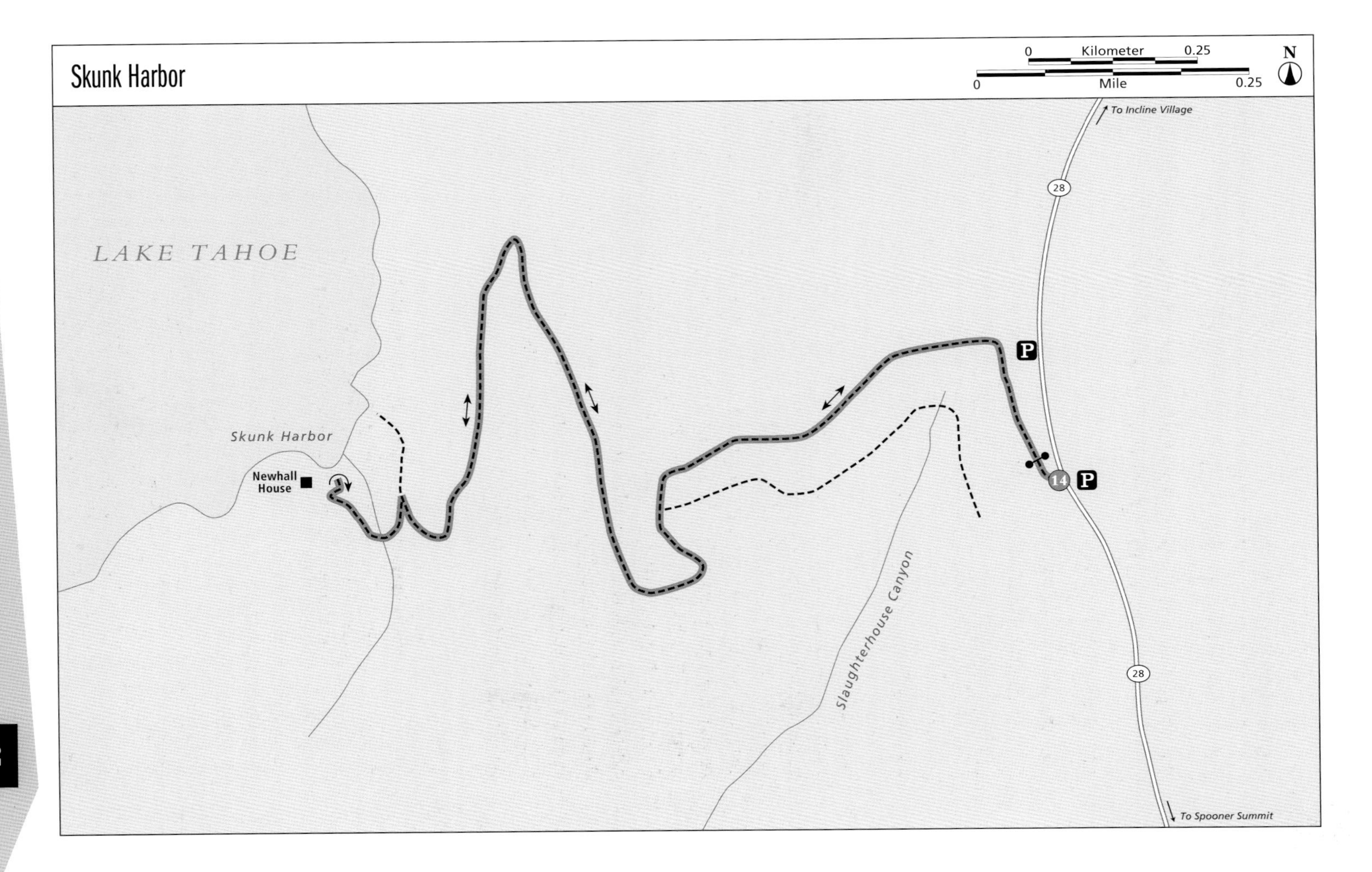
Skunk Harbor
0
Kilometer
0.25
0
Mile
0.25
N
To Incline Village
28
LAKE TAHOE
Skunk Harbor
Newhall House
P
14
P
Slaughterhouse Canyon
28
To Spooner Summit

15

Spooner Lake Loop

This splendid day hike circumnavigates the forested shoreline of Spooner Lake, once a water source for miners working the Comstock Lode near Virginia City.

Start: At the signed trailhead in the picnic area at Lake Tahoe–Nevada State Park
Distance: 2.1-mile loop
Hiking time: 1–2 hours
Difficulty: Easy
Trail surface: Singletrack; dirt roadway; pavement
Best seasons: Late spring, summer, and fall (when the aspens turn)
Other trail users: None on the loop itself; cyclists on the portions leading to and from the loop
Trailhead amenities: Restrooms, picnic sites, informational bill-boards, trashcans, a bike shop
Canine compatibility: Leashed dogs permitted
Fees and permits: A day-use fee is levied.
Schedule: The park is open 24 hours per day, 7 days a week, year-round to accommodate backcountry users. The entrance station is open from 8 a.m. to 9 p.m. from Memorial Day to Labor Day. From May 1 to Memo-rial Day, and from Labor Day to Sept 30, hours are from 8 a.m. to 7 p.m. From Oct 1 to Apr 30, hours are from 8 a.m. to 5 p.m.
Maps: USGS Glenbrook NV; state park map available at the entrance station; information signboard map at the trailhead
Trail contact: Lake Tahoe–Nevada State Park, PO Box 6116, Incline Village, NV 89452; (775) 831-0494; parks.nv.gov/parks/marlette-hobart-backcountry

Finding the trailhead: From the junction of NV 28 and Village Boulevard in Incline Village, follow NV 28 south for about 11 miles to the signed turnoff into Lake Tahoe–Nevada State Park. Turn left (east) into the park and follow the park road to the trailhead. From South Lake Tahoe/Stateline, follow US 50 north for about 12 miles to the junction with NV 28. Go left (west) onto NV 28 for 0.5 mile to the park entrance on the right. GPS: N39 06.369' / W119 54.963'

THE HIKE

Glades of quaking aspen, bright green in spring and vivid gold in fall, crowd the first mile of this flat, easy circuit around Spooner Lake. The aspen groves, including some gnarly old specimens with trunks scarred by graffiti, blend into the otherwise evergreen woodland on the lake's shoreline. Wildflowers bloom among meadow grasses in small clearings, and breaks in the trees open to views across the water. Ducks and other waterfowl may be seen swimming along the shoreline, and if you are lucky you may spot an osprey.

The large information sign at the trailhead shows the extensive trail system that explores the Marlette-Hobart backcountry, anchored by Marlette Lake and Hobart Reservoir. Spooner Lake offers a kindler, gentler sampling of what you find farther in.

The other backcountry reservoirs, like Spooner Lake, were integral to the development of the Comstock Lode and the exploitation of the landscape and forests surrounding Lake Tahoe that resulted from the mining enterprise. Interpretive signs along the route detail Spooner Lake's role in the complex delivery system that moved resources from the Sierra to the silver mines near Virginia City. An array of railroads, haul roads, and flumes (one 17 miles long) originated around the lake; these carried water and timber to the mines. Spooner Lake, then part of Spooner Ranch, was strategically located near a relatively low pass in the Carson Range. Ranch owner Michel Spooner, along with a partner, established Spooner Station in 1860, with a mill, hotel, saloon, and other accommodations serving the miners, lumberjacks, and travelers that crossed the pass.

From the trailhead follow the signed paved path (North Canyon Road; lined with interpretive signs) down to the signed Spooner Lake trail at the base of the hill. The loop begins on the lakeshore and is described in a counterclockwise direction; turn right onto the path.

Green Tip:

Many people visit natural areas for quiet, peace, and solitude, so avoid making loud noises and intruding on others' privacy.

Montane ecotones—meadow, aspen forest, evergreen forest—merge seamlessly as you follow the well-maintained singletrack around the lake. Highway noise from US 50 can be a distraction at the outset, but it fades as you reach the woods on the northern shoreline, and trees screen the highway from view.

Near the halfway point you'll reach the junction with the Tahoe Rim Trail (TRT); the route follows a portion of the long-distance trail back to the lake's earthen dam. Anglers become more common as you approach the dam, with rocky beaches suitable for fishing and picnicking surrounding the sloping structure. The bugs can be brutal in season in marshy areas around the dam; walk with your mouth closed!

The loop closes on the far side of the dam. From the signed junction with North Canyon Road (which leads to Marlette Lake and other destinations in the backcountry), climb up through the woods and back to the picnic area, parking lot, and trailhead.

MILES AND DIRECTIONS

0.0 Start at the trailhead next to the restrooms, signed for all trails. Follow the paved path past the large information sign, descending on the North Canyon Road to the lakeside. Turn right onto the signed Spooner Lake trail. Alternatively, you can go right from the paved path at the top of the hill, walking through the split-rail fence. Stay left (northeast) to a picnic area surrounded by boulders, and follow the dirt path down to a gravel road. Turn right (south); in 25 yards you will meet the signed Spooner Lake Loop.

0.6 Pass through a meadow on boardwalks. At the junction stay left (straight) on the Spooner Lake Loop; an access trail breaks right toward US 50. The trail descends into quaking aspen groves.

1.0 Cross a boardwalk over the inlet stream and climb to the junction with the Tahoe Rim Trail. Go left (southwest) on the signed TRT/Spooner Lake Loop.

1.6 At the junction with the link to North Canyon Road and Marlette Lake, stay left (south), following the shoreline.

1.8 Arrive at the dam and a trail junction. Cross the dam and go down through the spillway. Pass a signboard listing angling regulations, then cross the gravel road to the sign that points uphill to the parking area. Two paths lead through the woods; pick one and start the short climb.

2.1 Arrive back at the trailhead.

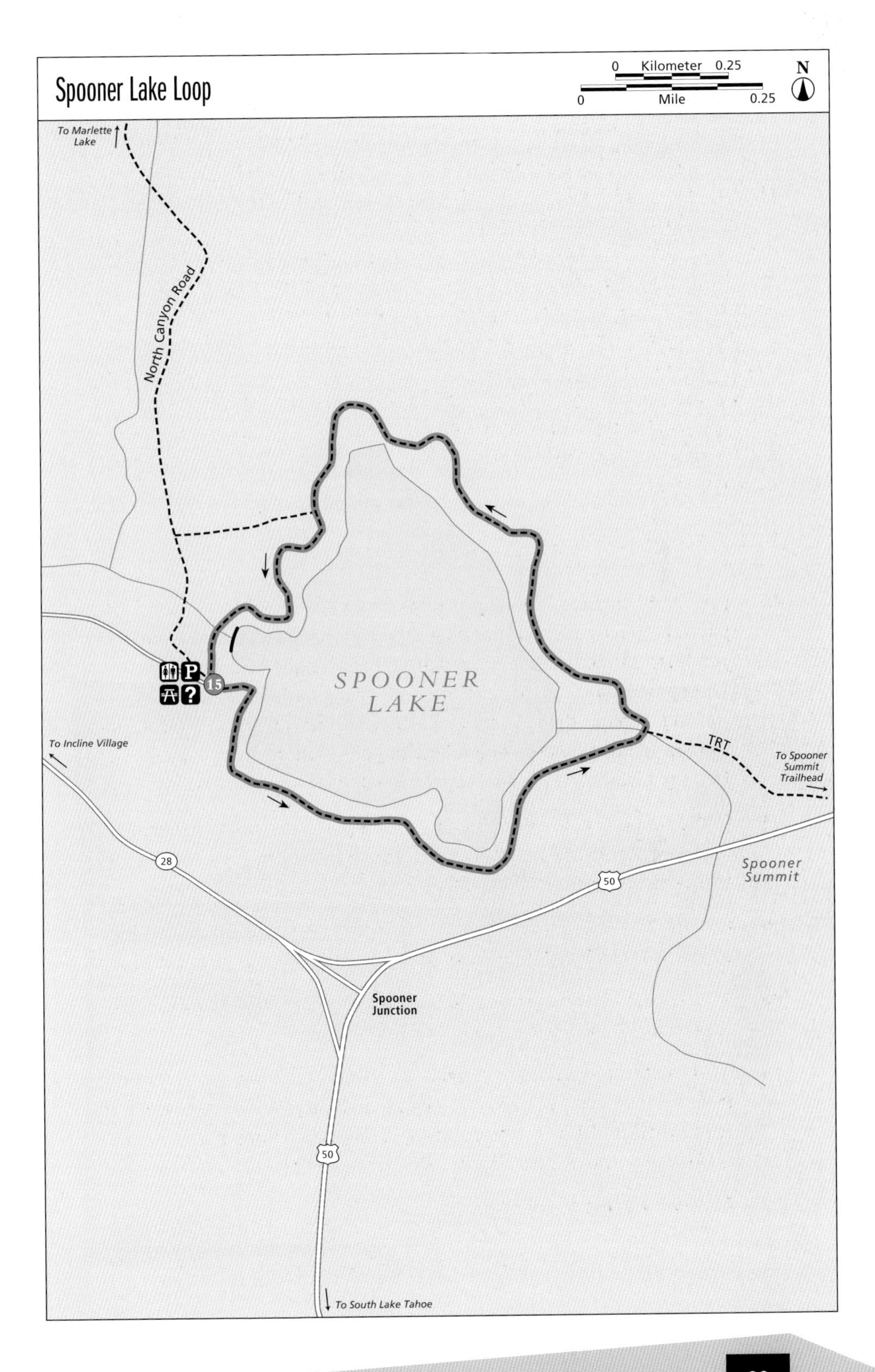
Spooner Lake Loop
0 Kilometer 0.25
0 Mile 0.25
N
To Marlette Lake
North Canyon Road
SPOONER LAKE
15
To Incline Village
TRT
To Spooner Summit Trailhead
28
50
Spooner Summit
Spooner Junction
50
To South Lake Tahoe

HIKE INFORMATION

Local information: Incline Village Crystal Bay Visitors Bureau provides information about lodging, recreation, and dining for the Nevada side of north Lake Tahoe. Contact the visitors bureau by calling (775) 832-1606 or (800) GoTahoe, or visit www.gotahoenorth.com. For information on lodging, restaurants, and activities in South Lake Tahoe, contact the Lake Tahoe South Shore Chamber of Commerce. The chamber is located at 169 US 50, 3rd Floor, Stateline, NV 89449; call (775) 588-1728; visit www.tahoechamber.org.
Services: Spooner Lake Outdoor Company operates the full-service Flume Trail Bike Shop in Incline Village, which offers shuttles for one-way travelers on the Marlette Flume Trail and the Tahoe Rim Trail. Call (775) 298-2501 or visit www.flumetrailtahoe.com.
Camping: The park maintains three primitive walk-in camps in the backcountry with a 14-day camping limit within a 30-day period. Contact the park at (775) 831-0494 for more information.

Anglers use the beaches and trails along Spooner Lake to find just the right place to cast a line.

Marlette Lake

Take the trail to Marlette Lake when the aspens turn in the autumn. Gorgeous stands of the golden-leaved trees light up a good stretch at the start of this long, easy trek, begging for pictures and enticing hikers to linger. Marlette Lake, as blue as Tahoe, sits in a wooded bowl that is a delight at any time of year.

Start: At the trailhead in Lake Tahoe–Nevada State Park
Distance: 10-mile lollipop loop
Hiking time: 5–7 hours
Difficulty: Moderate
Trail surface: Singletrack; gravel service road
Best seasons: Late spring, summer, fall
Other trail users: Mountain bikers, trail runners
Trailhead amenities: Restrooms, picnic sites, informational billboards, trashcans, a bike shop where you can get trail information
Canine compatibility: Dogs not permitted
Fees and permits: A fee to enter Lake Tahoe–Nevada State Park
Schedule: The park is open 24 hours per day, 7 days a week, year-round to accommodate backcountry users. The entrance station is open from 8 a.m. to 9 p.m. from Memorial Day to Labor Day. From May 1 to Memorial Day, and from Labor Day to Sept 30, hours are from 8 a.m. to 7 p.m. From Oct 1 to Apr 30, hours are from 8 a.m. to 5 p.m.
Maps: USGS Glenbrook NV; state park map available at the entrance station; information signboard map at the trailhead
Trail contact: Lake Tahoe–Nevada State Park, PO Box 6116, Incline Village, NV 89452; (775) 831-0494; parks.nv.gov/parks/marlette-hobart-backcountry
Special considerations: North Canyon Road can be a busy place, particularly on weekends. While on the road be sure to stay right. Speed limits are posted but cyclists don't always adhere, so it's best to stay clear. Sharing the route is typically not a problem, as the track is plenty wide, but courtesy and an awareness of others is mandatory.

Finding the trailhead: From the junction of NV 28 and Village Boulevard in Incline Village, follow NV 28 south for about 11 miles to the signed turnoff into Lake Tahoe–Nevada State Park. Turn left (east) into the park and follow the park road to the trailhead. From South Lake Tahoe/Stateline, follow US 50 north for about 12 miles to the junction with NV 28. Go left (west) onto NV 28 for 0.5 mile to the park entrance on the right. GPS: N39 06.369' / W119 54.963'

THE HIKE

Marlette Lake is the most accessible destination in the backcountry of Lake Tahoe–Nevada State Park, a scenic target for hikers and mountain bikers on the Tahoe Rim Trail (TRT) and the Flume Trail (aka the Marlette Flume). Cyclists use North Canyon Road, a graded gravel service road, to reach the scenic lake from the trailhead near the park entrance, but there is a separate trail for hikers that skims the slopes above the road. This lollipop incorporates both trail and road, but you can minimize encounters with wheeled recreationalists by sticking to the trail both out and back.

The hike up to the lake, though steep in sections, is fairly straightforward. The lower reaches of the route are enlivened both by stands of aspen, firing gold in autumn, and by miners' cabins, one in fairly good shape and the second a shambles. You will also pass the signed access trails for backcountry cabins that can be rented as bases for cross-country skiing.

The Marlette Lake Trail, for hikers and equestrians, departs from North Canyon Road after about 1 mile, and swings via easy switchbacks onto the east-facing hillside above the cycling track. Voices of wheeled travelers drift up into the woods, mingling with the screeches of jays and the wind in the treetops.

A steady but easy climb leads to a bridge that spans a year-round stream. A bench about halfway along offers a nice streamside respite near the remnants of a woodcutter's cabin. Round a series of switchbacks until you are several hundred feet above the valley floor, with awesome views opening east onto the stony slopes of Snow Valley Peak.

Timber for miners working the Comstock Lode was harvested from the slopes of the Carson Range year-round. High stumps, which can be spotted throughout the backcountry but are highlighted near the woodcutter's cabin along the Marlette Lake Trail, indicate the snow depth at the time the trees were cut in winter.

Trails converge in the wooded saddle at the top of the climb. Follow a short unsigned path to the signed Marlette Lake Trail; the bike trail can be seen through the trees to the right, and Chimney Beach lies far down the trail on the left. A relatively steep descent leads across several bridges to the shoreline of Marlette Lake, where the trail ends on the service road near the spawning station.

You can retrace your steps to the trailhead from here, or complete the lollipop by following the service road (offering access to the Marlette Flume Trail) to the right. The lakeshore road leads to a staging area used by cyclists at the junction with North Canyon Road. A restroom is available here. Though unsigned, the return route is obvious, climbing steeply uphill, away from Marlette Lake and to the trail junction in the saddle above.

North Canyon Road drops steeply from the saddle at first, passing a link onto Snow Valley Peak and to the Tahoe Rim Trail (TRT) before the pitch eases on the valley floor. Pass the North Valley backcountry camp (with a restroom and link to the TRT) and the trail to the Wild Cat Cabin (used by cross-country skiers). Reach the junction with the lower end of the Marlette Lake Trail at the 9-mile mark and retrace your steps to the trailhead.

The last stretch of trail offers tantalizing views of the destination: Marlette Lake.

MILES AND DIRECTIONS

0.0 Start on the paved interpretive Beetle Discovery Trail, following the sign for all trails including the Spooner Lake Trail and the Marlette Flume Trail. Head down the dirt road; at its base the Spooner Lake Loop trail breaks right. Stay left on the signed North Canyon Road.

0.4 Pass the access trail to the Spooner Lake Cabin. Stay left on the roadway.

0.8 Pass Spencer's Cabin.

1.0 Reach the start of the signed Marlette Lake Trail and go left, leaving the roadway to the cyclists for now.

2.1 Cross a bridge over a year-round stream.

2.75 Pass a bench that perches above another stream, which is funneled under and through a jumble of granite boulders.

3.5 Round switchbacks to views of Snow Valley Peak.

4.4 Reach the signed trail junction at the top of the climb. Continue on an unsigned path to the signed Marlette Lake Trail. The bike route is to the right; a trail to Chimney Beach departs to the left. The Marlette Lake Trail drops down a narrow drainage spanned by a couple of bridges.

5.0 Arrive at the service road on the shoreline of Marlette Lake. Turn right on the service road.

5.25 Reach the staging area and restroom. Go right and uphill on the unsigned North Canyon Road.

6.0 Back atop the saddle, pass the junction with the Marlette Lake Trail and continue downhill on North Canyon Road.

6.1 Pass the junction with the Snow Valley Peak trail to the Tahoe Rim Trail, remaining on North Canyon Road.

7.0 Pass North Canyon Camp (with a restroom and TRT trail link); stay on the obvious North Canyon Road.

8.1 Pass an overgrown road leading to the creek; again, stay on the obvious main route.

8.3 Pass the trail to Wild Cat Cabin, remaining right on the roadway.

9.0 Reach the junction of North Canyon Road and the lower end of the Marlette Creek Trail. Retrace your steps from here.

10.0 Arrive back at the trailhead.

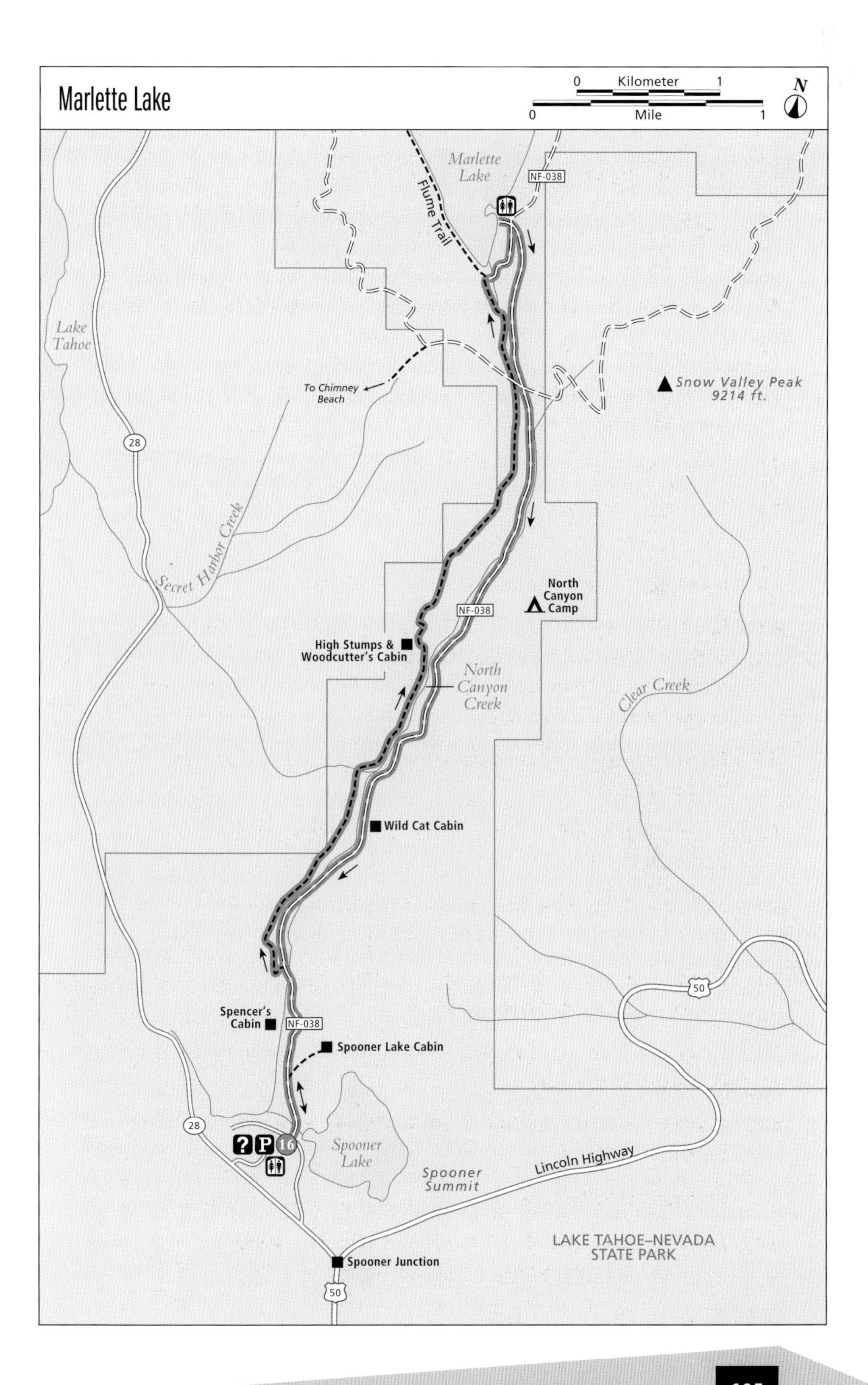

Marlette Lake
0 Kilometer 1
0 Mile 1
N
Marlette Lake
NF-038
Flume Trail
Lake Tahoe
To Chimney Beach
Snow Valley Peak 9214 ft.
28
Secret Harbor Creek
North Canyon Camp
NF-038
High Stumps & Woodcutter's Cabin
North Canyon Creek
Clear Creek
Wild Cat Cabin
50
Spencer's Cabin
NF-038
Spooner Lake Cabin
28
16
Spooner Lake
Spooner Summit
Lincoln Highway
LAKE TAHOE–NEVADA STATE PARK
Spooner Junction
50

Local information: Incline Village Crystal Bay Visitors Bureau provides information about lodging, recreation, and dining for the Nevada side of north Lake Tahoe. Contact the visitors bureau by calling (775) 832-1606 or (800) GoTahoe, or visit www.gotahoenorth.com. For information on lodging, restaurants, and activities in South Lake Tahoe, contact the Lake Tahoe South Shore Chamber of Commerce. The chamber is located at 169 US 50, 3rd Floor, Stateline, NV 89449; call (775) 588-1728; visit www.tahoechamber.org.

Services: Spooner Lake Outdoor Company offers shuttle service to one-way travelers on the Flume Trail. For more information call (775) 298-2501 or visit www.flumetrailtahoe.com.

Camping: The park maintains three primitive walk-in camps in the backcountry with a 14-day camping limit within a 30-day period. Contact the park at (775) 831-0494 for more information.

The Marlette Cabins

Two cabins that were part of massive wood-harvesting efforts in the Tahoe basin during the gold and silver rushes lie along the route to Marlette Lake.

Gleaning precious metals out of the Comstock Lode and other mining enterprises required a lot of timber, which was used to build flumes, tunnels, mine shafts, and the structures of boomtowns themselves. The slopes surrounding Lake Tahoe supported thick stands of old-growth pine and fir, and men were dispatched into the high country to render that timber into serviceable lumber. Cabins throughout the region provided shelter for the lumberjacks, who worked year-round. Blasted by time and harsh winters, one remnant is the so-called woodcutter's cabin, little more than a stack of logs alongside the creek at about the midpoint of the Marlette Lake Trail. Perhaps dating back to the late nineteenth century, the cabin housed three to four workers, likely immigrants from China.

Spencer's Cabin, built in the 1920s as part of the Carson Tahoe Lumber & Flume Company's operation in the Carson Range, sits in a stand of aspen bordering a lovely meadow alongside North Canyon Road. The cabin passed to the Whittel family before being leased by rancher Charlie Fulstone. Namesake Spencer was one of the rancher's caretakers.

Honorable Mentions

Sand Point Nature Trail

Take a break from the sun and water with a quick stroll along the boardwalk at Sand Point. With views across Lake Tahoe and into rocky coves along the shoreline, and interpretive signs describing some of the components that make the lake's environment so beautiful and unique, the 0.4-mile wheelchair- and stroller-accessible loop is perfect for families. After you've made the round, you can settle on lovely Sand Point Beach for a picnic and a swim.

Sand Point Nature Trail is part of Lake Tahoe–Nevada State Park. The recreation area is open from 8 a.m. to 9 p.m. daily in summer. A day-use fee is levied. The area is extremely popular, with kayaking, diving, and picnic facilities as well as a visitor center and gift shop. The park also hosts the annual Lake Tahoe Shakespeare Festival in July and August; the amphitheater is cupped inside the trail loop.

If you'd like to extend your exploration of the East Shore near Sand Point, you can follow a 0.6-mile path to Memorial Point, where you'll find more interpretive signage, restrooms, parking, and short paths that lead to overlooks.

To reach the trail from the junction of NV 28 and Village Boulevard in Incline Village, follow NV 28 south along Lake Tahoe's east shore for 4.8 miles to the signed park entrance on the right (west). The parking lots fill by midmorning on summer days, restricting access to the park and trail. Parking, water, restrooms, and a visitor center and gift shop are near the trailhead.

Tahoe Rim Trail at Spooner Summit

The Tahoe Rim Trail leads both north and south from Spooner Summit, with US 50 slipping between. Unless you plan to circumnavigate the lake, excursions both north and south are out-and-back affairs, leading as far into the backcountry as time, ability, and will allow.

Heading north from the summit, a hike of about 2 miles one way offers access to two overlooks with views of the Carson Valley, a panorama sublime in dusky and sienna hues. The contrast between the Tahoe basin and the high desert valley is striking. On one side of the divide lies the largest expanse of water in the Sierra Nevada; the landscape on the other side rolls high and dry for a thousand miles to the Rocky Mountains. You can turn around at either overlook, or continue on to Snow Valley Peak (about 5.5 miles one way from the trailhead) and beyond.

Heading south from the summit, the Tahoe Rim Trail climbs steeply via a series of switchbacks, then traverses a rolling ridgeline that offers expansive views of Lake Tahoe to the west and only fleeting views of the more austere Carson Valley to the east. The hiking mellows as you roller coaster along the ridgeline, with views of Mount Tallac and the Desolation Wilderness across the lake.

The trail passes through sections of woodlands that have been harvested; scars from the clearing are healing, and the relatively open spaces present nice options for picnic spots or turnaround points. At about 2.5 miles logging roads collide with the trail below Duane Bliss Peak; this is also an ideal turnaround point. No trail leads up Bliss Peak, but intrepid hikers with good route-finding skills might take on the challenge. Hikers with more time and energy can continue along the TRT to Kingsbury Grade and beyond.

The TRT trailheads at Spooner Summit lie on either side of US 50 as it crests Spooner Summit. From Incline Village follow NV 28 south to its intersection with US 50. Turn left on US 50, and go 0.7 mile to Spooner Summit. For the trailhead leading south, go right into the picnic area parking lot; there is also parking along US 50. The trailhead for the northern section of the TRT is on the north side of the highway.

To reach the trailheads from the intersection of US 50 and CA 89 in South Lake Tahoe, drive north on US 50 to the US 50/NV 28 intersection at the base of Spooner Summit. Follow US 50 an additional 0.7 mile to the summit and trailheads.

Marlette Lake is a scenic destination in the Marlette-Hobart backcountry on Lake Tahoe's east shore.

SOUTH SHORE AND BEYOND

Round Top Lake

South Lake Tahoe and its immediate neighboring city, Stateline, are the busiest resort locales at the lake. Yes, there is hiking here, but there is so much more. Casinos offer twenty-four-hour entertainment, including performances by well-known musicians, comedians, and magicians, as well as dining and, of course, gambling. High-class lodging, relatively inexpensive hotels, expensive boutiques, kitschy gift shops, supermarkets, big-box franchises, hardware stores and auto shops, and restaurants ranging from burger joints and taco shops to exclusive lounges cluster around the casinos. Expansive Nevada Beach offers fun in the sun and water, and year-round activities at Heavenly Valley Ski Resort ensure residents and visitors alike have plenty to do.

As engaging as the modern attractions of the twin towns straddling the California/Nevada border are, the backcountry puts all that to shame. The high Sierra and Desolation Wilderness are easily accessed from the South Shore. Fallen Leaf Lake, a finger of blue water stretched below the slopes of majestic Mount Tallac, serves as gateway to some of the most spectacular landscapes in the wilderness. Heading south into the Hope Valley and over Carson Pass, the mountains harbor trails less traveled that lead into alpine basins and through meadows thick with wildflowers.

Historic sites are plentiful along the south shore as well, with Vikingsholm, a Nordic mansion crooked in the elbow of sparkling Emerald Bay, being arguably the most impressive. The Tallac Historic Site houses other stunning lakeshore estates. And high above Fallen Leaf Lake the remnants of Glen Alpine Springs Resort remind hikers that the wilderness can quickly reclaim even the most beloved of Lake Tahoe's resorts.

Debris from mining operations in the high country surrounding Reno and Lake Tahoe is a relatively common sight.

Vikingsholm and Emerald Point

Ocean-green and opalescent, it's quite obvious how Emerald Bay, a gleaming fjord on Lake Tahoe's south shore, earned its name. As if the natural beauty weren't enough, spectacular Vikingsholm, huddled in the pines at the head of the bay, is another draw. Not so obvious is the jewel of a trail that leads along the bay's north shore to its narrow mouth.

Start: At the signed trailhead in the large paved parking area on CA 89
Distance: 5.2 miles out and back
Hiking time: 3–4 hours
Difficulty: Moderate due to trail length and the steep ingress and egress
Trail surface: Graded dirt road; pavement, singletrack
Best seasons: Spring, summer, fall
Other trail users: None
Trailhead amenities: Parking, a gift and information station in the trailhead lot; restrooms, a visitor center, and picnic facilities at Vikingsholm. The parking lots at the Vikingsholm and neighboring Eagle Falls and Bayview trailheads are congested during high season. Lots fill quickly, but additional parking is available along the roadway. Please be courteous and safe in selecting a parking space.
Canine compatibility: Leashed dogs permitted in the park; no dogs allowed on trails or beaches or at Vikingsholm
Fees and permits: A parking fee is levied.
Schedule: The trail is open from sunrise to sunset. Vikingsholm and the Emerald Bay State Park visitor center are open daily from Memorial Day to Sept 30 from 10 a.m. to 4 p.m. Tours of Vikingsholm are available for a fee; call (530) 541-3030.
Maps: USGS Emerald Bay CA; Emerald Bay park map and brochure available online and at the visitor center
Trail contact: Emerald Bay State Park, PO Box 266, Tahoma, CA 96142; (530) 541-3030 (summer only); www.parks.ca.gov
Special considerations: You will gain and lose more than 400 feet in elevation within the first mile. Heed the trailhead sign that warns you not to attempt the route if you have heart, respiratory, or knee problems.

Finding the trailhead: From the intersection of US 50 and CA 89 in South Lake Tahoe, head north on CA 89 for 10.7 miles to the large Emerald Bay State Park parking area on the right (southeast). From Tahoe City, take CA 89 south for 17.6 miles (parking is on the left). The signed trail begins to the left of the huge rock slab that overlooks Emerald Bay. GPS: N38 57.261' / W120 06.619'

THE HIKE

Of all the shoreline estates along Lake Tahoe, Vikingsholm is arguably the most spectacular, with striking Scandinavian architecture and views opening onto one of Lake Tahoe's most popular sights, sparkling Emerald Bay. Lora Josephine Knight built the home in 1929; it was designed by architect Lennart Palme, her nephew. The house, open for tours, features massive carved timbers, huge native granite boulders mortared into exterior walls, and a roof sewn with wildflowers. Mrs. Knight also rebuilt the structure atop Fannette Island (the only island in Lake Tahoe) as a teahouse. The island was also the home of Captain Dick Barter, "the Hermit of Emerald Bay," in the late 1800s.

Hiking down to the storied estate is quintessential Tahoe and massively popular. But stretch a bit beyond the mansion's grounds and you'll find yourself on the Rubicon Trail, where chances are good that you'll leave behind whatever crowds you met at Vikingsholm and enjoy Emerald Bay in relative solitude. In the off-season, whether spring or fall, if you walk quietly and watchfully as you near Emerald Point, you may see an eagle or osprey return to a lakeside nest, a tangle of twigs and branches perched at the top of a standing dead tree.

Begin by heading down the wide path (a human highway in the busy summer season). Two switchbacks broken with long traverses drop to a junction where a park map points you downhill and right through open woodland to Vikingsholm. Take some time to explore the grounds, check out the visitor center, take a tour of the house, and picnic on the beach. When you're ready to move on, pick up the signed Rubicon Trail on the northeast side of the main house (the right side as you face the building from the beach).

A series of bridges and boardwalks assist passage along the forested shoreline, which is pierced by drainages and lush with berries, ferns, and other verdant undergrowth. It's easy going to Parsons Rock, which overlooks the bay and Fannette Island just before the trail enters the Emerald Bay Boat Camp.

The Rubicon merges with the camp road for a stretch, then breaks back to the shoreline as a dirt singletrack at a trail sign. The easy rambling continues, with short timber stair steps leading down to small half-moon beaches. The mouth of the bay, pinched by Emerald Point on the north and Eagle Point on the south, remains in sight until the Rubicon begins to bend north toward Rubicon Bay, D. L. Bliss State Park, and Calawee Cove. A clearing just before the trail turns north is the turnaround point (though any of the little beaches would work just as well). Return as you came, enjoying sporadic views up into the stony Desolation Wilderness as you go.

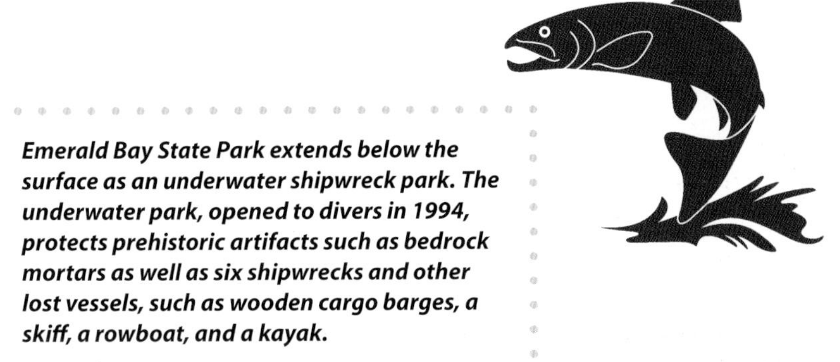

Emerald Bay State Park extends below the surface as an underwater shipwreck park. The underwater park, opened to divers in 1994, protects prehistoric artifacts such as bedrock mortars as well as six shipwrecks and other lost vessels, such as wooden cargo barges, a skiff, a rowboat, and a kayak.

Seen from the top of the trail leading down to Vikingsholm, Fannette Island, the only island in Lake Tahoe, anchors the center of Emerald Bay.

MILES AND DIRECTIONS

Note: Mileages include a 0.3-mile tour of the paved paths around Vikingsholm.

0.0 Start by descending the broad, well-graded trail.

1.0 Arrive at Vikingsholm and tour the grounds.

1.3 A signed trailhead for the Rubicon Trail is to the right (northeast) of Vikingsholm as you face it. Turn right (east) onto the flat path.

1.9 Enter the boat camp and follow the paved road through the sites.

2.1 At the east end of the camp, where the pavement begins to climb, the signed Rubicon Trail breaks to the right (east), turning to dirt and following the shoreline.

2.4 Pass a series of short staircases that lead down to tiny beaches.

2.6 Reach a clearing where trails appear to split, with the obvious Rubicon Trail breaking left (north). This is the turnaround point. The social tracks dead-end in the brush.

5.2 Retrace your steps to the trailhead.

Option: The Rubicon Trail continues through neighboring D. L. Bliss State Park to Rubicon Point, a 4.5-mile one-way journey from Vikingsholm.

HIKE INFORMATION

Local information: For the scoop on lodging, restaurants, and activities in South Lake Tahoe, look to the Lake Tahoe South Shore Chamber of Commerce. The chamber is located at 169 US 50, 3rd Floor, Stateline, NV 89449; call (775) 588-1728; visit www.tahoechamber.org. Or visit www.tahoesouth.com.

Local events/attractions: Guided tours of Vikingsholm, listed on the National Register of Historic Places, are available from Memorial Day through Sept. A fee is charged. Call the D. L. Bliss State Park office at (530) 525-9529 for more information.

Camping: D. L. Bliss State Park offers camping during the summer months (the park is closed in winter). There are 138 sites, all equipped with metal bear boxes, where all food should be stored. Some sites are suitable for RVs, but they cannot exceed 18 feet in length. Campers are free to use all park facilities. A fee is charged. For more information call (530) 525-7277 or (530) 525-3345 (in summer). Online reservations can be made by visiting the D. L. Bliss State Park page at www.parks.ca.gov; the link will take you to the park's ReserveAmerica (www.reserveamerica.com) page.

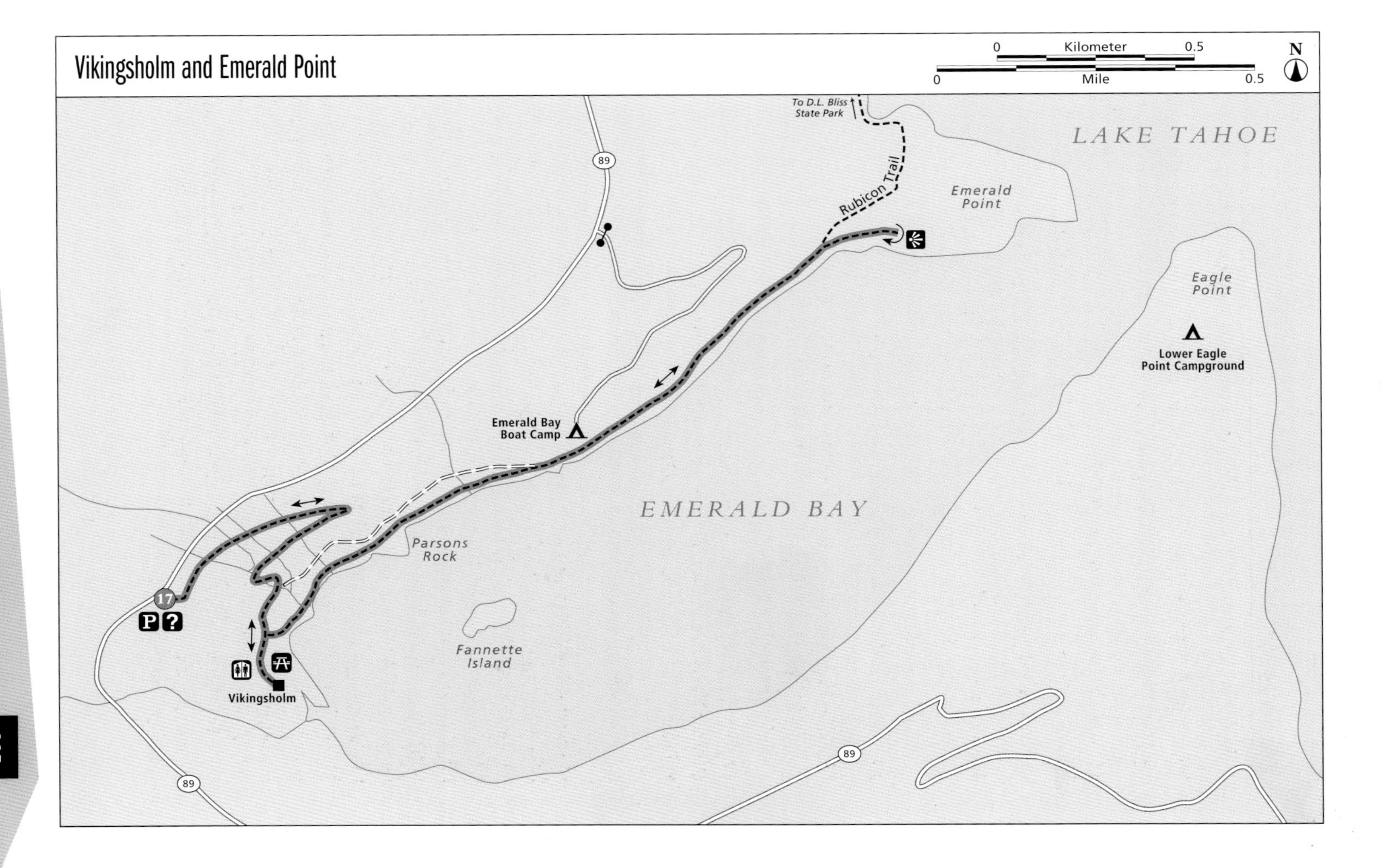
Vikingsholm and Emerald Point
Kilometer
0
0.5
Mile
0
0.5
N
LAKE TAHOE
Eagle Point
Lower Eagle Point Campground
Emerald Point
Rubicon Trail
To D.L. Bliss State Park
EMERALD BAY
89
Emerald Bay Boat Camp
Parsons Rock
Fannette Island
Vikingsholm
17

18

Eagle Lake

Dark and clear, Eagle Lake sits in a small basin bordered by steep granite aprons and great black-streaked cliffs. The classic Sierran setting and relative ease of access ensures this trail as one of the most popular around Lake Tahoe.

Start: At the well-signed trailhead in the Eagle Falls parking area off CA 89
Distance: 2 miles out and back
Hiking time: About 1 hour
Difficulty: Moderate due to some steep climbing
Trail surface: Dirt singletrack; granite stair steps
Best seasons: Summer and fall
Other trail users: None
Trailhead amenities: Parking, restrooms, picnic sites, trashcans, an information signboard, and wilderness permit site. The parking lots at Eagle Falls and neighboring Vikingsholm are congested during the high season. Additional parking is available along the highway. Please be courteous and safe in selecting a parking space.
Canine compatibility: Leashed dogs permitted. Because the trail is so popular, owners are asked to keep their pets under control and to clean up any messes.
Fees and permits: A vehicle parking fee is levied if you can find space in the trailhead lot. Parking along CA 89 is free. A free wilderness permit, available at the trailhead, is required.
Schedule: Sunrise to sunset daily
Maps: USGS Emerald Bay CA; a map on the signboard at the trailhead
Trail contact: US Forest Service Lake Tahoe Basin Management Unit, Forest Supervisor's Office, 35 College Dr., South Lake Tahoe, CA 96150; (530) 543-2600; www.fs.fed.us/r5/ltbmu
Special considerations: You will gain and lose about 400 feet in elevation, and you must climb and descend a stretch over granite steps, so be prepared for a moderate workout.

Finding the trailhead: From the intersection of US 50 and CA 89 in South Lake Tahoe, head north on CA 89 for 10.3 miles to the signed Eagle Falls parking area on the left (south). From Tahoe City follow CA 89 south for 18 miles, past the parking area for Vikingsholm, to the Eagle Falls parking lot on the right. GPS: N38 57.118' / W120 06.811'

THE HIKE

The naked, glacier-slick walls of a stark Desolation Wilderness cirque form the backdrop for Eagle Lake. The trail leading up to the lake is varied and moderately challenging but quite short, making it well within reach of any hiker seeking an alpine experience without excess effort.

Begin on stairs at the trailhead sign, staying on the signed Eagle Lake Trail where it connects with the shorter Eagle Loop. The trail climbs gently at first, allowing you to enjoy views of cascades on Eagle Creek and the soaring pinnacles and great gray domes of the Desolation Wilderness.

Nearing the bridge over the cascades at Eagle Falls, a twisting stone stairway leads up, then down, to a vista point and the sturdy bridge spanning the cataract. Enjoy the falls, then cross the bridge and climb granite stairs and rocky singletrack past the wilderness boundary sign and to a large, smooth, flat granite slab dotted with pine and cedar. The trail is worn into the slab; rocks line the track as well, keeping all but the most distracted hikers on route.

The trail skirts a rock outcrop overlooking the wooded creek valley below, then traverses above the drainage on a well-worn wooded path, with the jagged crowns of the canyon walls rising above the forest canopy. Gentle climbing

Storm clouds and mist drop onto Eagle Lake.

takes you to a trail junction at 0.9 mile; from here you can head deeper into the Desolation Wilderness. To reach Eagle Lake, however, bear right (west) toward the glacial cirque, following the arrow on the sign.

Scramble down to the shores of Eagle Lake at the 1-mile mark. A sprinkling of cedar, ponderosa, and Jeffrey pine provide shade from the vivid alpine sunshine. If you don't mind icy water, Eagle Lake invites a dip. There is no beach, however, so you'll have to dry off and/or enjoy the stunning views from a perch on a tree stump or a slab of sunbaked granite.

Return as you came, enjoying views of Emerald Bay and Lake Tahoe on the descent.

MILES AND DIRECTIONS

0.0 Start by climbing steps to the junction of the Eagle Lake Trail and the Eagle Loop. Stay left (southwest) on the Eagle Lake Trail.

0.2 Climb granite steps past the second Eagle Loop trail junction and stay left (south), crossing the bridge.

0.4 Pass the Desolation Wilderness boundary.

0.9 At the junction with the trail to the Velma Lakes, stay right (south) on the signed trail to Eagle Lake.

1.0 Arrive at Eagle Lake.

2.0 Retrace your steps to the trailhead.

Options: From the trail intersection just before Eagle Lake, you can head farther and higher into the Desolation Wilderness. The wilderness offers an abundance of backpacking possibilities, with Dicks Lake, Fontanillis Lake, and the Velma Lakes among the nearest destinations.

HIKE INFORMATION

Local information: For the scoop on lodging, restaurants, and activities in South Lake Tahoe, look to the Lake Tahoe South Shore Chamber of Commerce. The chamber is located at 169 US 50, 3rd Floor, Stateline, NV 89449; call (775) 588-1728; visit www.tahoechamber.org. Or visit www.tahoesouth.com.

Local events/attractions: Guided tours of historic Vikingsholm, located across CA 28 from the Eagle Falls trailhead, are available from Memorial Day through Sept. A fee is charged. Call the D. L. Bliss State Park office at (530) 525-9529 for more information.

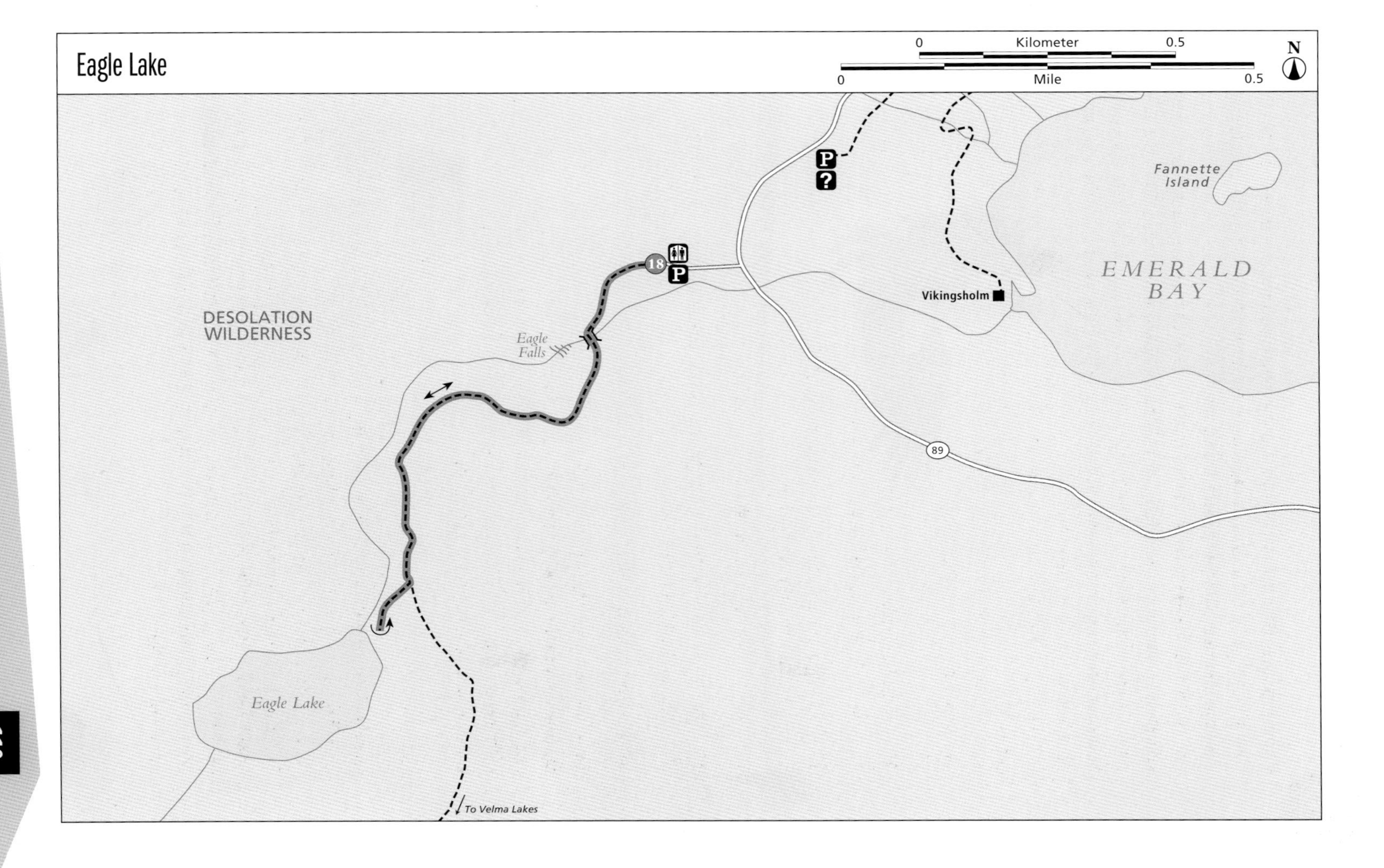
Eagle Lake
0
Kilometer
0.5
0
Mile
0.5
N
Fannette Island
EMERALD BAY
Vikingsholm
18
89
DESOLATION WILDERNESS
Eagle Falls
Eagle Lake
To Velma Lakes

Camping: D. L. Bliss State Park offers camping during the summer months (the park is closed in winter). There are 138 sites, all equipped with metal bear boxes, where all food should be stored. Some sites are suitable for RVs, but they cannot exceed 18 feet in length. Campers are free to use all park facilities. A fee is charged. For more information call (530) 525-7277 or (530) 525-3345 (in summer). Online reservations can be made by visiting the D. L. Bliss State Park page at www.parks.ca.gov; the link will take you to the park's ReserveAmerica (www.reserveamerica.com) page.

Eagle Lake is a popular destination in the Desolation Wilderness and is relatively easy to reach.

Velma Lakes

Uphill. And uphill. And . . . A long, stair-step climb into the Desolation Wilderness leads to the sparsely wooded alpine basin that holds the lovely Velma Lakes. Views on both the ascent and the descent are spectacular.

Start: The Eagle Falls trailhead near Emerald Bay
Distance: 9 miles out and back
Hiking time: 5–6 hours
Difficulty: Strenuous
Trail surface: Dirt singletrack
Best seasons: Summer and fall
Other trail users: None
Trailhead amenities: Parking, restrooms, picnic sites, information signboard, trashcans. The parking lots at Eagle Falls and neighboring Vikingsholm are congested during the high season. Additional parking is available along the highway. Please be courteous and safe in selecting a parking space.
Canine compatibility: Leashed dogs permitted. Because the trail to Eagle Lake is so popular, owners are asked to keep their pets under control and to clean up any messes.
Fees and permits: A free wilderness permit is required, available at the trailhead. A vehicle parking fee is levied if you can find space in the trailhead lot. Parking along CA 89 is free.
Schedule: 24 hours a day, 7 days a week, year-round
Maps: USGS Emerald Bay CA and Rockbound Valley CA
Trail contact: US Forest Service Lake Tahoe Basin Management Unit, Forest Supervisor's Office, 35 College Dr., South Lake Tahoe, CA 96150; (530) 543-2600; www.fs.fed.us/r5/ltbmu
Special considerations: The route involves more than 1,700 feet in elevation gain via steep trail and rock staircases.

Finding the trailhead: From the intersection of US 50 and CA 89 in South Lake Tahoe, head north on CA 89 for 10.3 miles to the signed Eagle Falls parking area on the left (south). From Tahoe City follow CA 89 south for 18 miles, past the parking area for Vikingsholm, to the Eagle Falls parking lot on the right. The well-signed trailhead is near the picnic area and restrooms. GPS: N38 57.118' / W120 06.811'

THE HIKE

Sequestered within the polished granite and sparse woodlands of Desolation's high country, you'll be happy to spend an hour (or a night) on the shores of any of the three Velma Lakes. No matter how you get there, you'll have come a long way and gained a lot of elevation; you'll need the respite.

You can approach the Velmas from the east, via either the Eagle Falls trailhead or the Bayview trailhead, or from the west, from Glen Alpine or the Pacific Crest Trail by way of Lake Aloha and Dicks Pass. The route described here is an out-and-back day hike starting at Eagle Falls. This allows you to take in spectacular views of Eagle Lake from above, as well as long-distance views of Lake Tahoe framed by the narrow granite walls of the Eagle Creek drainage.

Begin on stairs at the trailhead sign, following the signed Eagle Lake Trail. Climb a twisting stone stairway up, then down, to a vista point and the sturdy bridge spanning the cataracts of Eagle Falls. Cross the bridge and climb granite stairs and rocky singletrack past the wilderness boundary sign and across a large, smooth, relatively flat granite slab. The trail is worn into the slab, with smaller rocks lining the route.

A shallow, sparsely wooded basin high in the Desolation Wilderness cradles the three Velma Lakes.

Beyond the slab, the trail traverses above the Eagle Creek drainage on a shady path. Climb relatively gently to the signed trail junction at 0.9 mile. The trail to the right leads to Eagle Lake, cradled in its impressive granite cirque. The trail to Velma Lakes heads left, and uphill.

And uphill. And up some more. Beyond the junction the path makes an ascending traverse of the lower west-facing slopes of Maggies Peaks, which top out at about 8,500 feet. Eagle Lake lies below, surrounded by dramatic cliffs and polished granite aprons. Steady climbing leads into a steep woodland, where you'll cross a stream (dry in late season) and then climb alongside the drainage. The trail incorporates roots and boulders into staircases that assist in the ascent.

A few switchbacks lead up onto a saddle with great views across the granite spine of the wilderness. This is a good place for a rest before continuing to the three-way junction of trails to Velma Lakes, back to Eagle Lake, and to the Bayview trailhead. Head right on the relatively flat path signed for Velma Lakes.

At more than 8,100 feet, the widely spaced trees that find purchase among the granite outcrops are silvered and stunted by wind and snow. The views are high Sierra classic, of glacier-polished granite mountainsides that glimmer in brilliant sunshine and drop into seemingly bottomless gorges. This is the realm of the backpacker: The scents of sweat, bug juice, and camp stove fuel waft from them as they pass, before being cleared away by the constant breeze.

At the next trail junction, with a trail to Dicks Lake, stay right on the signed trail to Velma Lakes. The path begins to descend, and you'll catch sight of deep blue water in the distance through the trees. Continue down, crossing Eagle Creek (a challenge in early season when the water level is high with snowmelt) and passing a small lake/pond before reaching Middle Velma Lake, arguably the best destination for day hikers, and the junctions of the trails leading up to Upper Velma Lake and Fontanillis Lake. This is the turnaround point. The Velma Lakes are not located adjacent to the trail but are easily reached via short walks off the main track. Pick a spot on the shore of the Velma of your choice (Lower Velma Lake is a short cross-country walk east of Middle Velma), take a rest, and then return as you came.

Green Tip:

Keep to established trails as much as possible. If there aren't any, stay on surfaces that will be least affected, like rock, gravel, dry grasses, or snow.

MILES AND DIRECTIONS

0.0 Start by climbing steps to the junction of the Eagle Lake Trail and the Eagle Loop. Stay left (southwest) on the Eagle Lake Trail.

0.2 Climb granite steps past the second Eagle Loop trail junction and stay left (south), crossing the bridge.

0.4 Pass the Desolation Wilderness boundary.

0.9 At the junction with the trail to the Velma Lakes, stay left on the signed trail to Velma Lakes.

1.25 Dip across a streambed (dry in late season) and stay left at what appears to be a trail junction, climbing up alongside the drainage.

2.0 Round switchbacks onto a saddle. The trail descends via switchbacks, then traverses.

2.6 Arrive at a signed three-way junction. The left-hand trail leads back to the Bayview trailhead. Stay right on the trail to Velma Lakes.

3.4 At the junction with the trail to Dicks Lake, go right on the signed trail to Velma Lakes.

4.5 Reach the junctions with the trails to Upper Velma Lake, then Fontanillis Lake. This is the turnaround point, though you can choose to explore and rest on the shore of Upper, Middle, or Lower Velma Lakes. Return as you came.

9.0 Arrive back at the trailhead.

HIKE INFORMATION

Local information: For the scoop on lodging, restaurants, and activities in South Lake Tahoe, look to the Lake Tahoe South Shore Chamber of Commerce. The chamber is located at 169 US 50, 3rd Floor, Stateline, NV 89449; call (775) 588-1728; visit www.tahoechamber.org. Or visit www.tahoesouth.com.

Local events/attractions: Guided tours of historic Vikingsholm, located across CA 28 from the Eagle Falls trailhead, are available from Memorial Day through Sept. A fee is charged. Call the D. L. Bliss State Park office at (530) 525-9529 for more information.

Camping: Backcountry campsites are available around Middle Velma Lake and other destinations in the Desolation Wilderness. Backpackers must obtain permits to camp in the wilderness, with 50 percent of the permits available in advance and the remainder given out on a first-come, first-served basis. A fee is charged. Be sure to observe wilderness regulations, which limit groups to twelve

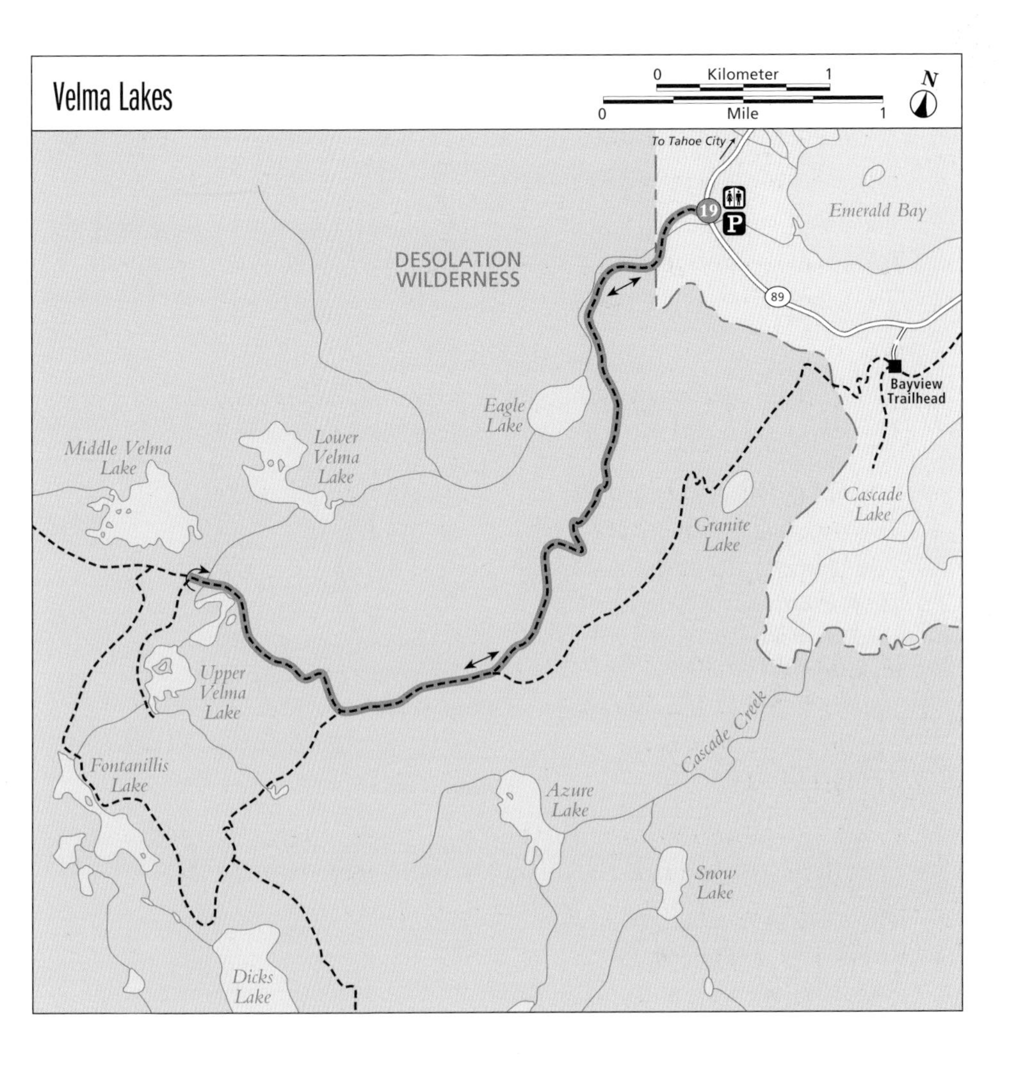

individuals, require campsites to be situated at least 100 feet from any water source, and request that proper precautions be taken to protect foodstuffs from black bears. For more information and permits contact the forest service's Lake Tahoe Basin Management Unit by calling (530) 543-2600 or visit www.fs.fed.us/r5/ltbmu.

Developed camping is available at D. L. Bliss State Park. There are 138 sites, all equipped with metal bear boxes for food storage. A fee is charged. For more information call (530) 525-7277 or (530) 525-3345 (in summer). Online reservations can be made by visiting the D. L. Bliss State Park page at www.parks.ca.gov; the link will take you to the park's ReserveAmerica (www.reserveamerica.com) page.

20

Cascade Falls

A brief walk through nicely spaced evergreens is a peaceful preamble to the rocky path and raucous creek at the end of the trail to Cascade Falls. Views of Cascade Lake and Lake Tahoe add to the hike's appeal.

Start: At the signed trailhead at the day-use parking lot in the Bayview Campground
Distance: 2 miles out and back
Hiking time: 1–2 hours
Difficulty: Moderate due to climbs and descents over rocky terrain
Trail surface: Dirt singletrack; granite
Best seasons: Late spring, summer, fall
Other trail users: None
Trailhead amenities: Parking, restrooms, trashcans, water, and informational signboards are available in the Bayview Campground.
Canine compatibility: Leashed dogs permitted
Fees and permits: None
Schedule: Sunrise to sunset daily
Maps: USGS Emerald Bay CA
Trail contact: US Forest Service Lake Tahoe Basin Management Unit, Forest Supervisor's Office, 35 College Dr., South Lake Tahoe, CA 96150; (530) 543-2600; www.fs.fed.us/r5/ltbmu

Finding the trailhead: From the intersection of US 50 and CA 89 in South Lake Tahoe, head north on CA 89 for 9.4 miles to a left (south) turn into the Bayview Campground. From Tahoe City follow CA 89 south for 18.9 miles, past the parking areas for Vikingsholm and Eagle Falls, to a right turn into the campground. Follow the campground road 0.3 mile to limited parking at the signed trailhead. Direct access to the trailhead may be difficult in high season; be prepared to park outside the campground or in safe pullouts along the highway. GPS: N38 56.607' / W120 06.000'

THE HIKE

Boisterous Cascade Creek feeds both Cascade Falls and Cascade Lake. The dark, still lake, cupped in a wooded bowl and surrounded by private property, is off-limits to hikers. The falls are off-limits too, rendered inaccessible by steep granite faces. But above the falls the creek is a friendly destination, coursing over smooth granite slabs. Settle in on the sunny rocks and enjoy the cooling mists while taking in vistas of Cascade Lake and Lake Tahoe.

To begin, walk behind the information kiosk and turn left (south) onto the signed Cascade Trail. The trail bends around two short trail posts, passing through a mixed evergreen forest, then climbs a short, stone stairway to an overlook of the falls in the distance, as well as Cascade Lake and Lake Tahoe.

At about the 0.5-mile mark, the trail begins a rocky downward traverse of the slope on the north side of Cascade Lake. Pick your way down to and then along the base of a granite cliff, taking care as the footing is uneven. You can catch glimpses of the falls tumbling toward the lake, but be sure to stop walking before you look.

Cross a relatively narrow ledge, then climb granite steps and broken rock to broad sun-splashed slabs that border the creek. A lovely granite bowl opens

A series of cascades spills out of the Desolation Wilderness into Cascade Lake.

upstream, stretching back into Desolation Wilderness. A maze of trails has been worked onto the landscape over the years, some marked by "ducks" (stacks of rocks also known as cairns) and others delineated by lines of rocks. Look left and downhill for a wooden trail marker that points the way to the falls overlook. Stay low (left and north) to get closer to the falls, but don't get too close as you don't want to take a tumble. Stay high (right and south) to reach stretches of the creek that permit water play and toe-dipping.

The whole terrace opens on wonderful views across Lake Tahoe. Take in the sights, cool your jets, then return as you came.

MILES AND DIRECTIONS

0.0 Start behind the informational signboard, turning left (south) at the sign pointing toward CASCADE FALLS.

0.5 Head up the stone steps to lake views and vistas of the falls.

0.7 Traverse across slabs and steps at the base of a granite wall.

0.8 The trail levels as you approach the creek, and the granite terrace opens uphill to the south.

1.0 Reach the creek above the falls. Enjoy the sun and views, then return as you came.

2.0 Arrive back at the trailhead.

Option: A right (southwest) turn at the Bayview trailhead puts you on the trail to Granite Lake and other destinations in the Desolation Wilderness, including the Velma Lakes. A wilderness permit for day use is required and available at the trailhead.

HIKE INFORMATION

Local information: For the scoop on lodging, restaurants, and activities in South Lake Tahoe, look to the Lake Tahoe South Shore Chamber of Commerce. The chamber is located at 169 US 50, 3rd Floor, Stateline, NV 89449; call (775) 588-1728; visit www.tahoechamber.org. Or visit www.tahoesouth.com.

Camping: Thirteen campsites are available on a first-come, first-served basis at the Bayview Campground. Recreational vehicles are limited to 20 feet in length. A fee is charged. For more information contact the forest service's Lake Tahoe Basin Management Unit by calling (530) 543-2600, or visit www.fs.fed.us/r5/ltbmu.

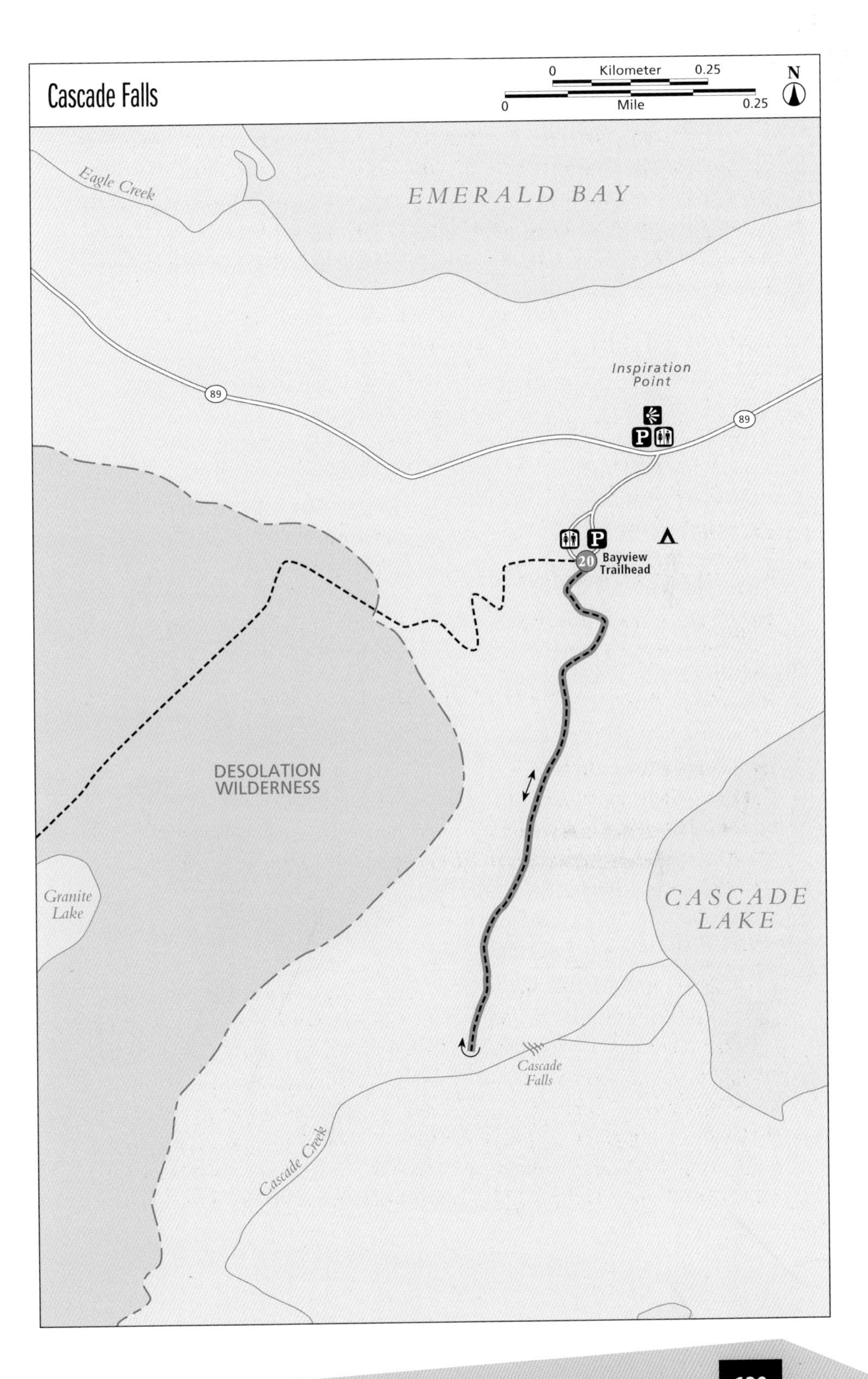
Cascade Falls
0
Kilometer
0.25
0
Mile
0.25
N
Eagle Creek
EMERALD BAY
Inspiration Point
89
89
20
Bayview Trailhead
DESOLATION WILDERNESS
Granite Lake
CASCADE LAKE
Cascade Falls
Cascade Creek

21

Cathedral Lake

Mount Tallac, at more than 9,700 feet in elevation, dominates nearly every South Lake Tahoe vista. It's also a powerful presence on the hike to Cathedral Lake, a peaceful tarn cupped among jumbled rock and thick-trunked evergreens that sits at the base of one of the peak's talus fields.

Start: At the Mount Tallac trailhead parking area off CA 89
Distance: 5.6 miles out and back
Hiking time: 4–5 hours
Difficulty: Strenuous due to an 1,100-foot elevation gain
Trail surface: Dirt singletrack
Best seasons: Late spring, summer, early fall
Other trail users: None
Trailhead amenities: Parking, an informational signboard
Canine compatibility: Leashed dogs permitted
Fees and permits: A free wilderness permit is required and available at the trailhead.
Schedule: Sunrise to sunset
Maps: USGS Emerald Bay CA; a map on the signboard at the trailhead
Trail contact: US Forest Service Lake Tahoe Basin Management Unit, Forest Supervisor's Office, 35 College Dr., South Lake Tahoe, CA 96150; (530) 543-2600; www.fs.fed.us/r5/ltbmu

Finding the trailhead: From the intersection of US 50 and CA 89 in South Lake Tahoe, head north on CA 89 for 4.1 miles to the turnoff for Camp Shelly and the Mount Tallac trailhead. Turn left (west) onto the trailhead road, and drive 0.4 mile to the first fork in the road, signed for the Mount Tallac trailhead and Camp Concord. Go left (southwest) for 0.2 mile to another intersection. Stay straight (right) on FR 1306, again signed for the Mount Tallac trailhead. The parking area is 0.5 mile ahead. GPS: N38 55.283' / W120 04.086'

THE HIKE

Though separated from the gray-green flanks of Mount Tallac by a narrow glacial valley for most of its distance, every foot of the trail to Cathedral Lake is shadowed by the mountain's daunting ramparts. The elevation gain is significant, but the climbing is never painfully steep and is mitigated by great views, shade, and a convenient refueling locale at Floating Island Lake, a tarn surrounded by a thick yellow pine forest that makes a logical turnaround spot for a shorter hike. Cathedral Lake is set above and beyond, in a talus-rimmed bowl near treeline on the mountain's southeast flank.

The trail begins by climbing through sunny scrubland scented with sage. Ascend a couple of switchbacks and wonderful views open of Fallen Leaf Lake below (east), and Lake Tahoe, behind and to the north.

The views improve atop the narrow ridgeback of the lateral moraine separating Fallen Leaf Lake from Mount Tallac, with the trail cruising along the spine of the moraine through Jeffrey pine and mountain hemlock. Drop off the ridge into a drainage, where the views are abandoned for shade.

Cathedral Lake stills in the morning light.

The trail roller coasters through forest and gully as it veers north. Climb up to and then alongside the creek that issues from Floating Island Lake. Pass the Desolation Wilderness boundary, then hitch up a final stretch to the flat, quiet shoreline of the little wooded lake. Take a break, then continue along the path, which skirts the south shore of Floating Island Lake.

At the edge of a small talus field just above Floating Island Lake, the trail veers right (west), resuming the climb via a short staircase composed of blocks of granite. Cross a small meadow and a creek (stay left on the main trail); beyond, the route traverses a hillside strewn with wildflowers and butterflies in early summer.

Drop to a second creek crossing, then meander up to the junction with a trail that descends to Fallen Leaf Lake. Stay right (southwest), climbing a last pitch up to Cathedral Lake. Rest on the shores of the small tarn, then return to the trailhead by the same route.

MILES AND DIRECTIONS

0.0 Start up the trail behind the informational signboard.

0.7 Reach the top of the lateral moraine, with views down to Fallen Leaf Lake and Lake Tahoe, and up to Mount Tallac.

1.2 Drop off the moraine.

1.8 Climb up along a creek to the boundary of the Desolation Wilderness.

1.9 Arrive at Floating Island Lake.

2.5 Cross a streamlet and stay right (west) around the talus field.

2.7 Arrive at the signed junction with the trail to Fallen Leaf Lake. Stay right (south) and up on the Mount Tallac Trail.

2.8 Arrive at Cathedral Lake. Rest, then retrace your steps.

5.6 Arrive back at the trailhead.

Options: If you have the will and strength, you can make the steep climb to the summit of Mount Tallac (9,735 feet; about 2.4 miles beyond Cathedral Lake). The trail also connects with other routes in the Desolation Wilderness, including a trail leading to Gilmore Lake and Glen Alpine.

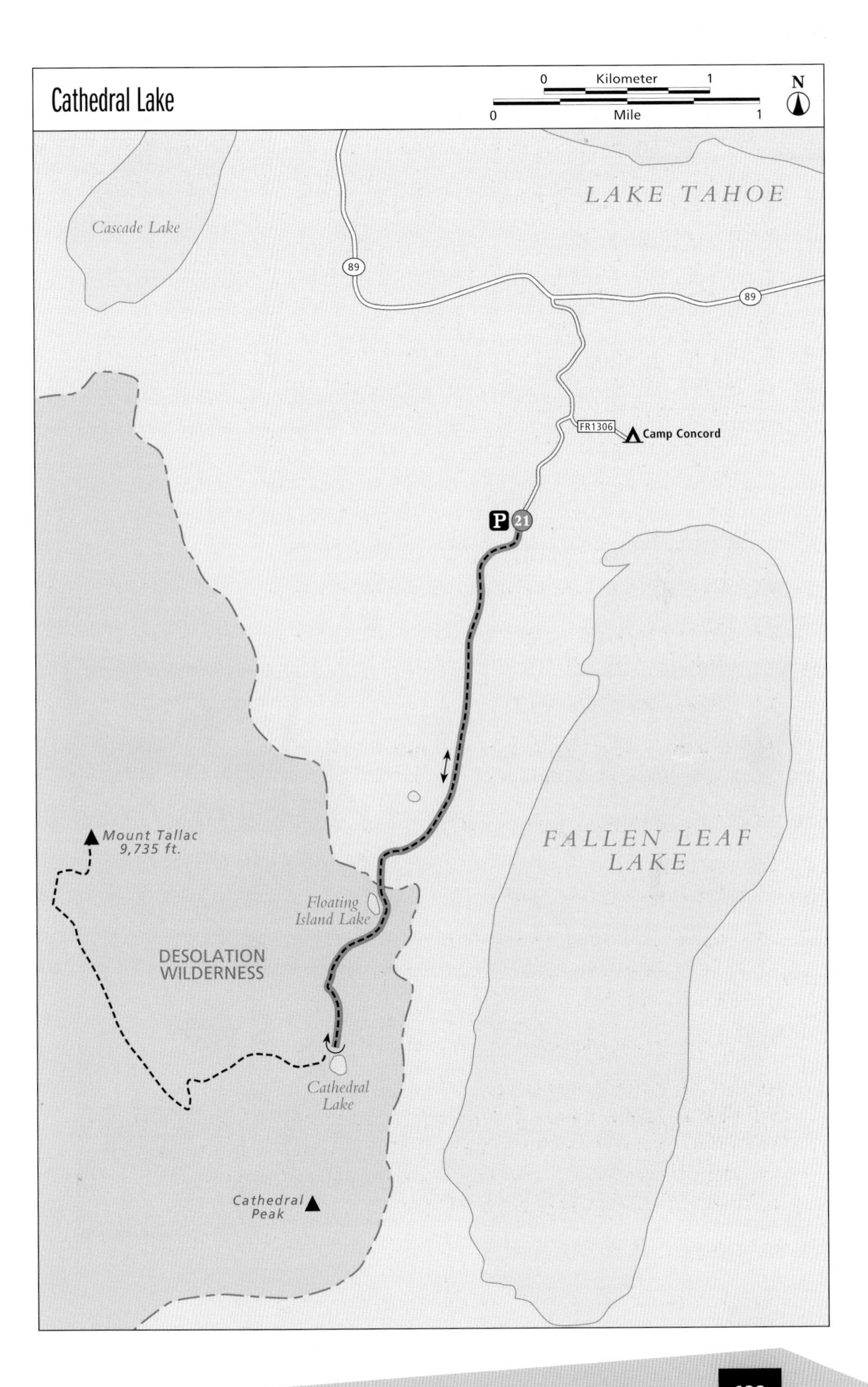

Cathedral Lake
0
Kilometer
1
0
Mile
1
N
LAKE TAHOE
Cascade Lake
89
89
FR1306
Camp Concord
P
21
FALLEN LEAF
LAKE
Mount Tallac
9,735 ft.
Floating
Island Lake
DESOLATION
WILDERNESS
Cathedral
Lake
Cathedral
Peak

HIKE INFORMATION

Local information: For information on lodging, restaurants, and activities in South Lake Tahoe, look to the Lake Tahoe South Shore Chamber of Commerce. The chamber is located at 169 US 50, 3rd Floor, Stateline, NV 89449; call (775) 588-1728; visit www.tahoechamber.org. Or visit www.tahoesouth.com.

Camping: While camping at Cathedral Lake is less than inviting, given the rocky terrain, backcountry campsites are available at other destinations in the Desolation Wilderness. Backpackers must obtain permits to camp in the wilderness, with 50 percent of the permits available in advance and the remainder distributed on a first-come, first-served basis. A fee is charged. Be sure to observe wilderness regulations, which limit groups to twelve individuals, require campsites to be situated at least 100 feet from any water source, and request that proper precautions be taken to protect foodstuffs from black bears. For more information and permits contact the forest service's Lake Tahoe Basin Management Unit by calling (530) 543-2600 or visit www.fs.fed.us/r5/ltbmu.

Stately pines and talus border Cathedral Lake.

Rainbow Trail

The Taylor Creek Stream Profile Chamber is the main attraction along this family favorite, but the Rainbow Trail has more to recommend it, including vistas across the Taylor Creek marshlands, bowers of quaking aspen, and comprehensive interpretive signage.

Start: At the signed trailhead outside the Taylor Creek Visitor Center
Distance: 0.6-mile lollipop
Hiking time: 45 minutes to 1 hour
Difficulty: Easy
Trail surface: Paved path
Best seasons: Spring, summer, and fall
Other trail users: None
Trailhead amenities: A large parking lot, restrooms, trashcans, water, a visitor center, and a gift shop
Canine compatibility: Dogs not permitted in the stream chamber or on Kiva Beach, but are otherwise allowed on leashes
Fees and permits: None
Schedule: The stream profile chamber is open Memorial Day to Oct 31 from 8 a.m. until a half-hour before the Taylor Creek Visitor Center closes. The visitor center is open from 8 a.m. to 4:30 p.m. from mid-May to mid-June and during Oct. It is open from 8 a.m. to 5:30 p.m. from mid-June through Sept.
Maps: USGS Emerald Bay CA; no map is needed
Trail contact: US Forest Service Lake Tahoe Basin Management Unit, Forest Supervisor's Office, 35 College Dr., South Lake Tahoe, CA 96150; (530) 543-2600; www.fs.fed.us/r5/ltbmu
Special considerations: The trail is wheelchair accessible. The Taylor Creek Visitor Center is staffed by rangers and offers information and gifts, including guidebooks.

Finding the trailhead: From the intersection of US 50 and CA 89 in South Lake Tahoe, go north on CA 89 for 3.2 miles to the signed turnoff for the Taylor Creek Visitor Center. Turn right (north) onto the visitor center road, and follow it to the parking area. The trailhead, with an arcing sign, is opposite the visitor center entrance. GPS: N38 56.133' / W120 03.243'

THE HIKE

If you visit the Taylor Creek Stream Profile Chamber in autumn, you can enjoy below-the-surface views of kokanee salmon, their scales lipstick-red as they prepare to spawn, doing laps in lovesick agitation. They mingle with their cousins: rainbow, brown, and Lahontan cutthroat trout, the latter species native to the deep waters of Lake Tahoe. Larger fish circle lazily in the stream scene behind the glass, while the smaller dart about, looking for food or perhaps practicing their moves to avoid becoming meals themselves.

Walkers on the Rainbow Trail pause for long stretches to take in this snapshot of life in a mountain stream. First-hand observation, coupled with the assistance of an interpretive naturalist and additional information from the accompanying interpretive display, enhance this unique hiking experience.

Green Tip:
Pass it down—the best way to instill good green habits in your children is to set a good example.

An interpretive arch announces the start of the Rainbow Trail.

Though the stream profile chamber is the Rainbow Trail's main draw, this pleasant path—easy enough for a toddler to manage—sports many other attractions. The marsh surrounding Taylor Creek is no scenic slouch, resplendent with wildflowers in spring and ringing with birdcall throughout the hiking season. Quaking aspen, turning a vivid gold in fall, provide yet another visual treat. The route is lined with interpretive signs and benches, where children of all ages can dawdle and contemplate.

The paved path begins just outside the visitor center, dropping to a marsh overlook and then to the trail junction where the loop begins. Go right (following the arrow), traveling in a counterclockwise direction. Meander through the meadow and skirt the marsh on boardwalks, taking in views toward Lake Tahoe. A bridge spans Taylor Creek, then the trail forks, with one branch leading down and through the stream profile chamber and the other going around it.

After your stream study, you'll emerge from the far side of the chamber into a stand of aspen. Pass a "pillow sensor" and rain gauge, along with the interpretive display that explains their functions. Beyond lies an alder spring, and then more of the tall grasses and wildflowers of the meadow. Once you return to the trail junction and close the loop, go right to the visitor center and parking area.

The scenic and educational Rainbow Trail is a family favorite and one of the most popular short routes on Lake Tahoe's south shore.

MILES AND DIRECTIONS

0.0 Start on the paved path under the Rainbow Trail arch.

0.1 Visit the marsh overlook, then return to the trail and drop to the start of the loop. Go right (counterclockwise) as indicated by the directional arrow.

0.3 Drop through the stream profile chamber.

0.4 At the Y outside the chamber, go left, past the monitoring station. Close the loop by circling back toward the visitor center.

0.6 Arrive back at the trailhead.

HIKE INFORMATION

Local information: For the scoop on lodging, restaurants, and activities in South Lake Tahoe, look to the Lake Tahoe South Shore Chamber of Commerce. The chamber is located at 169 US 50, 3rd Floor, Stateline, NV 89449; call (775) 588-1728; visit www.tahoechamber.org. Or visit www.tahoesouth.com.
Local events/attractions: The Camp Richardson Resort and Marina offers a wealth of recreational and lodging opportunities near the Tallac Historic Site, Rainbow Trail, and Fallen Leaf Lake. Among the amenities are a marina, lakeside cabins and camping facilities, a restaurant, and a sports center that offers bicycle rentals in summer and snowshoe rentals in winter. For more information contact the resort at (800) 544-1801 (local 530-541-1801) or visit www.camprichardson.com/the-resort.

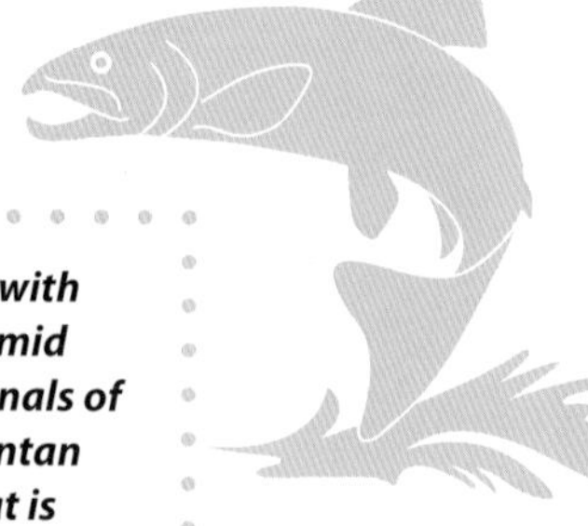

Explorer John C. Frémont is credited with being the first white man to see Pyramid Lake, where he made note in his journals of the presence of a subspecies of Lahontan cutthroat trout, the same species that is native to Lake Tahoe. Reports say Frémont encountered trout that weighed more than forty pounds, were up to 3 or 4 feet long, and of "excellent" flavor.

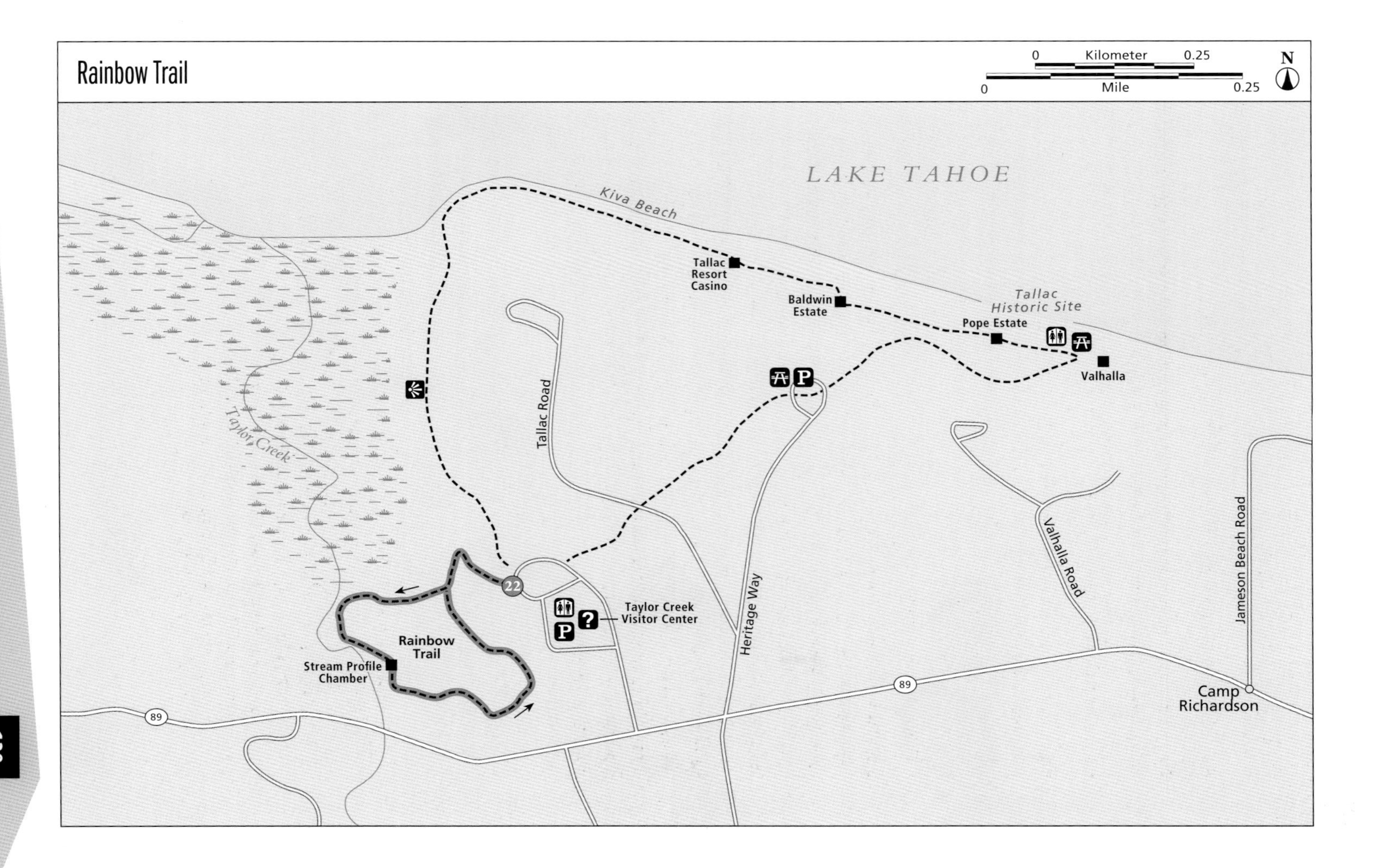

Rainbow Trail
0
Kilometer
0.25
0
Mile
0.25
N
LAKE TAHOE
Kiva Beach
Tallac Resort Casino
Baldwin Estate
Tallac Historic Site
Pope Estate
Valhalla
Taylor Creek
Tallac Road
Heritage Way
Valhalla Road
Jameson Beach Road
22
Taylor Creek Visitor Center
Rainbow Trail
Stream Profile Chamber
89
Camp Richardson

23

Lake of the Sky Trail and Tallac Historic Site

This scenic loop links the natural history of Lake Tahoe to its human history, from the wild creatures that inhabit the Taylor Creek marsh to turn-of-the-twentieth-century resort owners and their spectacular vacation homes.

Start: At the signed trailhead at the Taylor Creek Visitor Center
Distance: 2-mile loop
Hiking time: 2–3 hours
Difficulty: Easy
Trail surface: Singletrack, sand, pavement
Best seasons: Late spring, summer, fall
Other trail users: Cyclists, trail runners
Trailhead amenities: A large parking lot, restrooms, trashcans, water, a visitor center, and a gift shop
Canine compatibility: No dogs permitted on the portion of Kiva Beach west of Kiva Point. Leashed dogs are allowed on the section of beach that is part of the Kiva Picnic Area. Though leashed dogs are allowed on the trails, Tallac Historic Site is not dog-friendly. Leashed dogs are permitted on the beach west of Tallac Point.
Fees and permits: None
Schedule: The Taylor Creek Visitor Center is open from 8 a.m. to 4:30 p.m. from mid-May to mid-June and during Oct. It is open from 8 a.m. to 5:30 p.m. from mid-June through Sept. The trails can be used from sunrise to sunset daily.
Maps: USGS Emerald Bay CA
Trail contact: US Forest Service Lake Tahoe Basin Management Unit, Forest Supervisor's Office, 35 College Dr., South Lake Tahoe, CA 96150; (530) 543-2600; www.fs.fed.us/r5/ltbmu
Other: The link from the end of the Lake of the Sky Trail to the Tallac Historic Site is not a formal forest service trail.

Finding the trailhead: From the intersection of US 50 and CA 89 in South Lake Tahoe, go north on CA 89 for 3.2 miles to the signed turnoff for the Taylor Creek Visitor Center. Turn right (north) onto the visitor center road and follow it to the parking area for the visitor center. The signed trailhead is on the north side of the visitor center. GPS: N38 56.165' / W120 03.228'

THE HIKE

Lake Tahoe has provided bounty for residents and visitors for millennia, from the Washoe Indians and their ancestors, who summered on the lake's shores and harvested its fish and fauna, to turn-of-the-twentieth-century vacationers who built grand estates and party palaces. Wild creatures—deer, bear, eagles, and trout, to name a few—also have called the lake home for thousands of years. This trail loop offers glimpses into what each found and left on Tahoe's shores.

The tour begins on the Lake of the Sky Trail, which heads north from the Taylor Creek Visitor Center along the Taylor Creek Marsh to Kiva Beach. The trail is lined with interpretive signs describing the habitats that the route passes through and overlooks, and boasts a viewing deck on the border of Taylor Marsh.

Green Tip:
Don't take souvenirs home with you. This includes natural materials such as plants, rocks, shells, and driftwood as well as historic artifacts such as fossils and arrowheads.

Mount Tallac rises above the marshlands at the mouth of Taylor Creek on the Lake of the Sky Trail.

The formal trail ends at Kiva Beach, and an informal trail leads east along the gravelly beachfront toward developed trails in the Tallac Historic Site. Wander down along the water, enjoying wide lake views and the opportunity to watch water-skiers and wake-boarders, then hitch right (south) up one of the short staircases onto the doubletrack that leads into the historic site.

The first historic site you'll pass are the foundations of the Tallac Resort Casino, tucked in the woodland just off the shore. An interpretive sign describes the ballroom, gambling rooms, bowling alley, and stage that "Lucky" Baldwin built and operated here. Baldwin's purchase of the lakefront property in 1880 also resulted in the preservation of the grand old Jeffrey pines that shade picnic areas along the trail.

The trail bends right (south) at a gate to the signed TALLAC MUSEUM and Washoe Indian exhibit. Inside the Tallac Historic Site, you can wander at will through the grounds of the Baldwin, Pope, and Heller estates. Interpretive signs describe the buildings—cabins, homes, a museum, a boathouse theater—and exhibits preserved at the site, all of which have tree-screened lake views. Spend an hour here or the rest of the day, but be sure to visit the wonderful arboretum and garden before you head out to the parking lot to complete the loop.

A sign at the north end of the historic site's parking area directs you onto the singletrack trail that leads through scrub and woodland back to the visitor center and trailhead.

MILES AND DIRECTIONS

0.0 Begin on the signed, paved Lake of the Sky Trail on the north side of the visitor center. Pass the amphitheater; the trail turns to dirt.

0.2 Visit the viewing platform.

0.4 Reach the end of the Lake of the Sky Trail (with a map) at Kiva Beach. Turn right (east) along the beach.

0.6 Go right (south) up one of the short staircases onto the trail that parallels the beach. Go left (east) along the doubletrack past the Tallac Resort Casino.

0.9 The trail bends right (south) to the first buildings of the Tallac Historic Site. Go left, into the Washoe Indian exhibit, then wander through the historic site.

1.7 Complete your tour in the main parking lot. The signed singletrack back to the Taylor Creek Visitor Center is on the north side of the lot.

1.8 Cross the park road.

2.0 Arrive back at the trailhead.

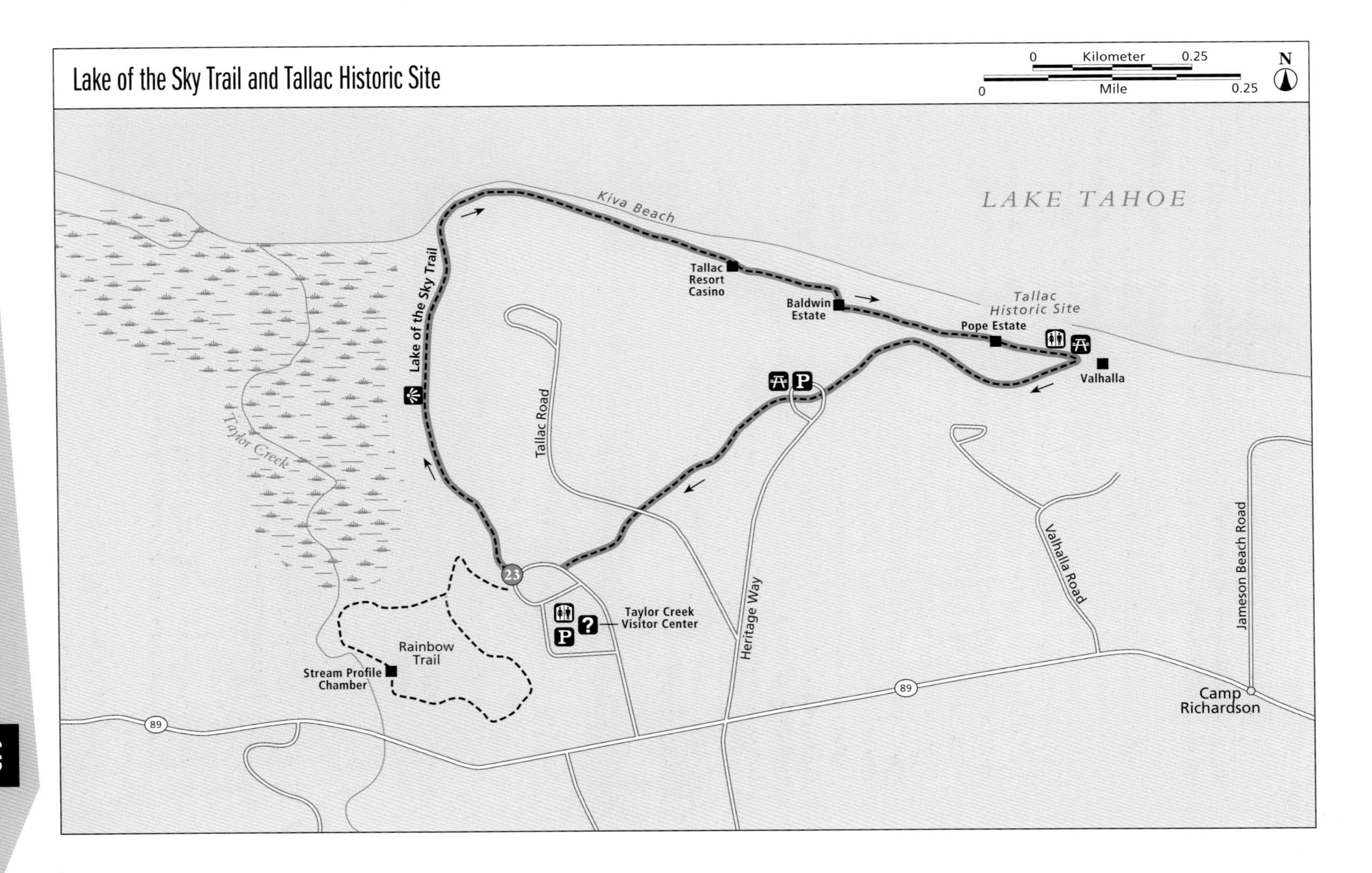
Lake of the Sky Trail and Tallac Historic Site
0 Kilometer 0.25
0 Mile 0.25
N
LAKE TAHOE
Kiva Beach
Tallac Resort Casino
Baldwin Estate
Tallac Historic Site
Pope Estate
Valhalla
Lake of the Sky Trail
Taylor Creek
Tallac Road
23
Taylor Creek Visitor Center
Rainbow Trail
Stream Profile Chamber
Heritage Way
Valhalla Road
Jameson Beach Road
Camp Richardson
89
89

HIKE INFORMATION

Local information: For information on lodging, restaurants, and activities in South Lake Tahoe, look to the Lake Tahoe South Shore Chamber of Commerce. The chamber is located at 169 US 50, 3rd Floor, Stateline, NV 89449; call (775) 588-1728; visit www.tahoechamber.org. Or visit www.tahoesouth.com.

Local events/attractions: The Tahoe Tallac Association hosts a number of cultural events at the Tallac Historic Site to benefit preservation and restoration efforts. For more information on events, which include concerts, theater, an annual holiday fair, and the Valhalla Arts & Music Festival, showcasing the art and music of different cultures and historical eras, call (530) 541-4975, write to PO Box 19273, South Lake Tahoe, CA 96151, or visit valhallatahoe.com.

Organizations: While the Tahoe Tallac Association (TTA) focuses on cultural events that assist in the preservation of Valhalla, the Tahoe Heritage Foundation works with the US Forest Service (and in conjunction with the TTA) to raise funds to support restoration, interpretation, and other programs at the Baldwin and Pope estates. Contact the foundation by writing PO Box 8586, South Lake Tahoe, CA 96158; call (530) 544-7383; or visit tahoeheritage.org.

The Lake of the Sky Trail empties onto Kiva Beach.

Angora Lakes

Pack your towels and bring the kids: The Angora Lakes Trail is short, sweet, and the perfect introduction to hiking in the mountains around Lake Tahoe.

Start: At the gate in the upper parking lot at the end of Forest Road 1214
Distance: 1 mile out and back
Hiking time: 45 minutes to 1 hour
Difficulty: Easy
Trail surface: Dirt access road
Best seasons: Summer and fall
Other trail users: Mountain bikers and the occasional automobile
Trailhead amenities: Parking, restrooms, information, a fee station. Food, water, restrooms, and information are available at the Angora Lakes Resort at trail's end.
Canine compatibility: Leashed dogs permitted; dogs may not swim in the lake
Fees and permits: A parking fee is levied.
Schedule: Sunrise to sunset daily. The resort is open daily from mid-June to mid-Sept.
Maps: USGS Echo Lakes CA; no map is needed
Trail contact: US Forest Service Lake Tahoe Basin Management Unit, Forest Supervisor's Office, 35 College Dr., South Lake Tahoe, CA 96150; (530) 543-2600; www.fs.fed.us/r5/ltbmu

Finding the trailhead: From the intersection of US 50 and CA 89 in South Lake Tahoe, go north on CA 89 for 3 miles to Fallen Leaf Lake Road. Turn left (west) onto Fallen Leaf Lake Road and go 2 miles to Tahoe Mountain Road. Turn left (southwest) onto Tahoe Mountain Road and follow it for 0.4 mile to unsigned FR 1214 (look for an open gate; the road appears to be dirt at the outset). Turn right (west) onto FR 1214 and travel 3 miles on the scenic, narrow, paved roadway to the parking area. The trailhead is beyond the gate at the south end of the upper lot. GPS: N38 52.261' / W120 03.788'

THE HIKE

After a short hike up a wide access road (with just enough elevation gain to get your heart pumping), you'll land on the sandy shores of Upper Angora Lake, replete with a spectacular alpine setting, cool water for swimming, rowboats for rent, and a snack bar that features some of the best lemonade money can buy. It's definitely not a wilderness experience, but the hike has a ton of charm, and the destination, framed by steep granite walls and featuring a sunny slip of beach, is a dream.

The route is straightforward: Follow the Angora Lakes access road as it loops in broad arcing turns up a boulder-strewn, forested hillside. After the short climb, the path flattens and is intersected by social paths that lead to private residences on Lower Angora Lake. Stay on the main track, tracing the north shore of the lower lake.

A second, exceptionally brief climb leads to the snack bar and cabins on the eastern shores of Upper Angora Lake, part of the Angora Lakes Resort. The west and north shores are contained by black-streaked terraced cliffs that form the lower reaches of Echo and Angora Peaks. The beach hugs the north shore; stake out a patch of sand, sip some luscious fresh-squeezed lemonade, and enjoy.

Three young hikers get ready to plunge into Upper Angora Lake.

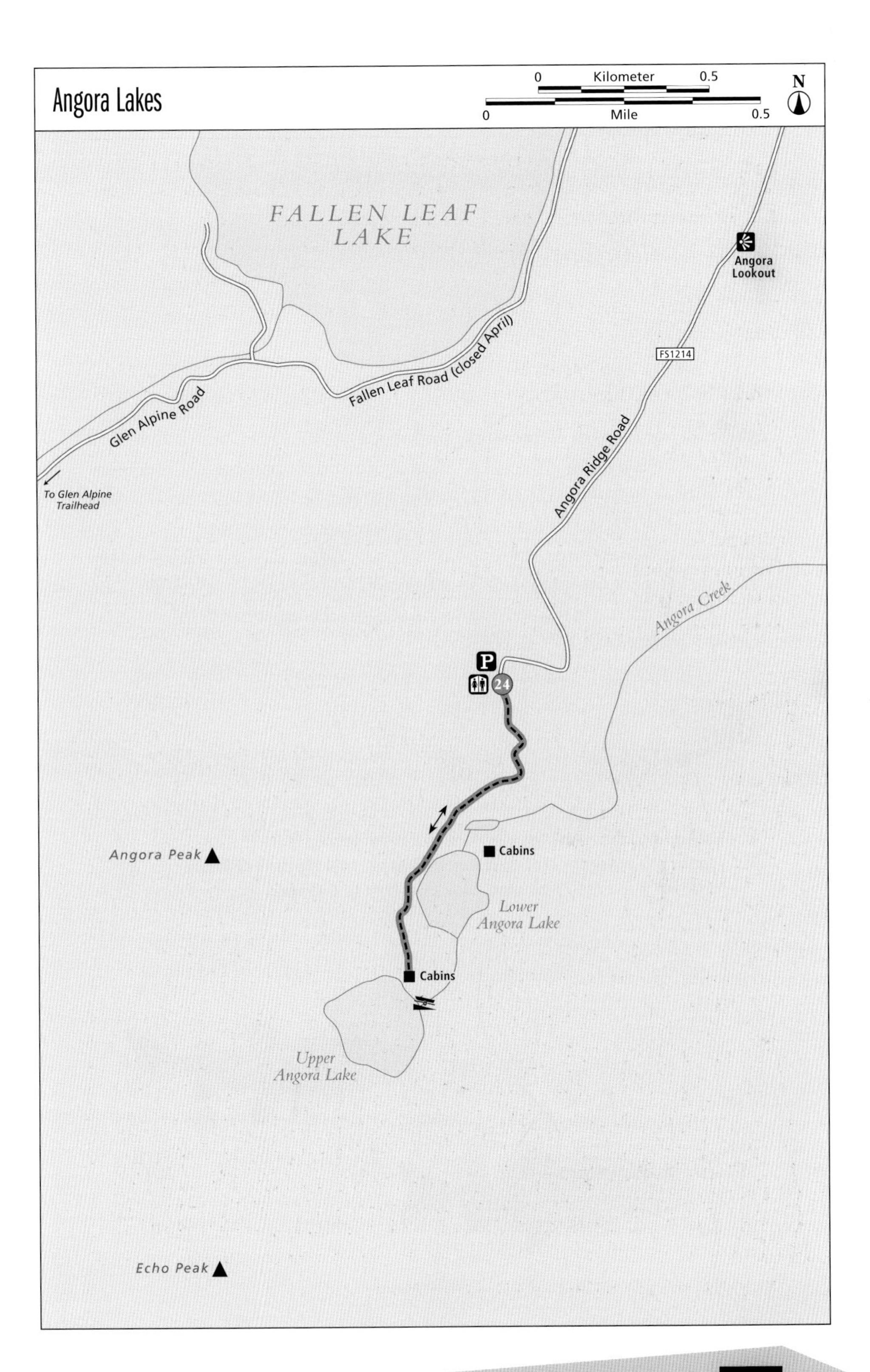
Angora Lakes
0
Kilometer
0.5
0
Mile
0.5
N
FALLEN LEAF
LAKE
Angora
Lookout
FS1214
Fallen Leaf Road (closed April)
Glen Alpine Road
To Glen Alpine
Trailhead
Angora Ridge Road
Angora Creek
P
24
Cabins
Angora Peak
Lower
Angora Lake
Cabins
Upper
Angora Lake
Echo Peak

MILES AND DIRECTIONS

0.0 Start by heading up the broad, busy dirt track.

0.2 Reach Lower Angora Lake.

0.5 Rest on the shores of Upper Angora Lake. Swim, boat, and enjoy, then retrace your steps.

1.0 Arrive back at the trailhead.

HIKE INFORMATION

Local information: For information on lodging, restaurants, and activities in South Lake Tahoe, contact the Lake Tahoe South Shore Chamber of Commerce. The chamber is located at 169 US 50, 3rd Floor, Stateline, NV 89449; call (775) 588-1728; visit www.tahoechamber.org. Or visit www.tahoesouth.com.

Local events/attractions: Angora Lakes Resort offers day-use access to the snack shack (where the lemonade is sold), as well as kayak and boat rentals. Cabins book far in advance; visit www.angoralakesresort.com or call (530) 541-2092 for more information.

Angora Lakes and Angora Peak got their names from the goats that prospector and Sierra Club partner Nathan Gilmore ran on the land. Their wool was exported to England.

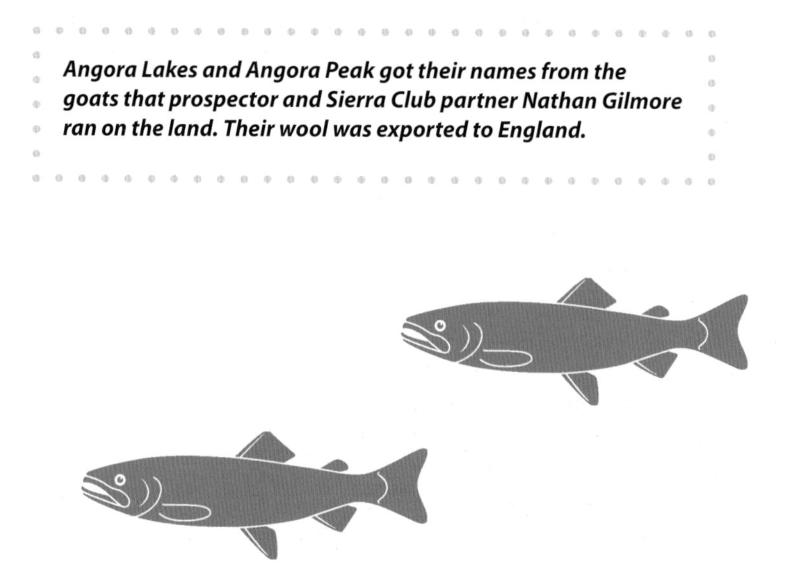

Gilmore Lake

Pass the remnants of Glen Alpine, once Lake Tahoe's premier resort, then climb into the rocky reaches of the Desolation Wilderness. Gilmore Lake, cupped in a bowl on the west side of Mount Tallac, is at trail's end.

Start: At the Glen Alpine trailhead at Lily Lake
Distance: 8.6 miles out and back
Hiking time: 5–6 hours
Difficulty: Strenuous
Trail surface: Cobblestone roadway, dirt singletrack
Best seasons: Summer, fall
Other trail users: None
Trailhead amenities: Parking, restrooms, information signboard, trashcans
Canine compatibility: Leashed dogs permitted
Fees and permits: A free wilderness permit is required and available at the trailhead.
Schedule: 24 hours a day, 7 days a week, year-round
Maps: USGS Emerald Bay CA
Trail contact: US Forest Service Lake Tahoe Basin Management Unit, Forest Supervisor's Office, 35 College Dr., South Lake Tahoe, CA 96150; (530) 543-2600; www.fs.fed.us/r5/ltbmu
Special considerations: Parking is limited at the Glen Alpine trailhead, though improvements/expansion are in the early stages of development. More parking is available in pullouts along the access road. Fallen Leaf Lake Road is one lane and busy in summer. Travel slowly and be courteous by stopping in wide spots to let oncoming traffic pass safely.

Finding the trailhead: From the intersection of US 50 and CA 89 in South Lake Tahoe, go north on CA 89 for 3 miles to Fallen Leaf Lake Road. Turn left (west) onto Fallen Leaf Lake Road. Pass the turnoff for Angora Lakes at about 2 miles, continuing on Fallen Leaf Lake Road for a total of 5 miles. Pass the lodge and marina, and at the fork just beyond stay straight, past the fire station, on FR 1216 to Lily Lake. The trailhead parking area is 0.6 mile ahead. The trailhead is at the northwest end of the parking lot, marked by a green metal gate. GPS: N38 52.627' / W120 04.836'

THE HIKE

If a hard line could be drawn in the woods, there would be one just above the site of the historic Glen Alpine Springs Resort. Where the gravel road ends and the trail begins, the personality of this trek to Gilmore Lake changes abruptly. Step onto the granite staircase, and you've left civilization behind. You are in the wilderness.

As with most trails in the Tahoe basin, the Glen Alpine changes with the seasons. In early season, or during heavy snow years, the route itself may be half submerged in flowing snowmelt. The stretch from Lily Lake to the Glen Alpine resort in particular can be soggy, but the pair of waterfalls spilling down the creek adjacent to the road are invigorating and entertaining.

At the outset, the trail is an access road surfaced in ankle-twisting cobbles. Gates and trail signs keep you on track at forks in the road, though the signs are inconspicuous, brown, and mounted above eye level on tree trunks. Parcels of private land line this section of the route, with rugged driveways leading to small cabins.

Patches of asphalt are interspersed with the cobbles on the road as you approach the first series of cascades on Glen Alpine Creek at 0.4 mile, the largest

An expansive shoreline presents plenty of space for relaxation after the climb to Gilmore Lake.

of which is about 30 feet in height. The display is best (and loudest) in June and early July. Past the falls, the trail climbs to another driveway intersection; go left (west), following the trail sign.

Continue past several more cabins, traveling through a lovely mixed evergreen forest with a lush understory of wild berries and flowers that bloom in spring, and deciduous trees and shrubs that turn hues of yellow and orange in fall. The cabins have all of Desolation Wilderness as a backyard.

Just beyond the old barn, a trail sign points you to the right (west) and into what is left of the Glen Alpine Springs Resort. Take a break and check out the remnants of what was once a thriving enterprise, including the soda spring, which still burbles and pops. Interpretive signs thoroughly describe the history of the resort, and a map directs you to the different structures that were part of the complex.

When you are ready, follow the last section of road to a trail marker. Climb the rustic granite staircase and up and around a granite outcrop, watching for lizards sunning themselves on the granite. A switchback leads up and over a granite hummock and the trail continues to climb westward, offering views across the valley to the steep cliffs that link the Angora Peaks to Keiths Dome and Cracked Crag.

The trail leading to Grass Lake, another wonderful hike, breaks off the Glen Alpine trail just beyond the Desolation Wilderness boundary sign. The climb to Gilmore Lake continues up stairs of granite and timber, nicely spaced if still steep and demanding. Switchbacks lead to moderately steep traverses as the trail climbs into the creek drainage that spills from a high saddle and feeds into Glen Alpine Creek. More stairs lead up the narrowing drainage; the trail crosses several small tributaries.

A creek crossing that may be treacherous in high water lies just below the saddle and the junction of trails leading to Lake Aloha (to the west) and Gilmore Lake (to the north). Depending on winter snowpack and water levels, the crossing can be negotiated via fallen logs or rock-hopping. In late season the creekbed may be dry.

From the trail junction, follow the trail signed for Gilmore Lake to the right. More climbing via timber-and-granite stairs lies ahead, first up to the trail junction with the path to Half Moon Lake, then up to the junction with the trail to Dicks Lake. From the last junction it's a short, relatively flat pitch to Gilmore Lake.

The lake sits in an almost perfectly round basin on the barren southwest flanks of Mount Tallac. At an elevation of about 8,200 feet, the tarn is below treeline, and the southern shore is shaded by firs and pines. The north shore is a scree slope, combed by rockfall and barren except for a few hardy evergreens. The upper slopes of Mount Tallac rise beyond the ridge on the east side of the lake.

Once you've taken in the views and fortified with food and water, return as you came.

MILES AND DIRECTIONS

0.0 Start by passing the green gate at the trailhead and walking up the cobbled roadway.

0.3 Cross a stream (dry in late season) and pass a gate and trail sign.

0.4 At the junction with a private access road stay right, follow the TRAILS sign. Check out the Glen Alpine falls before continuing up the cobbled trail.

0.5 At a second junction with a private drive, stay left, again following the TRAILS sign.

1.1 Pass the old barn and enter the Glen Alpine Springs Resort. Explore the site, then continue on the road.

1.3 The road ends at a trail sign for Susie Lake and Grass Lake. Head up the stone and log steps toward Susie Lake.

1.7 Pass the Desolation Wilderness boundary.

1.8 Reach the junction with the trail to Grass Lake. Stay straight (right) on the signed trail to Susie Lake and Mount Tallac.

2.75 Switchbacks and steps lead to a small creek crossing. Keep heading uphill.

3.1 Cross a streamlet that may be dry in late season.

3.3 Ford the main stream, which may be treacherous in early season. At the trail junction in the saddle above the creek crossing, go right (north) on the path signed for Gilmore Lake. The trail to the left (west) leads to Susie Lake and Lake Aloha.

3.6 Pass the junction with the trail to Half Moon Lake. Stay right on the signed trail to Gilmore Lake, climbing yet more stairs.

4.1 Pass the junction with the Pacific Crest Trail to Dicks Lake, staying straight on the signed trail to Gilmore Lake.

4.3 Reach the airy shores of Gilmore Lake. Enjoy the scenery, then return as you came.

8.6 Arrive back at the trailhead.

Gilmore Lake is named for Nathan Gilmore, prospector, founder of Glen Alpine Springs Resort, and Sierra Club co-founder.

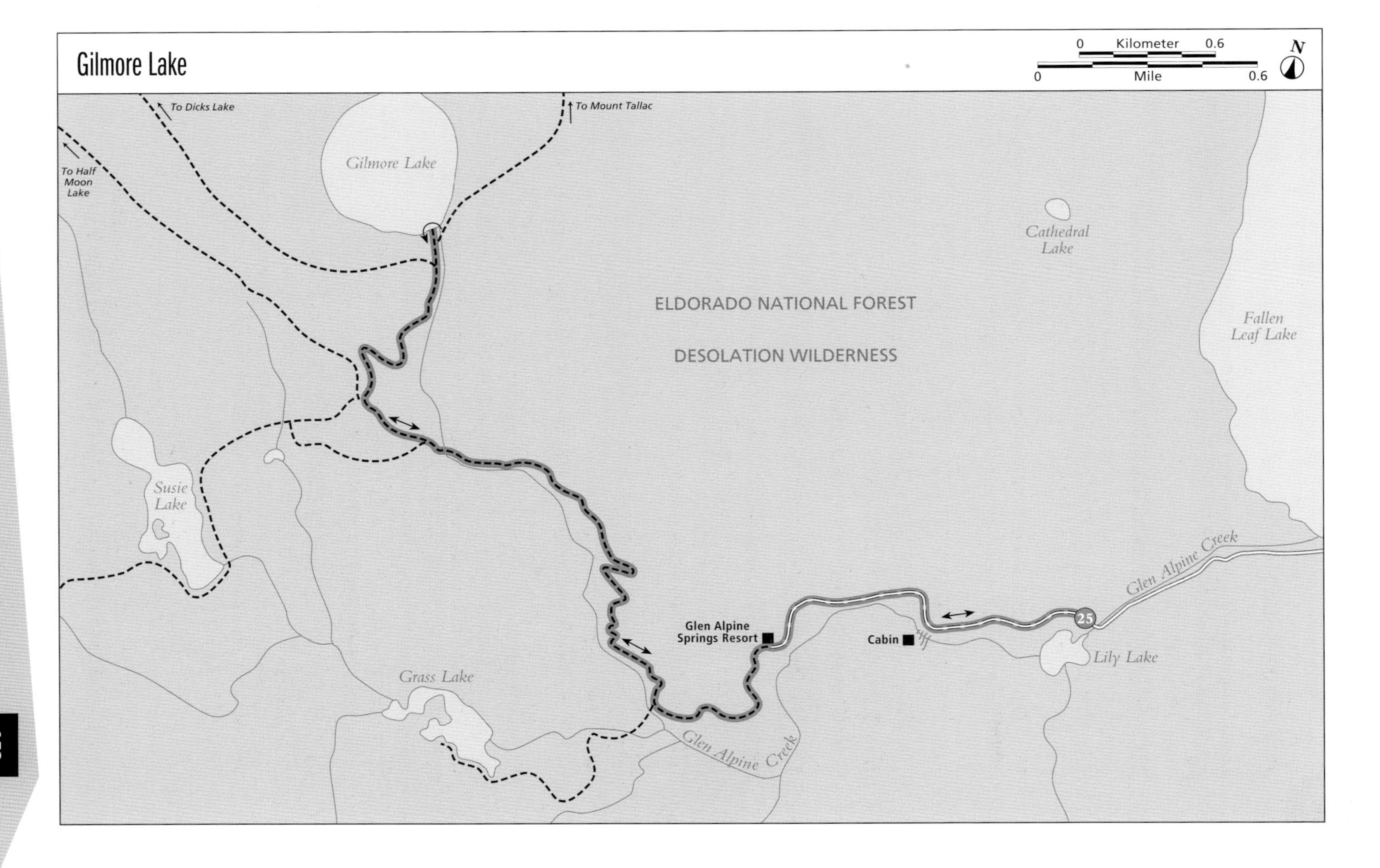

Gilmore Lake
0 Kilometer 0.6
0 Mile 0.6
N
To Dicks Lake
To Mount Tallac
To Half Moon Lake
Gilmore Lake
Cathedral Lake
ELDORADO NATIONAL FOREST
DESOLATION WILDERNESS
Fallen Leaf Lake
Susie Lake
Glen Alpine Creek
25
Glen Alpine Springs Resort
Cabin
Lily Lake
Grass Lake
Glen Alpine Creek

HIKE INFORMATION

Local information: For information on lodging, restaurants, and activities in South Lake Tahoe, contact the Lake Tahoe South Shore Chamber of Commerce. The chamber is located at 169 US 50, 3rd Floor, Stateline, NV 89449; call (775) 588-1728; visit www.tahoechamber.org. Or visit www.tahoesouth.com.

Camping: The campground at Fallen Leaf Lake features 205 sites and is open from Memorial Day through Oct, weather permitting. A fee is charged. Leashed pets are permitted. Recreation vehicles up to 40 feet can be accommodated. The camp is run by California Land Management Services Corp. under a special use permit from the US Forest Service. For reservations visit www.recreation.gov.

Glen Alpine Springs Resort

Though the native Washoe people were the first to enjoy the springs at what would become known as Glen Alpine Springs Resort, it was Nathan Gilmore, prospector and future co-founder of the Sierra Club, who would turn the area into Lake Tahoe's first bona fide upscale getaway.

Gilmore followed a game trail to Fallen Leaf Lake in 1859, according to a history of the resort posted on signboards at the site. His discovery of the soda spring followed in 1863, and he would eventually file deeds for 10,000 acres in the region, from Fallen Leaf Lake to the top of Mount Tallac. His intent was probably to take advantage of the mineral and timber resources of the land, but in the end his efforts resulted in the preservation of a large portion of what would one day become the Desolation Wilderness.

Glen Alpine Springs Resort was established by 1878, with its mineral water being enjoyed both on-site and bottled and sold elsewhere. Gilmore would eventually lose some of his extensive holdings in business transactions, and sell some of the land, including the resort itself, to his daughters and sister-in-law, Jennie Gray. The remainder was placed in the care of the Sierra Club, which he'd founded along with famed naturalist John Muir, University of California–Berkeley president Martin Kellogg, and Stanford University president David Starr Jordan. The land would be designated part of the Lake Tahoe Forest Reserve, established by President McKinley in 1899, and later the Desolation Wilderness, created in 1969.

The resort continued to operate, first under the guidance of Jennie Gray, then under her nephew Edward Gray Galt, and finally under the Garcia family, through the better part of the twentieth century. It was closed in 1966, after having been sold to a holding company. As with so many gorgeous California locales, the threat of development (in this case as condos) led to Glen Alpine's designation as a federal historic district in the 1970s.

Pacific Crest Trail at Echo Lakes

This leg of the fabled Pacific Crest Trail stretches from the granite slabs surrounding Lower Echo Lake to the forested shore of Upper Echo Lake. The hiking is easy and visually pleasing, especially at the outset where the route skirts the granite outcrops at the base of Flagpole Peak.

Start: At the signed trailhead on the north side of the Echo Chalet
Distance: 2.5 miles one way (with a boat taxi shuttle) or 5 miles out and back
Hiking time: 1.5 hours one way or 3 hours out and back
Difficulty: Moderate due to trail length and rocky terrain
Trail surface: Dirt and rock single-track
Best seasons: Summer and fall
Other trail users: None
Trailhead amenities: Parking, food, lodging, restrooms, information. Parking can be tight; if none is available at the chalet, scout a spot along the road or in the upper parking lot, and walk the short distance down to the chalet and trailhead.
Canine compatibility: Leashed dogs permitted
Fees and permits: There is no fee if you hike out and back; a fee is charged for the boat shuttle. You must fill out a free wilderness permit, available at the trailhead, if you hike into the wilderness area, regardless of whether you use the shuttle or not.
Schedule: The trail can be hiked 24 hours per day, 7 days per week, year-round. Boat shuttles are available until 6 p.m. in the summer months.
Maps: USGS Echo Lakes CA, maps on signboards at the trailhead
Trail contact: US Forest Service Lake Tahoe Basin Management Unit, Forest Supervisor's Office, 35 College Dr., South Lake Tahoe, CA 96150; (530) 543-2600; www.fs.fed.us/r5/ltbmu

Finding the trailhead: From the junction of US 50 and CA 89 in South Lake Tahoe, drive west on US 50 for 10 miles, over Echo Summit, to a right (north) turn onto Johnson Pass Road (with sign). Go 0.5 mile on Johnson Pass Road to Echo Lakes Road. Turn left (north) onto Echo Lakes Road and drive 1.2 miles to the Echo Chalet. The trailhead is on the north side of the chalet. GPS: N38 50.085' / W120 02.611'

THE HIKE

The granite basin that holds the Echo Lakes, at the edge of Desolation Wilderness and near the crest of the Sierra, provides the setting for this easy stretch of the combined Pacific Crest Trail (PCT) and Tahoe Rim Trail (TRT). The first part of the trail follows the shoreline of Lower Echo Lake, a broad expanse of water that is seldom quiet, its surface rippled by breezes spinning out of the high country. The upper lake is mostly hidden from the trail by a dense evergreen forest. To the north of the upper lake, the broad pass between Keiths Dome (on the northwest side) and Ralston Peak (on the southwest side) presents a headwall of great silvery terraces, at once beckoning and imposing, hinting at the alpine treasures that lie above and beyond.

The trail begins at the southern end of the lower lake, crossing the causeway atop the dam and the bridge that spans the spillway. The trail climbs past trail signs to a trail intersection. Head left (north) on Pacific Crest Trail, which traverses above the western shoreline, climbing through the manzanita before emptying onto granite slabs. The trail is etched in the bleached granite, narrow but well traveled, about 200 feet above the surface of the navy blue water.

Not far beyond a section of trail that has been augmented with asphalt, pass

A few miles of the border-to-border Pacific Crest Trail run alongside Echo Lake in the high Sierra.

the first of many small vacation cabins that line the shores of both lakes. Gentle climbing leads to a trail sign near some of those cabins, then two switchbacks lead up the steepest part of the hike, with the ascent moderating again as you approach the northeastern reaches of the lower lake.

The route drops through a rocky, brushy section in the shadow of an overhanging slab streaked with black, gray, and orange. Climb through the gap between the two lakes, where the trail and bordering hillside is stained orange with iron that has oxidized in the rock.

The trail bends back northward, offering brief views of the upper lake and the stony islands of the narrow passage between the two blue tarns. An easy traverse along the wooded shores of the upper lake reveals no views, but the dense forest shades colorful understory of brush, grasses, and wildflowers that ring with birdcall.

Crest a small rise. A TAXI sign has been nailed to the trunk of a big fir tree, where the narrow path to the boat dock branches off to the left (west). Drop about 50 yards to the boat dock, where you can pick up the phone and call for the boat taxi—the swift ride across both lakes is a treat for kids of all ages. Or, if you choose, take a break on the dock overlooking the lake, then retrace your steps to the trailhead.

A scenic stretch of the Pacific Crest Trail skims the shoreline of Lower Echo Lake.

MILES AND DIRECTIONS

0.0 Start by crossing the dam at the south end of Lower Echo Lake. At the Tahoe Rim Trail/Pacific Crest Trail signs and map, head up and right, then around left (north) to parallel the lakeshore.

0.3 Climb across a granite slab.

1.1 Pass a trail sign above a cluster of cabins. The trail switchbacks up the hillside.

1.6 Pass a black-streaked overhanging rock on the right, then the trail flattens. Pass more cabins.

2.0 Cross the red soils of the isthmus separating the upper and lower lake. The lake views disappear as the trail enters woodland.

2.3 Pass through an open area filled with wildflowers and birdsong.

2.5 At the TAXI sign nailed onto the tree, turn left (west) and drop to the boat dock. This is the turnaround point for an out-and-back hike or the place to pick up the boat taxi.

5.0 Arrive back at the trailhead (if on foot).

Options: The PCT and TRT continue into the high country of the Desolation Wilderness, where a wonderland of lakes, peaks, and rocky valleys awaits.

HIKE INFORMATION

Local information: For information on lodging, restaurants, and activities in South Lake Tahoe, contact the Lake Tahoe South Shore Chamber of Commerce. The chamber is located at 169 US 50, 3rd Floor, Stateline, NV 89449; call (775) 588-1728; visit www.tahoechamber.org. Or visit www.tahoesouth.com.

Camping: Backcountry campsites are available throughout the Desolation Wilderness above the Echo Lakes. Backpackers must obtain permits to camp in the wilderness, with 50 percent of the permits available in advance and the remainder distributed on a first-come, first-served basis. A fee is charged. Be sure to observe wilderness regulations, which limit groups to twelve individuals, require campsites to be situated at least 100 feet from any water source, and request that proper precautions be taken to protect foodstuffs from black bears. For more information and permits contact the forest service's Lake Tahoe Basin Management Unit by calling (530) 543-2600 or visit www.fs.fed.us/r5/ltbmu.

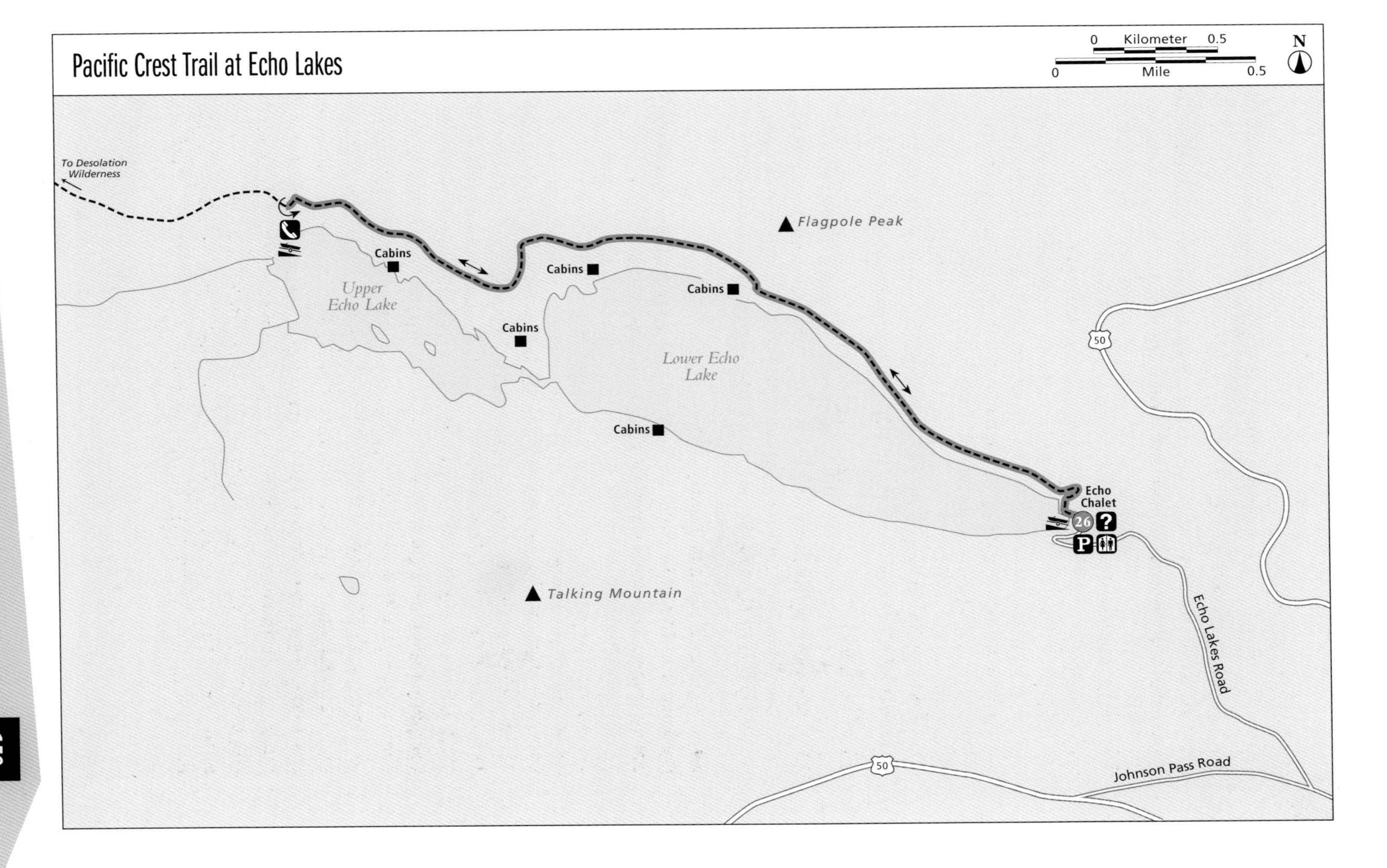

Pacific Crest Trail at Echo Lakes
0 Kilometer 0.5
0 Mile 0.5
N
To Desolation Wilderness
Flagpole Peak
Cabins
Upper Echo Lake
Cabins
Cabins
Cabins
Lower Echo Lake
Cabins
50
Echo Chalet
26
Talking Mountain
Echo Lakes Road
50
Johnson Pass Road

The Pacific Crest Trail

Stretching from the Mexican border to the Canadian border, and crossing the high country of the Sierra Nevada and the Cascade Range, hiking the length of the Pacific Crest Trail is an impossible dream for many hikers. But traversing sections of the cross-country route is entirely within reason.

One of only a handful of routes designated a National Scenic Trail, the PCT is in the company of the renowned, including the Appalachian Trail and the Continental Divide Trail. The PCT extends for 2,650 miles through the most stunning backcountry landscapes in the West: the Mojave Desert, the slopes of Mount Whitney, Sequoia and Kings Canyon National Park, Yosemite National Park, the Lake Tahoe area, Lassen Volcanic National Park, Crater Lake National Park, the volcano country along the spine of Oregon, the Mount Hood Wilderness, Mount Rainier National Park, and the Northern Cascades National Park.

Cobbling the trail together took more than sixty years, from its conception in the 1930s by Clinton C. Clarke, visionary preservationist, to its completion in 1993. The trail's route was scouted by relays of young men belonging to the YMCA, including ardent advocate Warren Rogers, who was a victim of polio. The Pacific Crest Trail Association and a number of public land managers pieced trail access together, and the variety of terrain it covers, from secluded wilderness to sections alongside highways and across private land, is testament to their determination.

Thru-hikers and thru-riders set out with the goal to travel the entire trail in a season. You may encounter one or a group of these long-distance hikers when you set out on any section of the route in the Lake Tahoe area.

For more information on the PCT, write to the Pacific Crest Trail Program Manager, US Forest Service, Pacific Southwest Regional Office, 1323 Club Drive, Vallejo, CA 94592. A nice trail brochure is available at www.pcta.org/pdf/2011-PCT-Map-Brochure.pdf. Call (888) 728-7245 (PC-Trail) for trail conditions. Several comprehensive guidebooks and trail maps are available. The trail's website is www.pcta.org.

Green Tip:

When hiking in a group, walk single file on established trails to avoid widening them. If you come upon a sensitive area, spread out so you don't cut one path through the landscape. Don't create new trails where there were none before.

Lam Watah Nature Trail

Wind through alternating meadow and open Jeffrey pine forest from Stateline's busy casino district to sunny Nevada Beach. Artifacts of the Washoe Indians lend the trail its name: "Lam" refers to the grinding stones used in food preparation, and "watah" refers to the water flowing through a portion of the meadow.

Start: At the signed trailhead on Kahle Drive in Stateline
Distance: 2.3 miles out and back
Hiking time: About 1.5 hours
Difficulty: Easy
Trail surface: Decomposed granite trail, asphalt, sand
Best seasons: Spring, summer, fall
Other trail users: Mountain bikers, trail runners
Trailhead amenities: Parking. Restrooms, water, and trashcans are available in the campground at Nevada Beach.
Canine compatibility: Leashed dogs permitted; no dogs (other than seeing-eye dogs) are allowed on Nevada Beach. Dogs are permitted in the "boat-in" picnic area at the south end of Nevada Beach.
Fees and permits: None
Schedule: Sunrise to sunset daily
Maps: USGS South Lake Tahoe CA
Trail contact: US Forest Service Lake Tahoe Basin Management Unit, Forest Supervisor's Office, 35 College Dr., South Lake Tahoe, CA 96150; (530) 543-2600; www.fs.fed.us/r5/ltbmu

Finding the trailhead: The trailhead is just northeast of Stateline's casino district at the corner of US 50 and Kahle Drive. Turn left onto Kahle Drive, then immediately right into the small parking lot with an informational signboard. GPS: N38 58.251' / W119 56.151'

THE HIKE

The Lam Watah Trail is a relatively peaceful interlude between always busy Stateline and the mostly busy campground at Nevada Beach. The trail's setting alternates between swatches of meadow and open pine woodland, a wide and gentle walk-and-talk route perfect for a sunset stroll or a break from the gaming tables.

The route never wanders far from civilization—houses are visible along Kahle Road along the trail's first section, and the towers of casinos and Heavenly Valley Ski Area's gondola rise against the mountain front on the return. Still, the trail showcases Tahoe's primary draw: the natural world, where wildflowers light the grasses in spring, and evergreen trees provide shade and a distinctive windblown song.

As the trail begins its gentle descent toward the beach, a variety of birds sing from the brush along a willow-bordered stream and pond to the right (north). Social trails cut right to the pond and left toward the homes through fragrant silver-leaved sages; stay straight on the obvious path. More birdsong emanates from a copse of aspen at the far edge of the pond—a bird magnet.

Purple lupine paint the grasses alongside the Lam Watah Nature Trail.

Cross the stream below the pond via a curving boardwalk, then enter the first stand of evergreens. The well-composed trail drops through meadows and rises through the woods in gentle undulations as it descends gently toward the lake. Benches placed along the track provide opportunities for rest and contemplation. In the distance the craggy peaks of the Desolation Wilderness cut the horizon.

The route ends at a signed trailhead in the Nevada Beach Campground. To reach the beach, follow the campground road around to the right (north, then southwest) to sandy access trails near the restrooms. No dogs are allowed on the beach, but it is the perfect place to cool your feet before retracing your steps to the trailhead. You can also follow the campground road to the left, to the Nevada Beach "boat-in" picnic area, where leashed dogs are permitted.

Green Tip:
When hiking at the beach, stay off dunes and away from nesting areas.

Winding boardwalks protect habitat and hikers' boots along the Lam Watah Trail.

MILES AND DIRECTIONS

0.0 Start by heading down the wide dirt track.

0.1 Pass the pond. Ignore social trails that break right and left, staying on the main track.

0.3 Cross the boardwalk.

0.4 Trails merge in the woods; remain on the main track heading west toward the lakeshore.

1.0 Arrive at the Lam Watah trailhead in the campground. Follow the campground road around right (north), then left (southwest) to the sandy beach access by the restrooms.

1.15 Reach the beach. Retrace your steps from here.

2.3 Arrive back at the trailhead.

HIKE INFORMATION

Local information: For details on lodging, restaurants, and activities in South Lake Tahoe, check out the Lake Tahoe South Shore Chamber of Commerce. The chamber is located at 169 US 50, 3rd Floor, Stateline, NV 89449; call (775) 588-1728; visit www.tahoechamber.org. Or visit www.tahoesouth.com.
Camping: The Nevada Beach Campground has fifty-four sites, both for tent camping and RVs. The campground offers a variety of amenities, including barbecues, restrooms, and easy access to both Nevada Beach and the attractions of Stateline and South Lake Tahoe. Reservations are available through reserve america.com; call (775) 588-5562 for more information.

Plans call for the Lam Watah trailhead on Kahle Drive to be expanded as part of the Nevada Stateline-to-Stateline Bicycle Path. A new restroom is in the works, and users will be able to access the footpath via the paved bikeway.

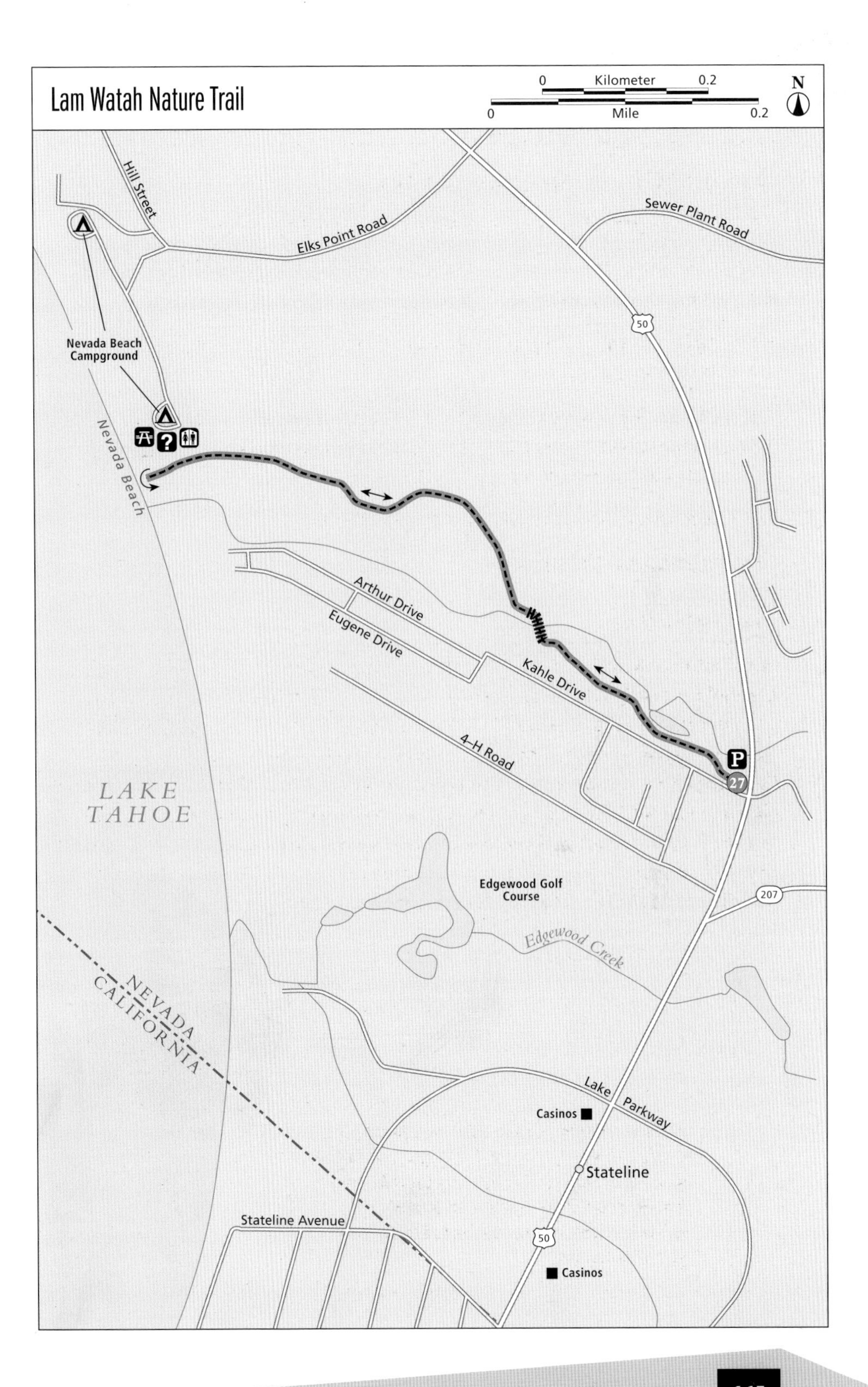
Lam Watah Nature Trail
0
Kilometer
0.2
0
Mile
0.2
N
Hill Street
Elks Point Road
Sewer Plant Road
50
Nevada Beach Campground
Nevada Beach
Arthur Drive
Eugene Drive
Kahle Drive
4-H Road
P
27
LAKE TAHOE
Edgewood Golf Course
207
Edgewood Creek
NEVADA
CALIFORNIA
Lake Parkway
Casinos
Stateline
Stateline Avenue
50
Casinos

Tahoe Rim Trail at Big Meadows

The seductions of a quiet mountain meadow are on display along this stretch of the Tahoe Rim Trail, which serves as a portal to "Meiss Country," named for an early pioneer family, and to Dardanelles Lake. A quick climb leads to Big Meadows, stuffed with wildflowers and solitude. And, like buttercream icing on a chocolate cake, a river (okay, a gurgling creek) runs through it.

Start: At the Tahoe Rim trailhead off CA 89 south of Meyers
Distance: 2 miles out and back
Hiking time: About 1 hour
Difficulty: Easy
Trail surface: Dirt singletrack
Best seasons: Late spring, summer, fall
Other trail users: Mountain bikers, equestrians
Trailhead amenities: Parking, an information signboard with maps, trashcans, restrooms
Canine compatibility: Leashed dogs permitted
Fees and permits: None
Schedule: Sunrise to sunset daily
Maps: USGS Freel Peak and Echo Lake CA; Tahoe Rim Trail map available at the trailhead
Trail contact: US Forest Service Lake Tahoe Basin Management Unit, Forest Supervisor's Office, 35 College Dr., South Lake Tahoe, CA 96150; (530) 543-2600; www.fs.fed.us/r5/ltbmu. Tahoe Rim Trail Association, 948 Incline Way, Incline Village, NV 89451; (775) 298-0233; www.tahoerimtrail.org

Finding the trailhead: From the intersection of US 50 and CA 89 in South Lake Tahoe, drive south on US 50/CA 89 for 4.7 miles to Meyers, where the two highways diverge. Turn left (southwest) onto CA 89 and go 5.1 miles to the signed Big Meadow trailhead on the left (north). Follow the short access road to the lower parking lot and the signed trailhead. GPS: N38 47.316' / W120 00.044'

THE HIKE

Mountain meadows witness the passage of the seasons in magical ways. In springtime and early summer, wildflowers are the main attraction, clustered in pockets of red, purple, white, and yellow, and busy with butterflies and bees. By late summer and autumn the flower display has diminished, but a glistening gold spreads through grasses that have absorbed the warmth of the summer sun. Even in winter, blanketed in thick snow, a mountain meadow is a calming, meditative place.

Big Meadows is all this, green and gold, easygoing and restful, delightful in all its incarnations.

The trail begins in the lower trailhead parking area, just beyond the information sign. Pass a blue-and-white Tahoe Rim Trail sign almost immediately; the trail runs alongside the highway until it climbs to the edge of the asphalt and crosses the road.

The path grows steeper on the other side of the pavement, climbing through a forest of stout mixed evergreens. Climb a log and granite staircase that doubtless presents a daunting obstacle to mountain bikers on the route. Highway noise filters through the forest, but the chatter of noisy Big Meadow Creek helps mask the sound.

The Tahoe Rim Trail cuts a rare straight line through Big Meadows.

The trail flattens as the highway noises fade; the boulder-strewn woodland is now full of birdsong and windsong. At the trail fork, go right (south), following the arrow that points to Meiss Meadow (aka Big Meadows). The left-hand trail leads to Scotts Lake.

Traverse a brief final stretch of woodland, then the step into the meadow. Worn deeply into the turf, the trail leads to a footbridge spanning the clear creek, then cuts a straight line through the grasses and wildflowers to the southern edge, where woodland hedges in the grassland and carpets the rolling mountains above.

The turnaround point is at the interface of the meadow and forest, though you can continue into the trees, where the trail leads to Dardanelles Lake and beyond. Sun-bleached stumps, once sturdy enough to provide restful seats, but grown cracked and rotting as the years have passed, mark the spot. Return as you came.

MILES AND DIRECTIONS

0.0 Start at the signed trailhead.

0.1 Cross CA 89.

0.6 At the trail intersection stay right (south) on the signed Meiss Meadow trail (aka Big Meadows).

0.7 Reach the edge of the meadow.

1.0 Arrive at the turnaround point at the southwest edge of the meadow.

2.0 Arrive back at the trailhead.

HIKE INFORMATION

Local information: For information on lodging, restaurants, and activities in South Lake Tahoe, look to the Lake Tahoe South Shore Chamber of Commerce. The chamber is located at 169 US 50, 3rd Floor, Stateline, NV 89449; call (775) 588-1728; visit www.tahoechamber.org. Or visit www.tahoesouth.com.
Restaurants: Naked Fish Sushi Bar, 940 Lake Tahoe Blvd. #3, South Lake Tahoe, CA 96150; (530) 541-FISH (3474); thenakedfish.com. There's a good chance you'll have to wait for a table in this small, hip sushi bar, but the food and atmosphere is invigorating. Specialty rolls, nigiri sushi, and traditional Japanese cooked cuisine are served.

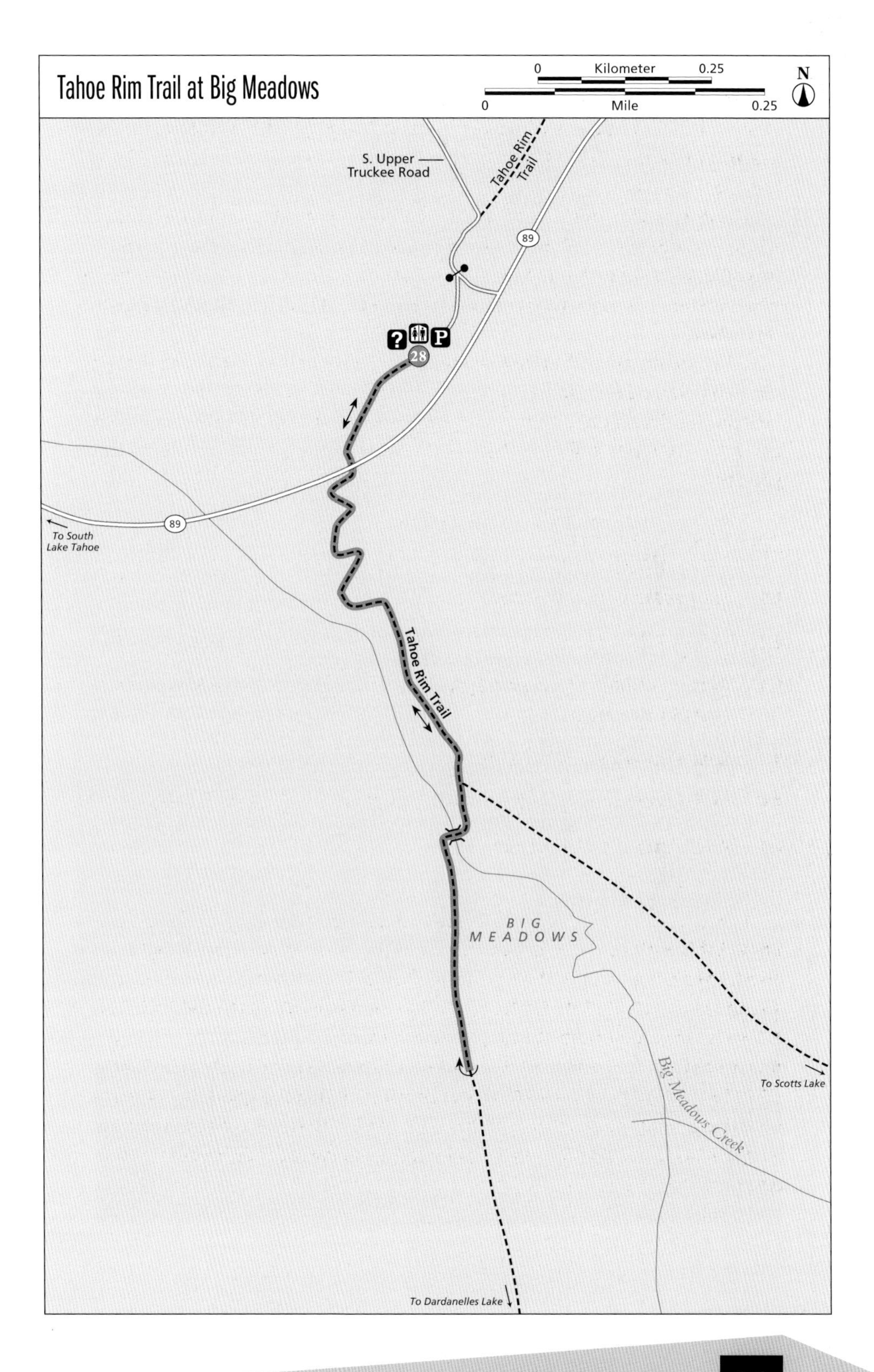
Tahoe Rim Trail at Big Meadows
0
Kilometer
0.25
0
Mile
0.25
N
S. Upper
Truckee Road
Tahoe Rim
Trail
89
28
To South
Lake Tahoe
89
Tahoe Rim Trail
BIG
MEADOWS
Big Meadows Creek
To Scotts Lake
To Dardanelles Lake

28

Tahoe Rim Trail

Anyone who hikes around Lake Tahoe will, at one time or another, find himself or herself on a section of the Tahoe Rim Trail (TRT). The product of sixteen years of hard work, the trail circumnavigates the lake basin in 165 miles, passing through some of the region's signature landscapes, including the Desolation Wilderness and the Marlette-Hobart backcountry of Lake Tahoe–Nevada State Park.

The TRT is multiuse, with hikers and equestrians able to use all trail segments, and mountain bikers allowed on portions that lie outside the Desolation Wilderness and other wilderness areas. Cyclists are also not permitted in parts of Lake Tahoe–Nevada State Park, and on segments of the TRT that overlap the Pacific Crest Trail. Mountain bikers are permitted only on the 9.2 miles between Tahoe Meadows and Tunnel Creek Road on even days.

Nearly 1,400 people are members of the 165 Mile Club to date, having hiked and/or ridden (on horseback or mountain bike) the entire trail. The overwhelming majority of club members are from the Tahoe Basin or from Reno and its environs, testament to how important the TRT is to those who call the Reno-Tahoe region home. A number of dogs have also completed the trail, as well as three llamas, a pair of goats, and a squirrel.

The Tahoe Rim Trail Association maintains a website that includes printable maps of the various segments of the TRT. While the trail can be traversed as a thru-hike, it's set up such that trekkers can tackle it in eight relatively short segments. The trail is marked on the ground with distinctive blue-and-white markers. The maps of trail segments on the website list significant landmarks and the distances between them. Guidebooks and comprehensive maps of the trail are also available. For more information, write to the Tahoe Rim Trail Association at 948 Incline Way, Incline Village, NV 89451; (775) 298-0012; www.tahoerimtrail.org.

Green Tip:

Toilet paper should be burned or packed out. To carry it with you, put a small piece of an ammonia-soaked sponge in your bag to help kill bacteria and odor.

Winnemucca and Round Top Lakes Loop

With so many reasons to recommend this hike, it is hard to know where to begin. The wildflower bloom below Winnemucca Lake must be seen to be believed. The setting of Round Top Lake, below a dark sawtooth ridgeline punctuated with permanent snowfields, is picture-book perfect. The trail blends challenge with reward splendidly. Make this a priority.

Start: At the Winnemucca Lake trailhead at Woods Lake
Distance: 5.25-mile loop
Hiking time: 3–4 hours
Difficulty: Strenuous due to nearly 1,100 feet in elevation change
Trail surface: Dirt singletrack
Best seasons: Spring for the wildflower bloom; autumn for fall color
Other trail users: None
Trailhead amenities: Parking, restrooms, an information signboard with a map, picnic tables
Canine compatibility: Leashed dogs permitted on the trails around Woods Lake; dogs not permitted in the wilderness
Fees and permits: A day-use fee is charged
Schedule: 24 hours a day, 7 days a week, year-round
Maps: USGS Caples Lake CA and Carson Pass CA; USDA Forest Service Lake Tahoe Basin Management Unit Map
Trail contact: Eldorado National Forest, Amador Ranger Station; (209) 295-4251; www.fs.usda.gov/Eldorado
Special considerations: This trail climbs into the subalpine zone above 9,000 feet. Be prepared to suck wind.

Finding the trailhead: From the intersection of US 50 and CA 89 in South Lake Tahoe, drive south on US 50/CA 89 for about 5 miles to Meyers, where the highways diverge. Go left (southwest) on CA 89, following it for 11 miles to its intersection with CA 88 in Hope Valley. Go right (northwest) on CA 88, toward Kirkwood Ski Area and Carson Pass. Drive 10.5 miles from the junction, over the scenic pass, to a left turn on the access road for Woods Lake Campground. Go 1.4 miles on the access road to the trailhead parking area, which is often full in the summer months. Overflow parking is available along the narrow roadway or in the overflow parking area located 1 mile from CA 88. GPS: N38 41.493' / W120 00.573'

THE HIKE

In early summer, during the height of wildflower season, this trek should top every Tahoe hiker's list. The northeast-facing hillside below Winnemucca Lake's basin is the site of a magnificent wildflower display. Indian paintbrush, in every shade of red from burgundy to antique rose, headlines the event, with a spectacular supporting cast of purple lupine and magenta penstemon, yellow and white yarrow, mountain aster, and the vivid green of mountain grasses. It's a vision best described by a painter or a photographer, not a wordsmith.

But don't write the hike off if wildflower season is over. Winnemucca Lake is a perfect alpine tarn, the setting and seclusion of Round Top Lake a noteworthy goal. The loop also boasts a glimpse of California's pivotal mining legacy at the Lost Cabin Mine, near trail's end.

Beginning at the overflow trailhead, where you are most likely to find parking, walk down the access road to the trailhead on the left side. Cross the bridge over Woods Creek and follow the stream, clear as glass, through the cedars and pines. At the trail fork go left on the signed trail to Winnemucca Lake.

The rocky summits of the Sisters loom above the trail to Winnemucca Lake.

The route ascends gently through a mixed evergreen forest dotted with boulders. Pass the remains of an "arrastra," a large basinlike structure used by early Mexicans to crush gold- and silver-bearing ore rocks. A steady, straightforward climb leads up stair-step roots and rocks onto the ascending traverse of the wildflower meadow. The trail gradually steepens as you approach the Winnemucca Lake basin, following the rollicking stream. Be prepared for wet conditions on the slope year-round, but more so in spring as the snow melts. The snowfields that cling to the rock faces of Round Top and the Sisters above are part of the source.

Enter the Mokelumne Wilderness at 1.5 miles and continue to climb. Top a final pitch and you'll be at the trail junction on the shoreline of Winnemucca Lake. The tarn sits in a craggy basin where snow lingers into late summer, caught in rocky crevices and shaded by steep cliffs. The wind at timberline can be fierce, as evidenced by the cropped hemlocks that huddle about the shore. But on a sunny autumn day, the setting is sublime.

To continue to Round Top Lake, return to the trail junction and go left (west). Cross the outlet stream, then begin a traversing climb. Circling west, head toward small twin waterfalls that flow until the snow melts away in late summer. Continue up and northwest on the steepening route, into the gap between the Winnemucca and Round Top basins. Round Top Lake and a trail crossing sit below, at 2.9 miles.

Shallow Round Top Lake, glittering turquoise below the ramparts of the sheltering Sisters and Round Top massif, is a peaceful place to rest before the descent to Woods Lake. Once you've hoarded an abundance of unfiltered sunshine and alpine splendor, return to the trail crossing and go down (north) on the broad signed path, enjoying wonderful views of Caples Lake and the west side of the Sierra crest. The trees quickly regain their stature as you drop in altitude; a steep pitch drops you into a willowy wetland interlaced with swift-flowing rivulets.

Pass the Mokelumne Wilderness boundary sign and continue down. The stream grows to a raucous cataract, which you will cross before bearing left (north), past a clearing. At the 4.0-mile mark lie remnants of the Lost Cabin Mine, including an old metal structure perched on a rock outcrop overlooking the stream and the remains of an old car that nearly block the trail.

Green Tip:

Hiking and snowshoeing are great carbon-free winter activities.

Switchbacks lead down past more mining structures to a stream crossing on logs and rocks. A trail sign keeps you on track. The trail broadens into a dirt road that lazily curves down past a gate to the campground road; go left (east) on the trail to return to the overflow parking area and trailhead.

MILES AND DIRECTIONS

0.0 Start at the upper trailhead. Walk down the road for 0.2 mile and pick up the signed trail to Winnemucca Lake

0.5 At the trail fork, go left to Winnemucca Lake. The right-hand trail goes to Woods Lake. Pass the Carson Pass Management Area sign.

1.1 Pass the "arrastra."

1.25 Begin the traverse of the wildflower slope.

1.5 Enter the Mokelumne Wilderness.

2.0 Reach the junction with the trail to Round Top Lake. Winnemucca Lake glitters just ahead. Take a rest on the lakeshore, then continue to Round Top by heading uphill from the trail junction.

2.9 Rest at Round Top Lake, then head down out of the basin on the signed trail to Woods Lake. Fourth of July Lake lies down the other trail.

3.7 Exit the Mokelumne Wilderness at the boundary sign.

4.0 Pass Lost Cabin Mine.

4.3 Cross the stream and pass a trail sign. The trail broadens to a dirt road.

4.8 Pass a gate and parking for the Woods Lake campground. Stay up and left on the singletrack trail.

5.25 Hitch down onto the access road for a short stretch before arriving back at the trailhead.

Options: Winnemucca and Round Top Lakes can be the first destinations on a longer exploration of the Mokelumne Wilderness, to Fourth of July Lake and beyond. Or, you can avoid the rigors of high-country trekking altogether by limiting your hike to a walk along the shoreline of Woods Lake.

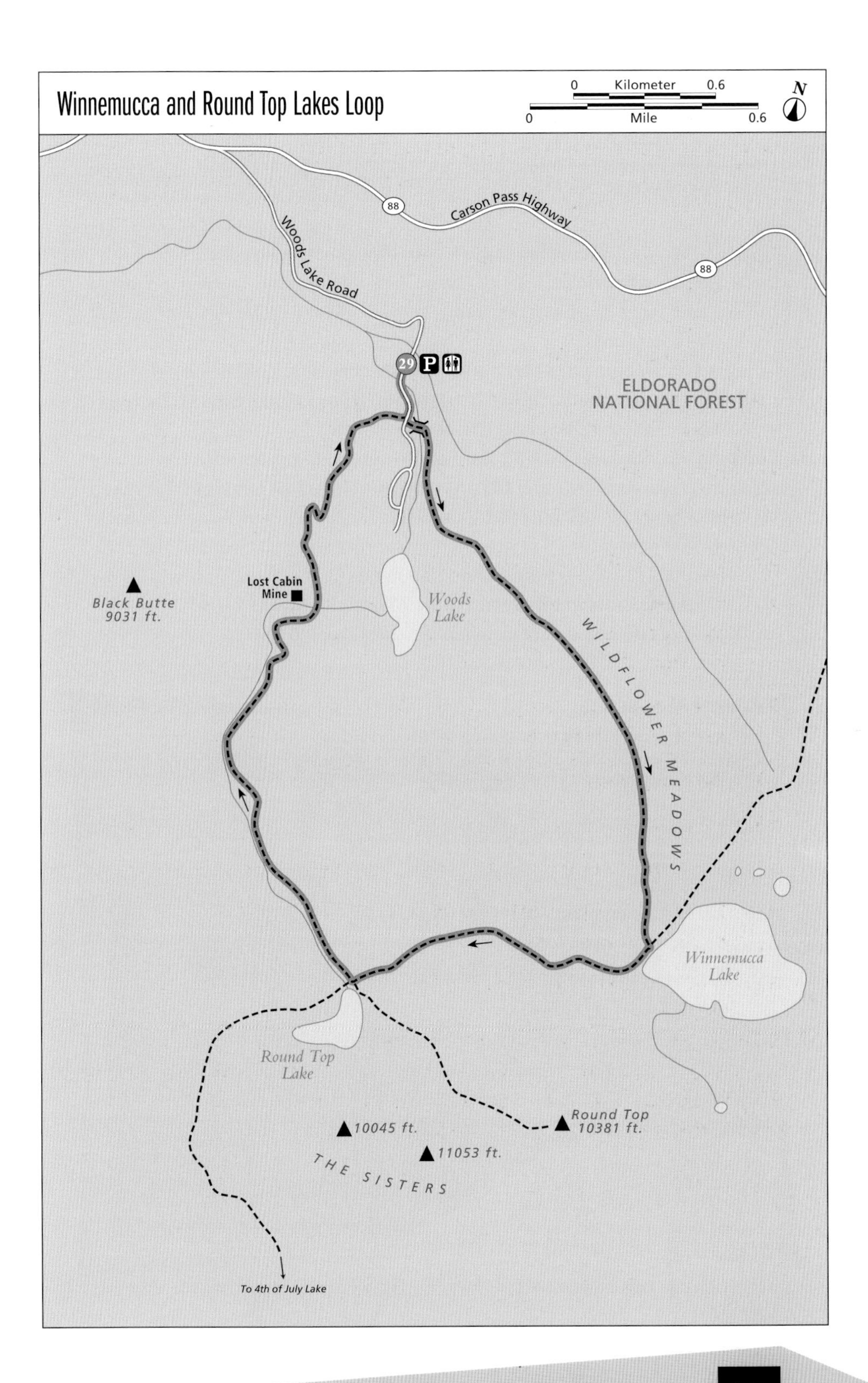
Winnemucca and Round Top Lakes Loop
0 Kilometer 0.6
0 Mile 0.6
N
88
Carson Pass Highway
Woods Lake Road
88
29
ELDORADO
NATIONAL FOREST
Lost Cabin
Mine
Black Butte
9031 ft.
Woods
Lake
WILDFLOWER MEADOWS
Winnemucca
Lake
Round Top
Lake
Round Top
10381 ft.
10045 ft.
11053 ft.
THE SISTERS
To 4th of July Lake

HIKE INFORMATION

Local information: For information on lodging, restaurants, and activities in South Lake Tahoe, contact the Lake Tahoe South Shore Chamber of Commerce. The chamber is located at 169 US 50, 3rd Floor, Stateline, NV 89449; call (775) 588-1728; visit www.tahoechamber.org. Or visit www.tahoesouth.com.

Local events/attractions: Nearby Caples Lake Resort offers lodging, a store, a marina, and other amenities. For more information call (209) 258-8888 or visit capleslakeresort.com.

Kirkwood Mountain Resort is a wintertime destination off the beaten Tahoe path. For more information about activities on the mountain, contact the resort at (209) 258-6000 or visit winter.kirkwood.com/site/.

Camping: Woods Lake, a US Forest Service campground, features twenty-five sites open between July 1 and Oct 15, snow permitting. All food must be stored in the bear boxes. A fee is charged. Camping in the Mokelumne Wilderness back-country is by permit only. For more information and permits, contact the Eldorado National Forest's Amador Ranger Station at (209) 295-4251, or visit www.fs.usda.gov/Eldorado. Information on the Mokelumne Wilderness is at www.fs.usda.gov/detail/eldorado/specialplaces/?cid=fsbdev7_019063.

Winnemucca Lake looks inviting on a clear summer day, but swimming requires a thick skin and strong heart.

Honorable Mentions

Desolation Wilderness Destinations

Grass Lake, a 5-mile out-and-back trek starting at the Glen Alpine trailhead, is a lovely day hike destination. Climb up and past the Glen Alpine Springs Resort, then to the trail junction at the boundary of the wilderness. A couple of creek crossings, each spanned by logs, present a bit of a challenge, then granite and timber staircases lead up to the lake. Contained by rolling expanses of granite and clusters of fir, pine, and brush, a spectacular waterfall spills off a red rock cliff to the west in early season; beyond and above the lake and falls, the arcing walls of the high glacial basin rise skyward.

Grass Lake is just one of a bonanza of alpine tarns—Aloha Lake, Susie Lake, Dicks Lake, Fontanillis Lake—that lie in Desolation's backcountry. The wilderness can be reached via the Glen Alpine trailhead, the Eagle Lake and Bayview trailheads near Emerald Bay, and from the Pacific Crest Trail (PCT) at Echo Lake. With a good map, a backpack, and several days to weeks, you can stitch together an excellent lake-to-lake high country excursion.

To reach the Glen Alpine trailhead, the closest for a hike to Grass Lake, from the intersection of US 50 and CA 89 in South Lake Tahoe, go north on CA 89 for 3 miles to Fallen Leaf Lake Road. Turn left (west) onto Fallen Leaf Lake Road and follow the narrow roadway for 5 miles. Pass the lodge and marina; at the fork stay straight, past the fire station, on FR 1216 to Lily Lake. The trailhead parking area is 0.6 mile ahead. Check hike descriptions for Eagle Lake, Cascade Falls (Bayview trailhead), and the PCT at Echo Lake for directions to those trailheads.

Pyramid Creek and Horsetail Falls

This short hike heads up Pyramid Creek to granite slabs at the base of Horsetail Falls, a spectacular spill that courses down the mountainside on the west side of Echo Summit, near Twin Bridges. At about 2.5 miles round-trip, this hike is not terribly long, but it does feature more than 400 feet in elevation gain. Great granite slabs define the route, making for a walk that is as engaging as the destination. Use caution and common sense as you travel alongside the creek and approach the falls, as route-finding on the slabs can be challenging. An easier loop trail option is also available. A fee is required at the trailhead parking area, and you'll need a free permit to enter the Desolation Wilderness.

To reach the Pyramid Creek trailhead at Twin Bridges from the intersection of US 50 and CA 89 in South Lake Tahoe, drive west on US 50 for 16 miles, over Echo Summit, to the parking lot on the right (northeast) side of the road just before the bridge at Twin Bridges.

Reno

Deep canyons like this, which cradles Whites Creek, define the east side of the Sierra Nevada above Reno.

The self-described Biggest Little City in the World has undergone a metamorphosis in the last quarter-century or so. Once known primarily as a gambling town, these days it is much more: The University of Nevada–Reno, a strong agricultural base, a growing service industry, and a revitalized recreational identity draw a variety of visitors to the city and enrich the lives of its residents.

Reno and its sister city, Sparks, are conjoined; it's hard to tell where one town ends and the other begins. Suburban enclaves buffer the city on all sides, with sprawl creeping south out of the Truckee Meadows toward the Washoe Valley. Two interstates, one brand-spanking new in 2012, serve the region, with I-80 stretching east-west and I-580/US 395 (portions of which were formerly just two-lane US 395) running south toward Carson City.

Reno's origins are linked to California's Gold Rush and the subsequent discovery of the Comstock silver lode. Its genesis was with a toll bridge over the Truckee River that served hopeful argonauts headed for the gold and silver mines around Virginia City. When the Central Pacific Railroad came through, the city of Reno was formally established and named for a hero of the Civil War. The year was 1868.

Mining and agriculture, Reno's staple industries, have long been subject to booms and busts. To counteract that instability the city looked to illicit trades that were always in demand: gambling and prostitution. It also became a place where divorces could be had, quick and easy.

While casinos are still integral to Reno's economy, these days recreation also plays a role. Washoe County has built an impressive system of parks and trails, many of which are known only to the locals. Cultural events, like the annual Great Reno Balloon Race, and cultural centers, like the university and the Wilbur D. May Center and arboretum, add depth to the city's recreational and occupational offerings.

For more information, contact the City of Reno, PO Box 1900, Reno, NV 89505; (775) 334-INFO (4636); www.reno.org.

Snowplant owes its distinctive red coloration to a lack of chlorophyll.

30

South Side Interpretive Trail at Swan Lake

A trail and a boardwalk lead through the Swan Lake Nature Study Area, where birds and hikers alike find a watery refuge in the desert.

Start: At the signed trailhead at the end of Lear Boulevard
Distance: 1.4 miles out and back on trail; 0.5 mile out and back on boardwalk (1.9 miles total)
Hiking time: 1.5–2 hours
Difficulty: Easy
Trail surface: Dirt and gravel singletrack; boardwalk
Best seasons: Spring and fall; avoid the unshaded trails on hot summer days
Other trail users: None
Trailhead amenities: Restrooms, a covered picnic shelter, trash receptacles
Canine compatibility: Leashed dogs permitted
Fees and permits: None
Schedule: Park hours are from 8 a.m. to 9 p.m. June to Sept; 8 a.m. to 7 p.m. Sept to Nov; 8 a.m. to 5 p.m. Nov to Mar; and 8 a.m. to 7 p.m. Mar to June
Maps: USGS Reno NV; www.nvtrailmaps.com
Trail contact: Swan Lake Nature Study Area, Washoe County Department of Regional Parks and Open Space, 2601 Plumas St., Reno, NV 89509; (775) 823-6500; www.washoecountyparks.com. Lahontan Audubon Society, PO Box 2304, Reno, NV 89505; (775) 324-BIRD (2473); www.nevadaaudubon.org.
Other: Bring binoculars and a guidebook to help you identify the birds that live near or visit the lake. The boardwalk section of the trail is handicapped accessible.

Finding the trailhead: From the intersection of I-80 and US 395 in downtown Reno, head north on US 395 for 8 miles to the Lemmon Drive exit. Go right (east) on Lemmon Drive for 1 mile to Military Road and turn left (north). Follow Military Road for 1.6 miles to Lear Boulevard. Turn right (east) on Lear Boulevard and go 0.4 mile to the end of the pavement. Head left (north) for 0.2 mile on the dirt road signed for the Swan Lake Nature Study Area to the trailhead and parking area. GPS: N39 39.024' / W119 51.395'

THE HIKE

The two prongs of this Swan Lake Nature Study Area tour venture into vastly different environments, though that won't be evident from the trailhead. Especially in dry years you'll see nothing but high desert scrubland stretching to the north and west, with no hint that Swan Lake exists at all.

The natural area has a distinctly unnatural setting, with warehouses on the south and west and wastewater treatment ponds on the east. The shallow lake and its surrounding wetlands, fed by meltwater from Peavine Peak to the southwest and treated wastewater (no swimming or fishing is permitted), can be as small as 100 acres or as large as 1,000 acres, depending on the amount of rainfall and runoff. Conditions will dictate whether the lake will be visible from the trailhead or trail, but generally the boardwalk passes over water.

The trail to the boardwalk is so easy that flip-flops can serve as appropriate footwear and is perfect for the elderly, those confined to wheelchairs, and small children. Constructed of recycled plastic boards, the floating walkway winds through a cattail-filled marsh to a viewing deck overlooking an expanse of dark water where ducks, geese, coots, swans, stilts, and avocets may be spotted.

The flat, easy South Side Interpretive Trail leads into a typical northern Nevada scrubland, with views of rolling brown hills to the north and east and Peavine Peak rising above the industrial complex to the southwest. Carpeted in bitterbrush,

The interpretive trail at Swan Lake leads to a stony hummock of a blind.

sages, and desert peach, the landscape is habitat for a variety of songbirds—swallows, blackbirds, and wrens—as well as raptors such as burrowing owls, northern harriers, and golden and bald eagles. Walk softly and quail are likely to scurry across the path in front of you, sparrows watch from perches atop the bushes, and garter snakes slither from trail's edge to the safety of nearby rocks.

Begin by following the raised gravel path to an information signboard ringed by benches, where the boardwalk and interpretive trail separate. You can do either or both: The interpretive trail is described first, then the boardwalk.

The interpretive trail leads first to a molded plastic blind in the form of a low rock wall. The mock-rock structure is posted with interpretive plaques and offers birders a chance to identify avian species without disturbing them.

From the blind the singletrack climbs gently into the scrub, with some sections white and alkaline, others sandy, and others paved in gravel. Turn around when you reach the dirt roadway that stretches north and south along the western boundary of the natural area, and return to the junction with the trail to the boardwalk.

As you head out onto the lake, the gravel path leads to a clump of cottonwood and willow, where you'll cross a bridge onto the recycled plastic boardwalk. Interpretive signs describe everything from how wastewater is used to maintain the marsh to the species of birds, mammals, and amphibians that are either permanent residents of the area or are likely to migrate through. Benches and viewing platforms offer places to rest and observe. The boardwalk ends at a platform overlooking the shallow lake where, depending on the season, a variety of ducks, coots, and other shorebirds play, feed, snort, and rumble on the water.

Enjoy the sights and sounds, then return to the trailhead via the same route.

MILES AND DIRECTIONS

0.0 Start by heading north on the gravel path.

0.1 The trail splits at the information signboard. Go left (west) on the singletrack South Side Interpretive Trail.

0.2 Arrive at the mock-rock blind. Continue west on the obvious singletrack.

0.7 Arrive at the dirt roadway; this is the turnaround point.

1.3 Return to the trail junction at the information signboard. Turn left (north) to reach the boardwalk.

1.5 Arrive at the observation deck at the end of the boardwalk overlooking the lake.

1.9 Return to the trailhead and parking area.

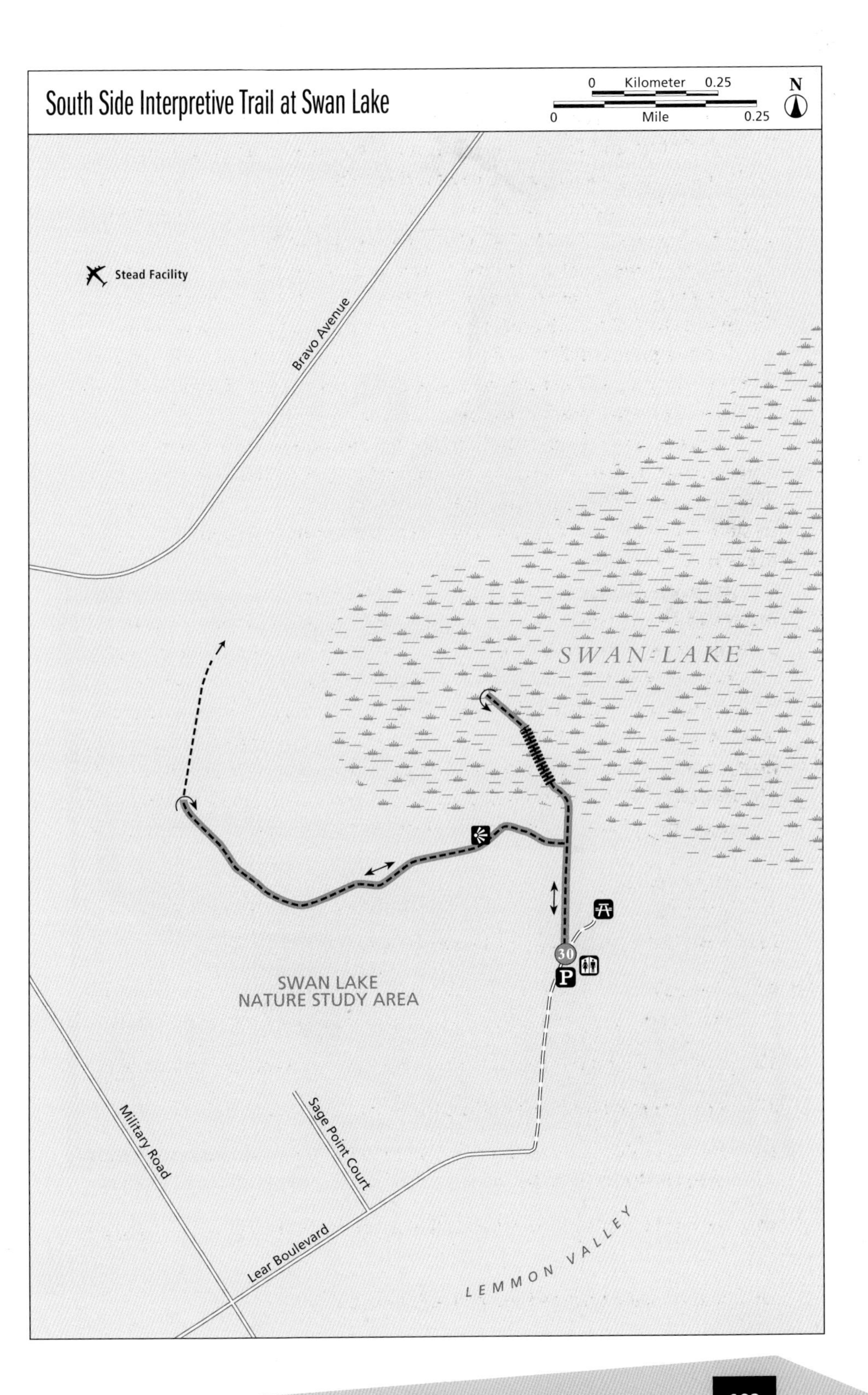
South Side Interpretive Trail at Swan Lake
0 Kilometer 0.25
0 Mile 0.25
N
Stead Facility
Bravo Avenue
SWAN LAKE
30
P
SWAN LAKE
NATURE STUDY AREA
Military Road
Sage Point Court
Lear Boulevard
LEMMON VALLEY

HIKE INFORMATION

Local information: The Chamber, serving Reno, Sparks, and northern Nevada, offers information and links to community events, government, and businesses including restaurants and lodging. The Reno office is at 449 S. Virginia St. 2nd Floor, Reno, NV 89501; (775) 636-9550; www.thechambernv.org. For information about the city of Reno, call Reno Direct at (775) 334-INFO or visit www.reno.gov/index.aspx?page=1.

A floating boardwalk allows hikers and birders to walk among the cattails, which harbor a bounty of birdlife.

Evans Canyon and Miner's Trail Loop

Follow Evans Creek through a steep-sided canyon, venturing into a cleft of high desert landscape embedded in suburban Reno.

Start: At the signed trailhead in the Reno Sports Complex
Distance: 3.5-mile lollipop
Hiking time: 2–3 hours
Difficulty: More challenging due to trail length and surface
Trail surface: Dirt singletrack
Best seasons: Winter, spring, late fall. Avoid the shadeless trail in the heat of summer.
Other trail users: Mountain bikers, trail runners
Trailhead amenities: Parking, restrooms, trashcans
Canine compatibility: Leashed dogs permitted
Fees and permits: None
Schedule: As a rule of thumb, Washoe County Parks are open from 8 a.m. to sunset. Formal hours are 8 a.m. to 9 p.m. from Memorial Day weekend to Labor Day weekend; 8 a.m. to 7 p.m. from Labor Day to the start of standard time; 8 a.m. to 5 p.m. from the start of standard time to the start of daylight savings time in spring; and 8 a.m. to 7 p.m. from the start of daylight savings time to Memorial Day weekend.
Maps: USGS Reno NV; www.nvtrailmaps.com
Trail contact: Rancho San Rafael Regional Park, Washoe County Department of Regional Parks and Open Space, 2601 Plumas St., Reno, NV 89509; (775) 823-6500; www.washoecountyparks.com
Special considerations: Do not venture onto this exposed trail without ample drinking water. Do not drink from the stream. Rattlesnakes are sometimes seen along the trail.

Finding the trailhead: From I-80 take the downtown Reno/Virginia Street exit. Go north on North Virginia Street for 1.2 miles, past the University of Nevada–Reno (UNR) campus and the junction with North McCarran Boulevard, to the left-hand (west) turnoff into the well-signed Reno Sports Complex. The trailhead is at the west end of the parking lot. GPS: N39 33.213' / W119 49.779'

THE HIKE

The massive abstract Basque monument, commemorating Basque sheepherders, is the first thing you'll see as you set off on the trail into Evans Canyon. Striking as the big blue sculpture is, little Evans Creek is just as appealing in its way, winding through a steep-walled desert canyon and watering small riparian gardens.

One of several streams that spill down and around Peavine Peak, Evans Creek meanders through high desert scrub that flowers beautifully in spring, with delicate pink blooms on the desert peach and pastel yellow flowers on the bitterbrush. Though the flow is relatively placid even in the runoff season, the creek has carved itself a relatively secluded canyon and is the focal point of a rare escape close to downtown Reno.

The trail begins and ends on an interpretive nature trail near the Basque monument and bordering a disk golf course. You can check out the Basque monument now or later, as the return leg of the loop will take you onto the nature trail that loops around it. Read the plaques and check out the views, then follow the nature trail down to the banks of the creek. Interpretive signs line this stretch of

The snow-capped peaks of the Carson Range highlight the return trek down the trail in Evans Canyon.

the route, and side trails carved by other users, including mountain bikers, wing out in different directions. The main trail is well trod and obvious; stick to it to avoid damaging the environment.

Leaving the nature trail for the Evans Canyon Trail, you will hike down into a steep-walled canyon with neighborhood homes perched above on the eastern edge. To the west, steep slopes climb up onto Peavine Peak, a dry, scrub-covered mountain dotted with power poles, slashed with the tracks of dirt roads, and painted with an "N" in honor of nearby UNR. On cool mornings and evenings, students in running shoes and on mountain bikes take to the trail in small swarms, so be prepared to share.

Pass several trail junctions and cross to the east side of the creek as you continue upstream. By the time you reach the junction with the Miner's Trail (the return route), you'll have lost sight of most signs of civilization, though they'll soon make encore appearances.

Toward the end of the trail the canyon widens, allowing the creek to pool and water springtime gardens of penstemon, aster, geranium, wild rose, and sage. Broken rock from small slides occasionally spills across the trail. Beyond the mile mark the creek spreads into a meadow and tailings piles—plant-free mounds of yellow- and red-streaked earth—hang from the canyon wall on the opposite side of the creek. At the head of the canyon, the route skirts the foundations of apartment buildings, crosses in front of a culvert, then meets the Miner's Trail. Take the Miner's Trail to begin a descent down the west side of the canyon.

The downstream stretch is highlighted by views of the peaks of the Carson Range. Snowcapped in springtime, they rise in striking contrast to the desert landscapes that dry up quickly around Reno. The Miner's Trail hooks up with the Evans Canyon Trail again at the 2-mile mark, and the Evans Canyon Trail meets the nature trail farther along. Lined with interpretive signs describing the area's geology, flora, and fauna, the nature trail closes the loop, circling a pond choked with cattails. Finish by climbing past the Basque monument to the trailhead.

The National Monument to the Basque Sheepherder, created by Basque artist Nestor Basterretxea and depicting a Basque sheepherder carrying a lamb beneath a moon, was damaged by vandals in 2011. The bronze plaques honoring Basque emigrants were removed in the crime; these have since been replaced by steel plaques more firmly affixed to the monument.

MILES AND DIRECTIONS

0.0 Start by passing through the gate and following the broad path toward the towering blue Basque monument.

0.1 Arrive at the monument. Circle around and head down the broad track, crossing over the Highland Ditch via a plank bridge as you descend.

0.3 Reach the junction with the nature trail at an interpretive sign in the creek drainage. Stay straight (right/northwest) on the main track. In less than 0.1 mile, cross Evans Creek, shallow and easy to ford in most seasons, then reach a second nature trail junction at a bench. Stay right (north) on the Evans Canyon Trail; the nature trail bends left (west). Climb into an open area filled with braided trails; the EVANS CANYON TRAILHEAD sign is obvious to the right (northeast).

0.6 At the intersection with an unsigned trail, stay right (north).

0.7 Reach the junction with the signed Updike Ravine Trail. Stay right (north) on the Evans Canyon Trail, with the stream now on the left (west) side.

1.0 Arrive at the intersection with the Miner's Trail. Stay right (north) on the Evans Canyon Trail.

1.5 Climb past the foundations of apartment buildings to the head of the canyon at a staircase and culvert. Pass in front of the culvert and pick up the Miner's Trail on the west face of the canyon atop a tailings pile.

1.8 Cross a second tailings pile.

2.1 Arrive at the junction with the Evans Canyon Trail. Cross the creek onto the Evans Canyon route and retrace your steps to the junction with the nature trail. (You can also stay on the Miner's Trail and rejoin the Evans Canyon Trail farther downstream.)

2.8 At the junction with the interpretive trail, go right (southwest), following the thoroughly signed route around the overgrown pond and through the riparian zone that thrives along the creek.

3.3 Arrive at the junction with the unsigned trail that climbs back east toward the Basque monument.

3.5 Arrive back at the trailhead.

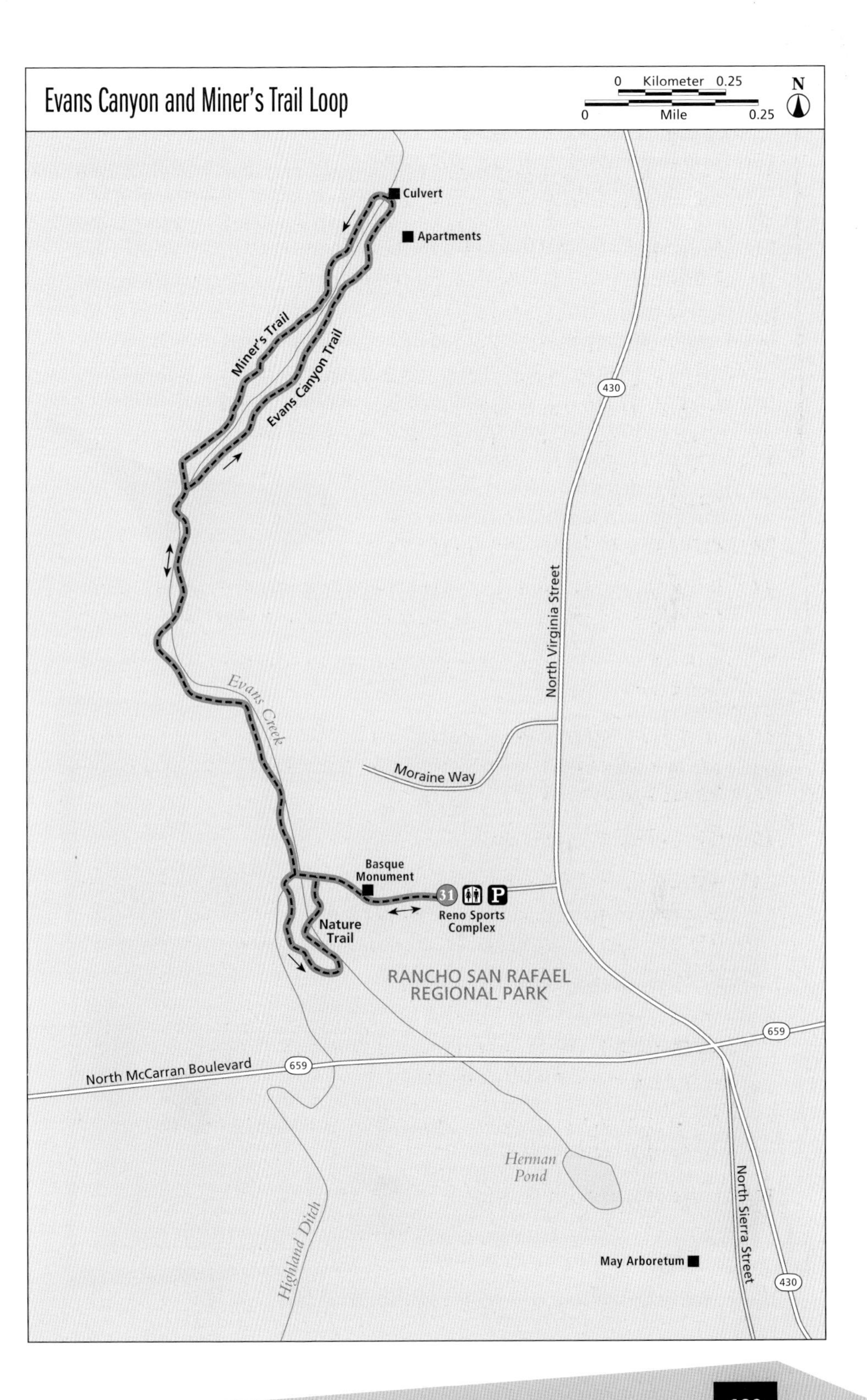
Evans Canyon and Miner's Trail Loop
0 Kilometer 0.25
0 Mile 0.25
N
Culvert
Apartments
Miner's Trail
Evans Canyon Trail
430
North Virginia Street
Evans Creek
Moraine Way
Basque Monument
31
P
Reno Sports Complex
Nature Trail
RANCHO SAN RAFAEL REGIONAL PARK
659
North McCarran Boulevard
659
Herman Pond
Highland Ditch
May Arboretum
North Sierra Street
430

HIKE INFORMATION

Local information: The Chamber, serving Reno, Sparks, and northern Nevada, offers information and links to community events, government, and businesses including restaurants and lodging. The Reno office is at 449 S. Virginia St. 2nd Floor, Reno, NV 89501; (775) 636-9550; www.thechambernv.org. For information about the city of Reno, call Reno Direct at (775) 334-INFO or visit www.reno.gov/index.aspx?page=1.

Local events/attractions: Rancho San Rafael Regional Park is ground zero for the Great Reno Balloon Race, touted as one of the largest, free hot-air ballooning events in the nation. According to the event website, the race started in 1982 with a paltry twenty balloonists; now that number tops one hundred. For more information about the race, including dates for the next event, visit the website at www.renoballoon.com or call (775) 826-1181.

Willows, reeds, and grasses thrive in the moisture provided by Evans Creek.

May Arboretum and Herman Pond

The May Arboretum and surrounding parklands provide a fine short hike within minutes of downtown Reno. The trails boast great views of the Carson Range and an enlightening botany lesson.

Start: At the arboretum entrance adjacent to the May Museum
Distance: 1.1-mile loop
Hiking time: 1 hour
Difficulty: Easy
Trail surface: Pavement; decomposed granite pathways
Best seasons: Spring and fall for blooms and autumn color, but the arboretum can be enjoyed year-round if you avoid extremes of summer heat and winter cold
Other trail users: None in the arboretum; mountain bikers near Herman Pond
Trailhead amenities: Parking, restrooms, water, and information are available at the trailhead. Visit the museum to pick up the booklet for the self-guided tree tour of the arboretum (a fee is charged).
Canine compatibility: No dogs permitted in the arboretum, but it's an off-leash dog paradise in the huge fenced pasture to the west. Dogs must be leashed in other areas of the park.
Fees and permits: None for the arboretum, but a fee is charged if you want to tour the May Museum.
Schedule: As a rule of thumb, Washoe County Parks are open from 8 a.m. to sunset. Formal hours are 8 a.m. to 9 p.m. from Memorial Day weekend to Labor Day weekend; 8 a.m. to 7 p.m. from Labor Day to the start of standard time; 8 a.m. to 5 p.m. from the start of standard time to the start of daylight savings time in spring; and 8 a.m. to 7 p.m. from the start of daylight savings time to Memorial Day weekend.
Maps: USGS Reno NV; wander at will on the arboretum trails, as you cannot get lost.
Trail contact: Rancho San Rafael Regional Park; Washoe County Department of Regional Parks and Open Space, 2601 Plumas St., Reno, NV 89509; (775) 823-6500; www.washoecountyparks.com. The garden's direct line is (775) 785-4153; the website is www.maycenter.com.

Finding the trailhead: The arboretum's address in Rancho San Rafael Regional Park is 1595 N. Sierra St. From I-80 take the downtown Reno/Virginia Street exit. Go north on North Sierra Street for 0.8 mile to Putnam Drive. Go left (west) on Putnam Drive for 0.1 mile to the signed entrance to Rancho San Rafael Regional Park. Follow the park road to the visitor center/museum/arboretum parking areas on the right (northeast). Park near the May Museum and the Wilbur D. May Great Basin Adventure; the signed arboretum entrance is between the two. GPS: N39 32.760' / W119 49.548'

THE HIKE

Wilbur D. May, whose name graces the arboretum, museum, and Great Basin discovery center in Rancho San Rafael Regional Park, was a renaissance man who arrived in Reno in 1936. Rancher, artist, sportsman, composer, world traveler, philanthropist—his legacy is preserved in this collection of public treasures.

Though May's name is synonymous with this metropolitan park, the land on which the arboretum sits has been utilized or owned by many people, according to park literature. First were the Washoe Indians, who split their time between the fruitful desert and alpine highlands of the Sierra Nevada. European ranch owners included the Pincolini brothers, who arrived in 1896, then the Jensen family, and also the Herman family, for whom the pond passed near the end of the route is named. Products of the ranch helped sustain Reno's casino industry around the turn of the twentieth century. A multifaceted preservation effort that stretched from 1976 to 1979 resulted in what is now one of the most popular regional parks in the Reno area.

The arboretum consists of interwoven trails lined with small gardens. The plants in each garden are meticulously identified and consist of natives and exotics alike. Wander at will; the route described here makes a vague counterclockwise tour of the gardens, passing willows and pines, snowberries and roses, sages and oaks, overlooks and gazebos, and shaded benches, nooks and crannies in xeriscape and cultivation. The gardens are named, providing benchmarks for route-finding, but the arboretum is contained and easy to navigate.

The Irwin Overlook, near the Carl Santini garden, is perched near the top of the arboretum grounds. Interpretive signs identify the main components of the panoramic views: the Virginia Range and its geology and history, including a description of the Comstock Lode; Slide Mountain and Mount Rose; the Carson Range and the high Sierra; and Crystal Peak and Peavine Peak to the northwest. Below them sprawls Reno, occupying the Truckee Meadows, with its signature high-rise casinos front and center.

From the overlook, a path drops rather steeply to the trail that skirts Herman Pond, a stock pond created by the damming of Evans Creek in 1954. Floods overran the pond twice, in 1986 and 1997—hard to envision from a seat on a waterside bench on a hot summer's day, as friendly ducks ply the quiet waters and the distant Carson Range looks like a picture. The pond is open for fishing, but swimming is not permitted.

From the pond, the trail hitches past the pasture, where dogs romp free of leashes. The route ends near the May Museum and the Great Basin Adventure, nice places for a visit following a nice hike.

Rancho San Rafael Regional Park, home to the May Arboretum, also hosts play fields.

MILES AND DIRECTIONS

0.0 Start by heading down the paved path beside the May Museum through the various gardens.

0.2 Drop left (north) to the Evans Creek Bridge and the May Grove. The arboretum paths are paved with decomposed granite on the north side of the bridge.

0.3 Stay on the highest paths to reach Fannie's Garden, then continue up to the Irwin Overlook, where you'll enjoy expansive views and interpretive signs.

0.7 Descend rather steeply from the overlook to the baseline trail and go right (north) toward Herman Pond. The trail circles the pond in a counterclockwise direction.

0.8 Cross the pond's inlet via a boardwalk. At the junction of the Pasture Loop Trail and the Evans Canyon Trail stay left (northwest) on the Evans Canyon Trail, skirting the dog-romping pasture.

1.0 Reach the T junction with the trail into the pooch play area and the arboretum/museum parking area. A park map confirms your location. Go left (southeast) to close the loop.

1.1 Arrive back at the trailhead.

HIKE INFORMATION

Local information: The Chamber, serving Reno, Sparks, and northern Nevada, offers information and links to community events, government, and businesses including restaurants and lodging. The Reno office is at 449 S. Virginia St. 2nd Floor, Reno, NV 89501; (775) 636-9550; www.thechambernv.org. For information about the city of Reno, call Reno Direct at (775) 334-INFO or visit www.reno.gov/index.aspx?page=1.

Local events/attractions: Rancho San Rafael Regional Park offers options galore. The May Museum houses art galleries and historical displays that include Wilbur May's collections from his world travels. Museum hours vary with the seasons, so be sure to call ahead or check the website. A fee is charged. For more information contact the Wilbur D. May Center at Rancho San Rafael Regional Park, 1595 N. Sierra, Reno, NV 89503; (775) 785-5961; www.washoecounty.us/parks/mc_home.

The Great Basin Adventure area, complete with log flume rides and a children's petting zoo, is popular with families. Playgrounds and other areas of the park are free; a fee is charged for other attractions. For more information contact Great Basin Adventure Park at Rancho San Rafael Regional Park, 1595 N. Sierra, Reno, NV 89503; (775) 823-6501; www.washoecounty.us/parks/rsrp.htm.

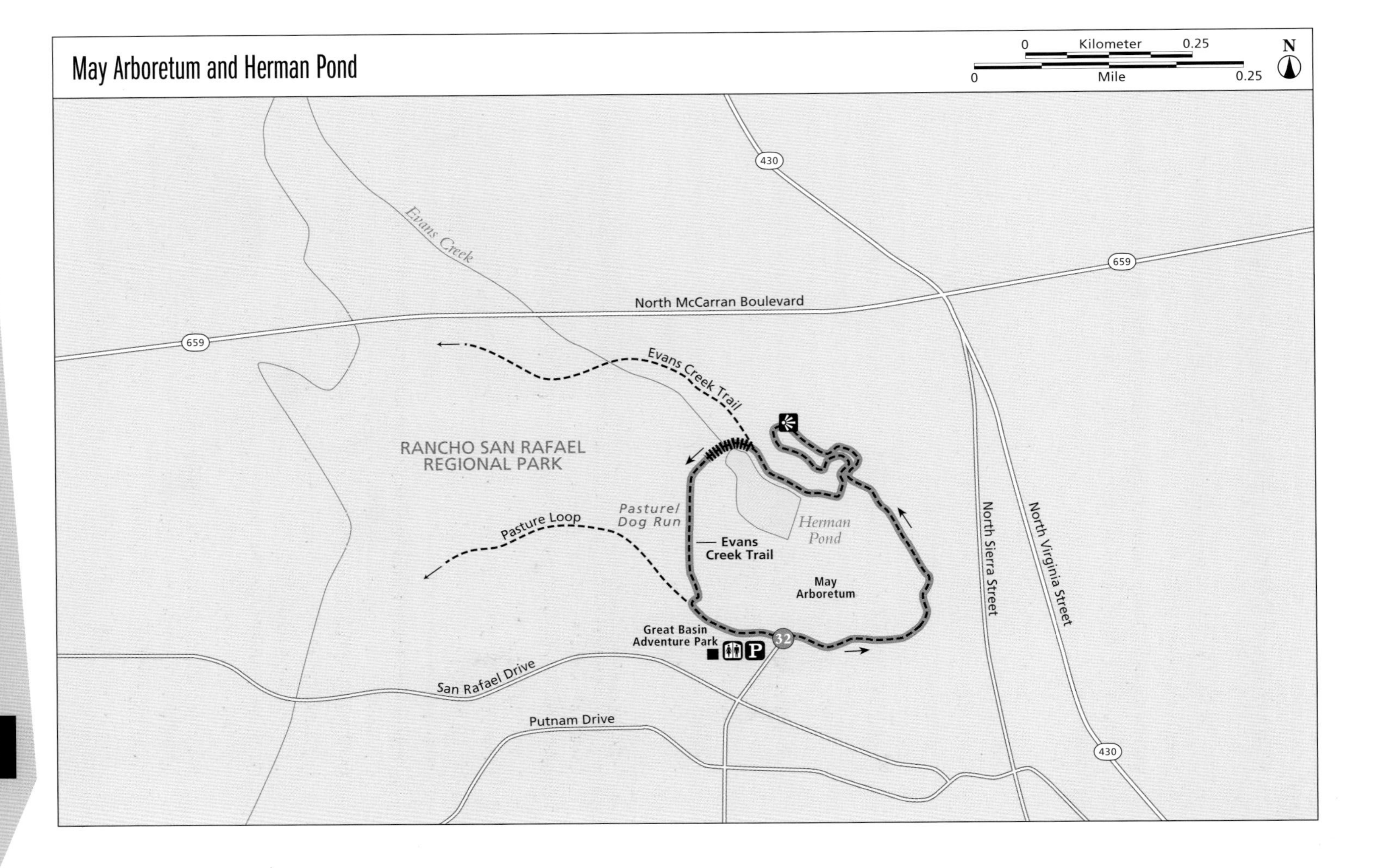
May Arboretum and Herman Pond
0
Kilometer
0.25
0
Mile
0.25
N
430
Evans Creek
659
North McCarran Boulevard
659
Evans Creek Trail
RANCHO SAN RAFAEL REGIONAL PARK
Pasture/ Dog Run
Pasture Loop
Herman Pond
Evans Creek Trail
May Arboretum
North Sierra Street
North Virginia Street
Great Basin Adventure Park
32
P
San Rafael Drive
Putnam Drive
430

Steamboat Ditch and the Hole in the Wall

Reno's Hole in the Wall is not an outlaw hideout. It's literally a hole in a rock wall: a narrow tunnel gushing snowmelt into Steamboat Ditch. The trail to the hole begins alongside the cooling flow of the Truckee River, then climbs to a ditchside walk with great views.

Start: On the Truckee River Parkway in Mayberry Park
Distance: 5.6 miles out and back
Hiking time: 3–4 hours
Difficulty: Moderate
Trail surface: Paved bike path, dirt singletrack, dirt roadway
Best seasons: Winter, spring, and fall. Avoid the trail on hot days, as it is completely exposed to the desert sun.
Other trail users: Mountain bikers, equestrians, trail runners
Trailhead amenities: Though there are plenty of spaces in the paved lot at Mayberry Park, these fill quickly on warm spring and summer weekends. The park also has restrooms, trashcans, picnic greens, and easy river access.
Canine compatibility: Leashed dogs permitted (but be warned: many run free)
Fees and permits: None
Schedule: As a rule of thumb, Washoe County Parks are open from 8 a.m. to sunset. Formal hours are 8 a.m. to 9 p.m. from Memorial Day weekend to Labor Day weekend; 8 a.m. to 7 p.m. from Labor Day to the start of standard time; 8 a.m. to 5 p.m. from the start of standard time to the start of daylight savings time in spring; and 8 a.m. to 7 p.m. from the start of daylight savings time to Memorial Day weekend.
Maps: USGS Verdi NV, Mount Rose NW NV; www.nvtrailmaps.com
Trail contact: Mayberry Park is managed by the Washoe County Department of Regional Parks and Open Space, 2601 Plumas St., Reno, NV 89509; (775) 823-6500; www.washoecountyparks.com. Other trail segments are maintained by City of Reno Parks, Recreation & Community Services, City Hall, 1 E. First St., Eleventh Floor, Reno, NV 89501; (775) 334-2260; www.cityofreno.com. The US Forest Service also manages some of the land along the route, and the trail crosses parcels of private land as well.

Special considerations: The Steamboat Ditch Trail crosses some parcels of private property, so remain on the ditchside track. Social paths intersecting the Tom Cooke Trail should be avoided, as shortcutting causes erosion, degrades the environment, and creates unsightly scars on the landscape.

Other: Mayberry Park is often crowded in spring, summer, and fall. Parking can be difficult; a second lot is east of the main lot down the dirt road.

Finding the trailhead: From I-80 westbound from Reno, take the West McCarran Boulevard exit. Go left (south) on West McCarran for 0.7 mile to West Fourth Street. Turn right (west) on West Fourth Street and travel 1.9 miles to Woodland Avenue. Turn left (south) and follow Woodland Avenue for 0.4 mile to its end in a driveway between warehouses; the driveway leads into Mayberry Park and to the Truckee River Parkway. GPS: N39 30.171' / W119 53.700'

THE HIKE

Linking the Truckee River Parkway, the Tom Cooke Trail, and the Steamboat Ditch Trail, hikers are treated to a short tour of the Truckee's thick riparian corridor, a long exploration of the high desert below the steep slopes of the Carson Range, and great views of Peavine Peak and the Truckee Meadows.

The path to the Hole in the Wall begins among the cottonwoods that shade the Truckee River in Mayberry Park, which on hot summer days is populated with picnicking families and young people carrying tubes and small rafts to take onto the river. Dirt tracks lead to narrow beaches along the Truckee, where rafters put in or spread picnic blankets.

Follow the paved Truckee River Parkway right (west) through the river's bottomlands, with warehouses bordering on the right (north) and steep, undeveloped canyon walls on the left (south). The pavement ends behind the Patagonia warehouse at a metal bridge and a rustic picnic shelter. Crossing the bridge is a bit exciting (especially for kids and dogs); spaces between the planks that make up the floor of the span are separated just enough for you to look down onto the swift flow of the water below.

On the other side of the bridge, the trail climbs left (southwest) to a wooden footbridge spanning the Last Chance Ditch. Like the Steamboat Ditch, which cruises along the hillside above, the Last Chance carries Sierra snowmelt to thirsty high desert ranches. The signed Tom Cooke Trail begins on the south side of the ditch.

The well-built singletrack uses switchbacks to ascend a steep, rocky fold in the scrub-covered hillside. Practice good stewardship of the open space by avoiding the social routes carved by careless hikers and cyclists cutting switchbacks.

The Tom Cooke Trail tops out on an open hillside with views up and across the grass- and sage-covered foothills of the Carson Range. Views north across the Truckee River valley are of sprawling Peavine Peak. Subdivisions and business parks fill the valley itself, and the whistle of a passing train (along with highway noise from the adjacent interstate) may waft up to the vista point.

The Tom Cooke Trail widens to doubletrack before it reaches its junction with the Steamboat Ditch Trail. At the T intersection with the ditch trail, go right (west) on the obvious, well-used dirt roadway. Heading left on the Steamboat Ditch Trail will take you east into the Hunter Creek drainage.

Sections of the Steamboat Ditch Trail are very popular with hikers, mountain bikers, and trail runners. The trail crosses private land but has been in public use a very long time. It's likely you won't see a fence or sign noting property boundaries or forbidding passage. Still, some land managers are uncomfortable with public use for obvious (and unfortunate) liability issues. Efforts are underway to formalize public access to the entire trail. Meanwhile, trail lovers continue to

Water from the High Sierra spills from the Hole in the Wall.

follow the ditch, enjoying a distinctive stripe of riparian greenery on the otherwise brown and scrubby mountainsides.

Traverse several gullies as you wind westward along the ditch. It's a gentle, almost imperceptible climb to the Hole in the Wall, and the path winds in and out of creases in the topography, offering different views depending on the orientation. Sometimes you gaze down on the Truckee River Valley and Peavine, sometimes across the Truckee Meadows across Reno's skyline and into distant blue-gray ranges of the Great Basin, sometimes up into the stony heights of the Carson Range. Occasionally, a diversion gate marks the head of one of the ravines.

You can't help but note the lone pine tree along the track as you approach the Hole in the Wall. The trail slips through a cut in the yellow and brown hillside, then through a spindly bower of shade trees to where, in spring and early summer, water erupts with whitewater force into the ditch through the hole. Unsigned use trails continue into the hills from this point, but the flat open area near the small pool at the mouth of the tunnel makes a nice picnic spot and a logical turnaround point. To retrace your steps to the trailhead, just go with the flow.

The flat trail alongside Steamboat Ditch offers views out into the Truckee Meadows.

MILES AND DIRECTIONS

0.0 Start on the paved Truckee River Parkway heading right (west).

0.3 Cross the bridge to the south side of the Truckee, then bear left (southwest) to cross the Last Chance Ditch and arrive at the signed start of the Tom Cooke Trail.

0.7 Reach the top of the climb at a vista point.

0.9 Arrive at the T junction with the Steamboat Ditch Trail. Go right (west) on the dirt road; the ditch trail also branches left (east) toward Reno.

1.4 Curl through a gully with a ditch gate.

2.3 Reach the junction with a dirt road leading right (north) away from the ditch. Stay left (southwest) on the obvious ditch trail. Less than 0.1 mile farther, cross a concrete diversion dam/gate in a gully.

2.5 Pass a lone pine.

2.8 Arrive at the Hole in the Wall and turnaround point.

5.6 Arrive back at the Mayberry Park trailhead.

HIKE INFORMATION

Local information: The Chamber, serving Reno, Sparks, and northern Nevada, offers information and links to community events, government, and businesses including restaurants and lodging. The Reno office is at 449 S. Virginia St. 2nd Floor, Reno, NV 89501; (775) 636-9550; www.thechambernv.org. For information about the city of Reno, call Reno Direct at (775) 334-INFO or visit www.reno.gov.

The Steamboat Ditch, completed in the early 1880s, stretches for about 47 miles from the foothills near Verdi to the farms and ranches on the dry desert flatlands surrounding Reno. The Steamboat Ditch Company maintains the ditch. Whatever water is not used for irrigation funnels back into the Truckee again at the end of the ditch run.

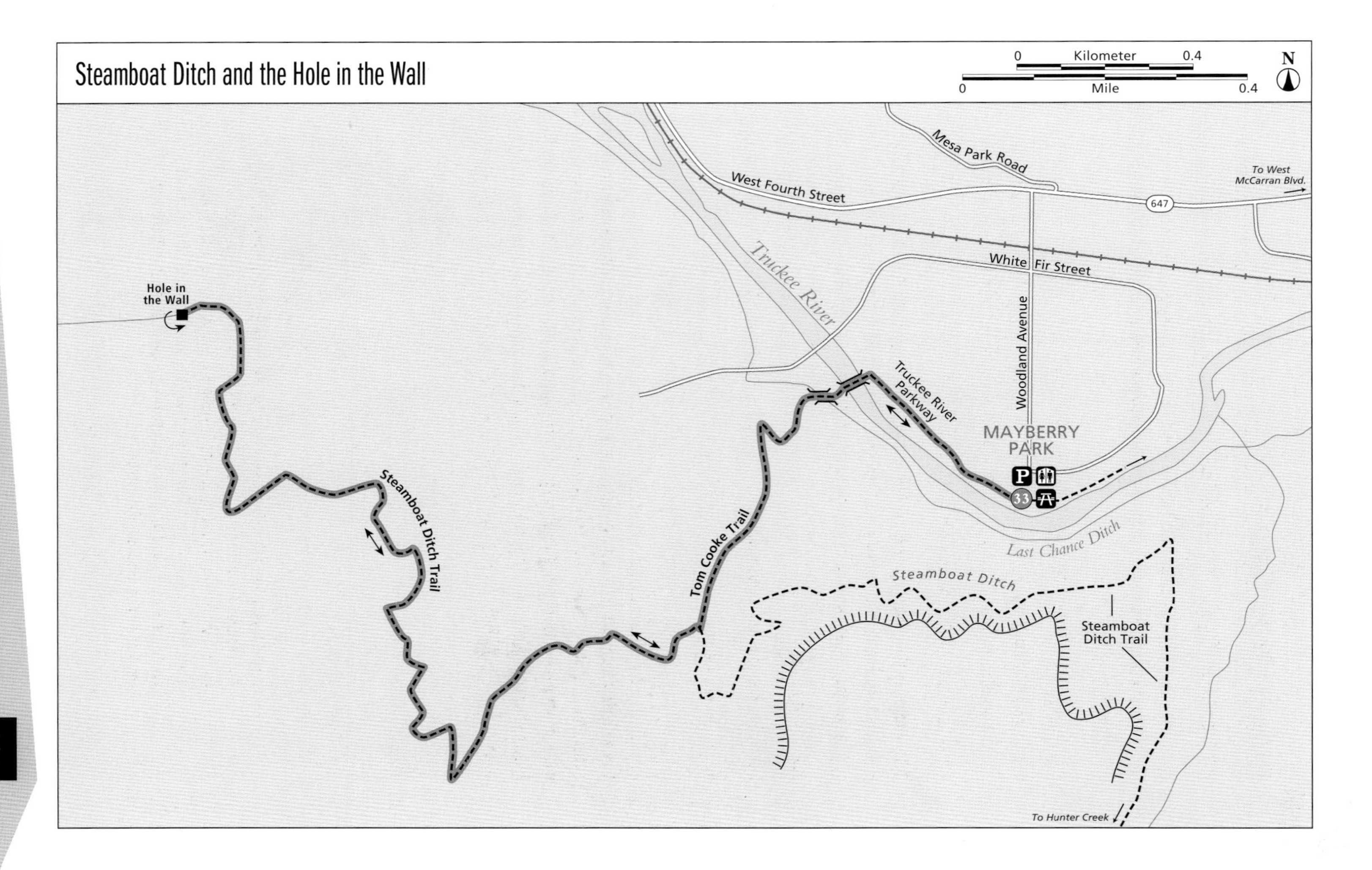
Steamboat Ditch and the Hole in the Wall
0
Kilometer
0.4
0
Mile
0.4
N
Mesa Park Road
West Fourth Street
To West McCarran Blvd.
647
White Fir Street
Truckee River
Woodland Avenue
Hole in the Wall
Truckee River Parkway
MAYBERRY PARK
33
Steamboat Ditch Trail
Tom Cooke Trail
Last Chance Ditch
Steamboat Ditch
Steamboat Ditch Trail
To Hunter Creek

34

Hunter Creek Falls

A narrow, deceptively strenuous trail ascends from dry desert to a waterfall on Hunter Creek that remains vigorous into the dry months of late summer and fall.

Start: At the Michael D. Thompson trailhead west of Reno's Juniper Ridge subdivision
Distance: 6 miles out and back
Hiking time: 4–5 hours
Difficulty: Strenuous
Trail surface: Dirt singletrack
Best seasons: Spring, late autumn
Other trail users: Mountain bikers, trail runners
Trailhead amenities: Parking, restrooms, picnic tables, trashcans, information signboard
Canine compatibility: Dogs permitted; leashes are required at the trailhead and within 1 mile of the trailhead.
Fees and permits: None
Schedule: Sunrise to sunset daily
Maps: USGS Mount Rose NW NV
Trail contact: Washoe County Department of Regional Parks and Open Space, 2601 Plumas St., Reno, NV 89509; (775) 823-6500; www.washoecountyparks.com. Humboldt-Toiyabe National Forest, 1200 Franklin Way, Sparks, NV 89431; (775) 331-6444; www.fs.usda.gov/detailfull/htnf/home/?cid=stelprdb5238686&width=full.
Special considerations: The first 2 miles of this trail traverse exposed scrublands with little shade. Avoid hiking in the heat of a summer day. Bring plenty of water. Rattlesnakes may be present on and adjacent to the trail during the hiking season.

Finding the trailhead: From I-80 westbound out of Reno, take the McCarran Boulevard West exit. Follow McCarran Boulevard right (south) for 1.6 miles to Caughlin Parkway. Turn right on Caughlin Parkway and go 1.2 miles to Plateau Road. Turn right onto Plateau Road and go 0.6 mile to Woodchuck Circle. Go left on Woodchuck Circle and climb 0.8 mile to the Michael D. Thompson trailhead. GPS: N39 29.577' / W119 53.669'

THE HIKE

Extremes of ecotone are showcased on the trail to Hunter Creek Falls. To begin, the route climbs with deceptive steepness for more than 2 miles through shadeless desert scrub, with rock outcrops jutting from steep parched hillsides. You can count the shade trees on one hand.

But by trail's end you are immersed in a montane yellow pine forest, shady and cooling. The route follows ridgebacks between creek drainages, with the water sometimes obvious and sometimes hidden below and shielded by trees. Hunter Creek Falls are a striking destination, rumbling down a steep face at a flat spot in the woods, with fallen logs offering perfect benches for resting and regrouping before the return leg or continuing into the high country.

The route begins by dropping away from the trailhead via a broad dirt road. Pass the connector to the Steamboat Ditch Trail; just beyond is the Hunter Creek crossing, either via a plank bridge located upstream of the road ford, rock-hopping, or wading if the water is low enough.

The trail continues streamside, with side trails branching left toward Hunter Creek. The main trail is obvious, wide at first, then narrowing as it climbs south into a steep, scrub-coated canyon. Pass a sign for the Humboldt Wilderness

Lush and vigorous, Hunter Creek Falls are a welcome destination along a trail that starts out hot and dry.

boundary and cross a rockslide; the upward traverse is exposed and hot in season, so take advantage of the sparse shade offered by the few stands of trees along the route.

A rightward bend in the trail (to the southwest) takes you up into the Hunter Creek drainage, and away from twin ramparts of dark rock, resembling flatirons, that guard the entrance to a neighboring canyon. The climb is gentle, roller coaster–like, and relentless, so set your pace and enjoy.

At about 2.5 miles, the path leads into woodlands, a nice respite from the scrub. No respite from the climbing, however: Continue up, crossing several side streams and following the ridgebacks between the stream drainages as you ascend.

The waterfall is at the 3-mile mark. A rather large clearing, with fallen logs serving as benches, makes a perfect lunch or snack spot, and affords great views of the falls. A bit of rock-hopping across the creek brings you right up to the spill, which tumbles down a narrow cleft split by a fallen log. But the creek should be negotiated with care, and only when water flows are safely low. The clearing also makes a nice camping spot for those planning longer treks into the backcountry.

When you've taken it all in, return as you came.

MILES AND DIRECTIONS

0.0 Begin at the Michael D. Thompson trailhead, heading down the broad dirt road.

0.1 Pass the Steamboat Ditch Trail connection, staying left on the Hunter Creek Trail. Cross Hunter Creek about 50 feet beyond the trail junction.

1.0 Pass a solitary pine that offers creekside shade.

1.3 Two switchbacks lead up the dry slope above the creek. Pass a second lone pine.

2.1 The trail bends southwest into the Hunter Creek drainage, bypassing the dark sentinel rocks of a neighboring canyon.

2.5 Enter the woods.

2.7 Cross side streams on log bridges.

3.0 Cross a last log bridge and reach the clearing at the waterfall. Take a break, then return as you came.

6.0 Arrive back at the trailhead.

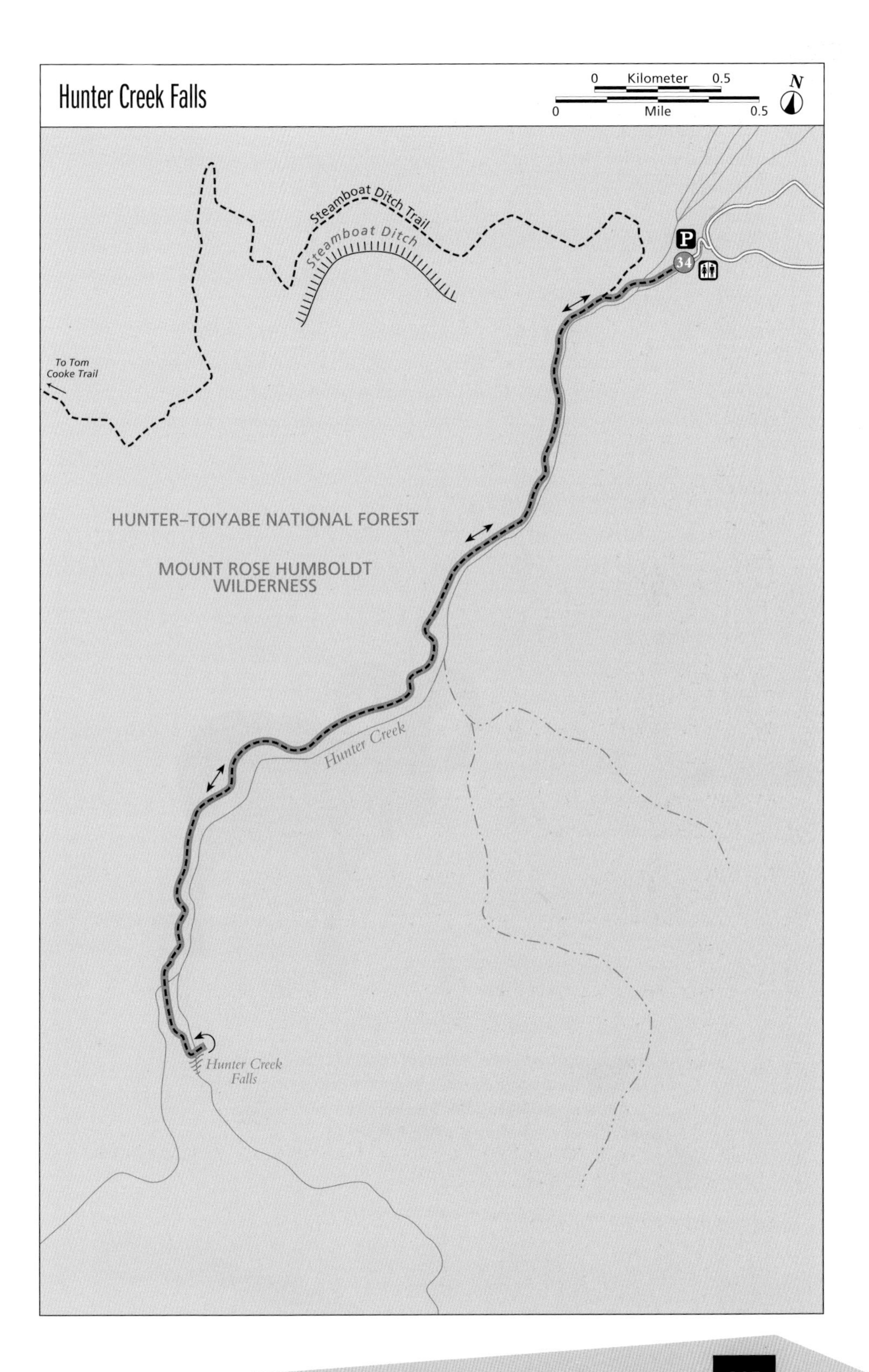
Hunter Creek Falls
0 Kilometer 0.5
0 Mile 0.5
N
Steamboat Ditch Trail
Steamboat Ditch
P
34
To Tom Cooke Trail
HUNTER–TOIYABE NATIONAL FOREST
MOUNT ROSE HUMBOLDT WILDERNESS
Hunter Creek
Hunter Creek Falls

HIKE INFORMATION

Local information: The Chamber, serving Reno, Sparks, and northern Nevada, offers information and links to community events, government, and businesses including restaurants and lodging. The Reno office is at 449 S. Virginia St. 2nd Floor, Reno, NV 89501; (775) 636-9550; www.thechambernv.org. For information about the city of Reno, call Reno Direct at (775) 334-INFO, or visit www.reno.gov/index.aspx?page=1.

Restaurants: Bangkok Cuisine, 55 Mount Rose St., Reno, NV 89509; (775) 322-0299; bangkokcuisinereno.com. Satisfy your post-hike cravings with traditional dishes such as pad Thai, or try something a bit more exotic, such as spicy crispy duck, a stuffed Thai omelet, or stir-fried bean thread noodles with shrimp or squid.

Camping: Undeveloped camping is permitted in the Hunter-Toiyabe National Forest and the Mount Rose Wilderness Area. For more information, contact the Carson Ranger District, 1536 Carson St., Carson City, NV 89701-5291; (775) 882-2766; www.fs.usda.gov/main/htnf/passes-permits

The Humboldt-Toiyabe National Forest is the largest in the contiguous United States. It encompasses more than six million acres and 1.2 million acres of wilderness in twenty-three designated wilderness areas.

Downtown River Walk

The Truckee River flows right through the glitz of downtown Reno, and the town has dressed up the promenade along its banks with colorful landscaping, sculpture, artificial waterfalls, bridges, and a whitewater park.

Start: On the paved path in Barbara Bennett Park
Distance: 2 miles out and back (with optional extensions)
Hiking time: About 1 hour
Difficulty: Easy
Trail surface: Pavement
Best seasons: Year-round
Other trail users: Cyclists, trail runners, skaters
Trailhead amenities: Parking available in Barbara Bennett Park (space permitting), and along roadways bordering the trail. Bennett Park also has restrooms, informational signage, and offers access to the whitewater park.
Canine compatibility: Leashed dogs permitted
Fees and permits: None
Schedule: 24 hours a day, 7 days a week, year-round
Maps: USGS Reno NV; no map is necessary
Trail contact: City of Reno Parks, Recreation and Community Services Department, 190 E. Liberty St., Reno, NV 89501; (775) 334-6265; www.cityofreno.com

Finding the trailhead: From I-80 take the downtown Reno/Virginia Street exit. Head south on Virginia Street for about 0.5 mile, through downtown, to West Second Street. Go right (west) on Second Street for 2 blocks to North Arlington Avenue. Go left (south) on North Arlington, over the Truckee River, and turn right (west) into signed Barbara Bennett Park. Parking is available on city streets in this area, too. GPS: N39 31.434' / W119 49.019'

THE HIKE

Whether you're a gambler working a blackjack table or a Reno resident working a casino shift, the Truckee River Parkway offers an escape from your labor. The paved trail, artfully built along the sparkling Truckee adjacent downtown Reno, provides a convenient and entertaining outdoor experience.

In addition to letting you stretch your legs and breathe fresh air, the riverside path overflows with people-watching potential. Cyclists, skaters, dog walkers, waders, rafters, kayakers, picnickers, dancers, basketball players, jugglers, and other street performers—they are all here, sharing the waterfront pathway with moms pushing strollers and couples holding hands. The kayakers are arguably the most fun to watch, spinning in whitewater created by artificial rock bars that pinch the river's flow. The kids are fun to watch, too, jumping from the rocks into the water and floating gently downstream.

Getting clear of the crowds is as easy as melding with them. A few blocks west of downtown the trail enters a greenbelt in a quiet neighborhood, where painted benches overlook the river in the shade of spreading cottonwoods. Impressive homes perch on the high south-side embankment; more modest homes line the north side.

An urban trail follows the Truckee River through downtown Reno.

You can access this popular 13-mile long trail—and all its amenities—from a variety of points along its length, so feel free to improvise on the tour described here. The walk begins in busy Bennett Park on the south side of the river near the whitewater park. Head east (downstream) to Wingfield Park, an island reached by arcing pedestrian bridges. The park is outfitted with an amphitheater and grassy greens.

The trail continues down the north side of the river, offering access to shopping and restaurants as well as the casinos. Continue east (downstream), crossing the next bridge to the south side of the Truckee (alongside Island Avenue). Here you'll enter the waterfall and sculpture garden, where colorful flowerpots and small gazebos mingle with sculptures of eagles, deer, bear, mountain goats, and other creatures being showered in sheets of water.

You can continue east on the parkway all the way to Reno's sister city of Sparks, but to reach the greenbelt stretch, circle back to the west at Virginia Street, crossing again to the north side of the river and returning to Wingfield Park. Cross North Arlington Avenue, pausing on the bridge to check out the river antics, then continue west, past little Lundsford Park, into a quiet neighborhood.

The trail is lined with sturdy cottonwoods shading a linear green that borders the riparian zone along the riverbanks. The homes on the north side, along Riverside Drive, are charming, but the mansions on the south side are to be envied. Benches along the trail look across the river to the palatial houses and their lovely gardens.

Though the trail continues westward toward the Carson Range, a likely turnaround point is the Keystone Avenue Bridge, just beyond the McKinley Arts and Culture Center and interpretive signs about Reno's origins and local arts and culture. Unless you choose to explore farther, retrace your steps to the trailhead.

The Truckee River Parkway is 13 miles long and can be picked up at a number of locations within Reno. Extend your walk east from the Reno whitewater park to the whitewater park in neighboring Sparks, or continue west through quiet neighborhoods toward the mountain front.

MILES AND DIRECTIONS

0.0 Start at Bennett Park heading east. Cross the intersection of West First Street and North Arlington Avenue to Wingfield Park.

0.1 Pass an interpretive sign about Reno's origins, then cross the bridge to the south side of the river and explore the waterfall and sculpture garden.

0.4 Circle back to Wingfield Park, cross North Arlington Avenue, and head left (west) on the north side of the river.

0.6 Enter the neighborhoods bordering Riverside Drive.

0.8 Reach the greenbelt section, with benches and views of riverside estates.

1.0 Pass the McKinley Arts and Culture Center before the turnaround point under the Keystone Avenue Bridge. Retrace your steps toward Wingfield Park.

2.0 Arrive back at the Bennett Park trailhead.

HIKE INFORMATION

Local information: The Chamber, serving Reno, Sparks, and northern Nevada, offers information and links to community events, government, and businesses including restaurants and lodging. The Reno office is at 449 S. Virginia St. 2nd Floor, Reno, NV 89501; (775) 636-9550; www.thechambernv.org. For information about the city of Reno, call Reno Direct at (775) 334-INFO, or visit www.reno.gov/index.aspx?page=1.

Restaurants: Campo Restaurant, 50 N. Sierra St., Reno, NV 89501; (775) 737-9555; www.camporeno.com. Looking for a good old carbo load before or after a long day on the trail? Campo is the spot. Located in downtown Reno, the restaurant features a variety of pizzas and pastas, with a few other entree and lunch selections.

Organizations: The Truckee River Parkway is part of a larger entity, the Tahoe-Pyramid Bikeway, which will, when completed, link Lake Tahoe to Pyramid Lake. The bikeway vision cobbles together trails, roads, and bridges as it drops from the headwaters of the Truckee to its end. For more information visit the Tahoe-Pyramid Parkway website at www.tpbikeway.org or call (775) 825-9868.

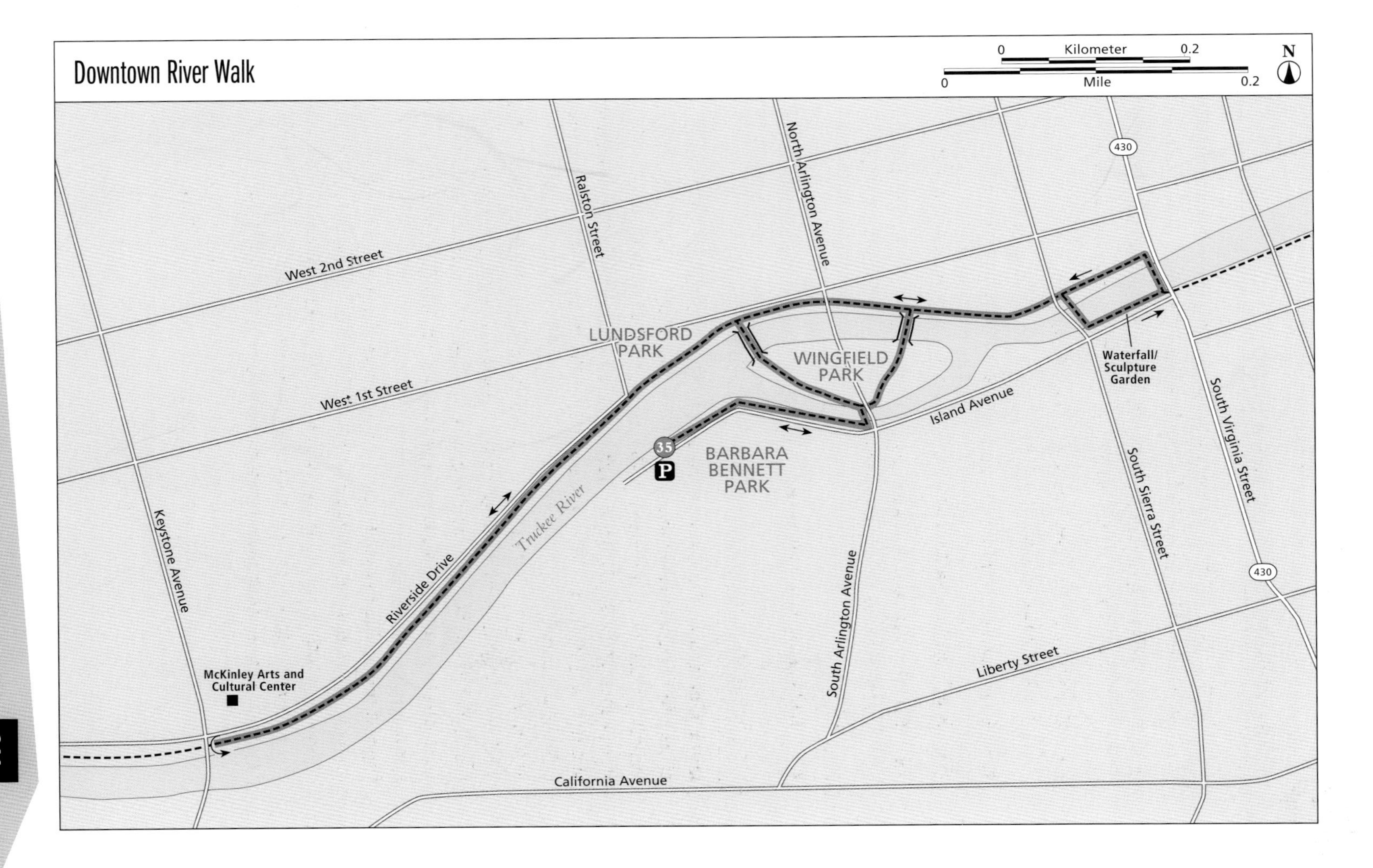
Downtown River Walk
0
Kilometer
0.2
0
Mile
0.2
N
West 2nd Street
Ralston Street
North Arlington Avenue
430
LUNDSFORD
PARK
WINGFIELD
PARK
West 1st Street
Waterfall/
Sculpture
Garden
Island Avenue
South Virginia Street
35
P
BARBARA
BENNETT
PARK
Truckee River
Keystone Avenue
Riverside Drive
South Sierra Street
South Arlington Avenue
Liberty Street
McKinley Arts and
Cultural Center
California Avenue

36

Oxbow Nature Study Area Loop

A nearly pristine pocket of riparian wildland has been set aside along the Truckee River within Reno's city limits. The nature trail that winds through this tiny preserve bears witness to how nature recovers after fire and flood.

Start: At the signed trailhead adjacent to the Oxbow interpretive center
Distance: 1-mile lollipop
Hiking time: 45 minutes to 1 hour
Difficulty: Easy
Trail surface: Wide gravel and dirt trail; boardwalk
Best seasons: Year-round
Other trail users: None
Canine compatibility: Dogs not permitted
Fees and permits: None
Schedule: Gates open at 8 a.m. daily. In winter the park closes at 4 p.m.; in summer it closes at sunset. During spring, summer, and fall the interpretive center is scheduled to be open from Monday to Friday from 8 a.m. to 5 p.m., but, according to land managers, there are no guarantees.
Trailhead amenities: Limited parking, restrooms, water, picnic facilities, an interpretive center
Maps: USGS Reno NV; no map is necessary
Trail contact: City of Reno Parks, Recreation, and Community Services Department, 190 East Liberty St., Reno, NV 89501; (775) 334-2260; www.cityofreno.com. Nevada Department of Wildlife (NDOW), 1100 Valley Rd., Reno, NV 89512; (775) 334-3808; www.ndow.org. The contact number for school groups is (775) 334-3808.

Finding the trailhead: From I-80 just west of downtown Reno, take the Keystone Avenue exit. Go left (south) on Keystone Avenue for 0.5 mile to West Second Street. Go right (west) on West Second Street for 0.4 mile; it turns into Dickerson Road. Continue another 0.6 mile to the end of Dickerson Road at the park gate. GPS: N39 31.117' / W119 50.774'

THE HIKE

Restoration and evolution are tangible in the Oxbow Nature Study Area. Its setting is distractingly urban, with railroad tracks running down one side of the preserve and apartment buildings visible through the trees and brush along the riverside on the other. But within the natural area itself you are insulated by greenery, birdsong, and the soothing rumble of the Truckee River rushing over its rocky bed. And if you return year-after-year, you can watch the land heal itself.

Oxbow has been in a state of transition since a human-caused fire burned about eighteen of the park's twenty-two acres in April 2008, killing some of the old cottonwoods that had thrived in the dense riparian zone and destroying man-made aids to study including a boardwalk and interpretive signs. A new loop trail and fledgling plantings were in place by spring of the following year, and the ravages of the blaze were softened even then by the vibrant greens of new growth. Recovery is a process best appreciated over time, and locals who keep Oxbow in their back pockets will witness the restorative process as it proceeds.

Fire isn't the only natural force that has transformed Oxbow since it was established in 1991. In 1997, the Truckee overflowed its banks—not for the first time and not for the last—filling the parcel with boulders, sand, and other debris. Nearly 5 feet of sand was deposited in the park during that event.

The loop through the Oxbow Nature Study Area allows hikers to explore a pocket of urban wildland.

But unless your visit coincides with another episode in the Oxbow drama, the study area is a rejuvenating place. Though charred snags can be spied throughout, willows thrive along the riverbanks. Sparrows, woodpeckers, robins, and other songbirds flit and chit in the brush. If you pass quietly and softly, you're likely to see other woodland creatures as well, and you might be treated to a rarer sighting of deer or coyote, a mink or a muskrat.

Begin your tour by reading the interpretive signs at the trailhead and checking out the viewing platforms. Stairs lead up to an overlook of the Truckee and the small pond that borders it. There is also a short trail that leads right (west) to the pond, which is frequented by ducks and also occasionally hosts a heron or muskrat. Beyond the small picnic green to the left (east) of the park's information building, another boardwalk leads out onto the Truckee itself, willows crowding the edges of the cold, rumbling water.

The trail proper begins at the base of the elevated viewing platform. You'll quickly enter the burn zone, and the Truckee comes into view to the left (south). The brush is thin enough to see the urban borders of the greenbelt, the railroad on one side and apartments across the river.

When the trail splits to form a loop, head to the right (northwest) to travel in a counterclockwise circuit. The path winds through recovering grasslands and woodland. Meet the wide gravel trail (the return path) at a T junction and walk a bit farther right (west) to explore a small meadow at the park's boundary. Then follow the gravel trail back toward the trailhead. Pass a bench and interpretive sign before tracing the shoreline of the Truckee back to the first trail junction. Short side trails head riverside, where you might find a pocket of beach upon which to rest and contemplate the river. From the trail split, retrace your steps to the trailhead.

MILES AND DIRECTIONS

0.0 Start by visiting the viewing platforms and pond, then set off down the signed main trail.

0.3 Go right (northwest) on the fenced trail through the meadow.

0.5 Meet a wide gravel path (the return route). Go right (west) into the meadow at the park's edge, then return to the trail junction and go right, following the gravel track.

0.75 Reach the first trail junction; stay right (straight) to retrace your steps to the trailhead.

1.0 Arrive back at the trailhead.

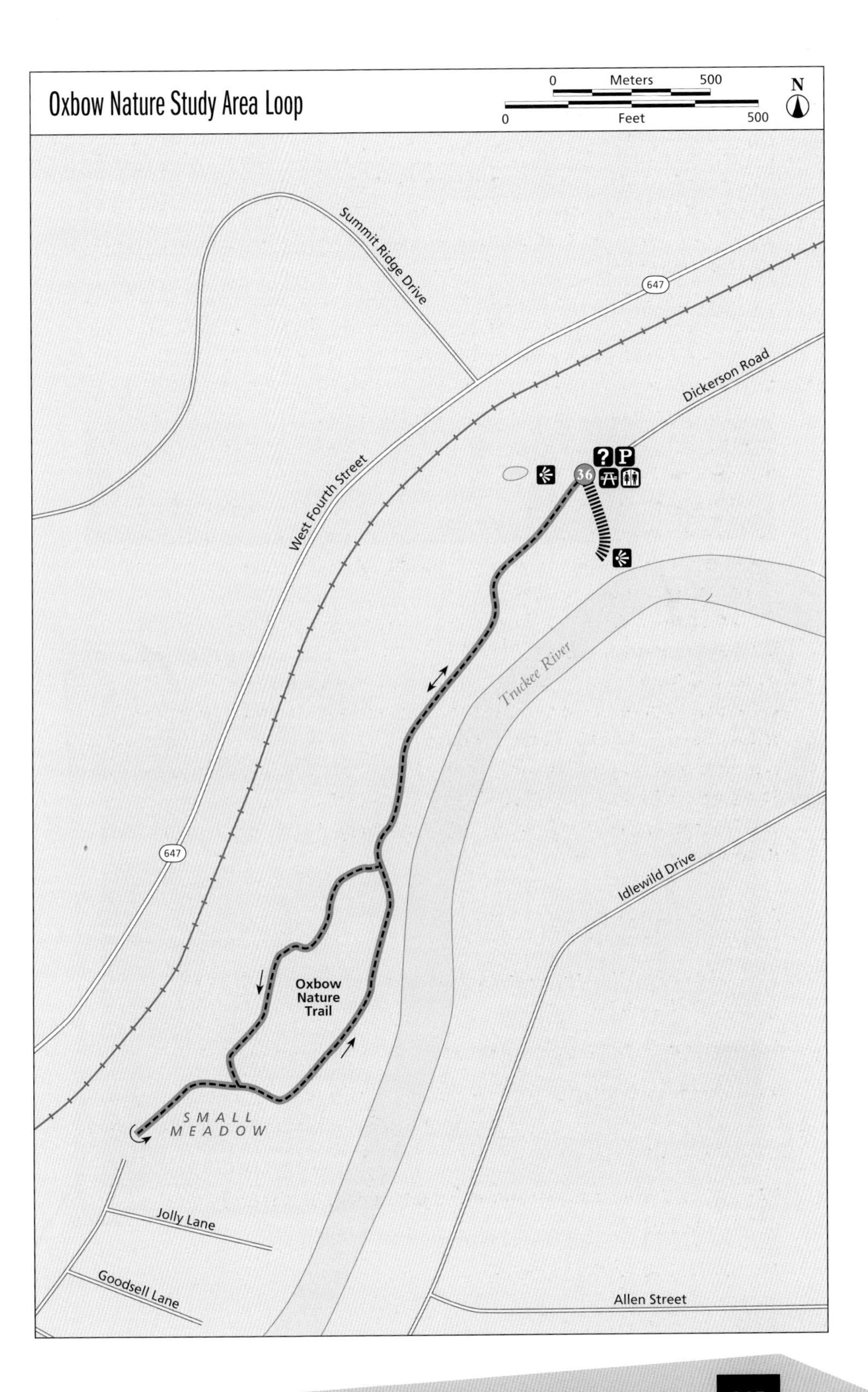

Oxbow Nature Study Area Loop
0
Meters
500
0
Feet
500
N
Summit Ridge Drive
647
Dickerson Road
West Fourth Street
36
Truckee River
647
Idlewild Drive
Oxbow Nature Trail
SMALL MEADOW
Jolly Lane
Goodsell Lane
Allen Street

HIKE INFORMATION

Local information: The Chamber, serving Reno, Sparks, and northern Nevada, offers information and links to community events, government, and businesses including restaurants and lodging. The Reno office is at 449 S. Virginia St. 2nd Floor, Reno, NV 89501; (775) 636-9550; www.thechambernv.org. For information about the city of Reno, call Reno Direct at (775) 334-INFO, or visit www.reno.gov/index.aspx?page=1.

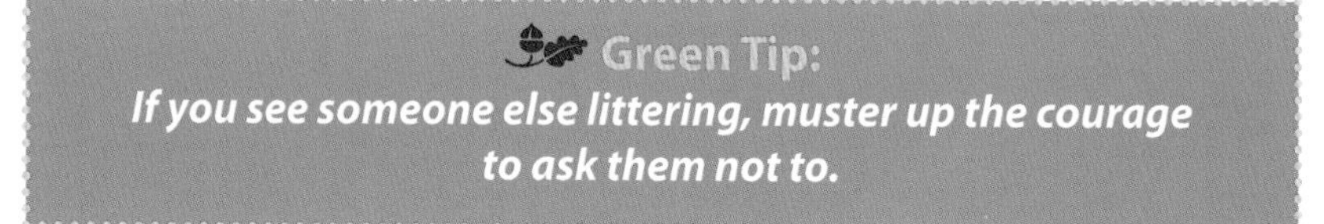

Green Tip:

If you see someone else littering, muster up the courage to ask them not to.

Viewing platforms in the Oxbow Nature Study Area overlook the Truckee River.

Bartley Ranch Regional Park Loop

Remnants of Nevada's ranching heritage are preserved in this large suburban park. The trail begins next to a charming one-room schoolhouse, rides for a stretch atop a wooden flume, and meanders among farm equipment near trail's end.

Start: At the signed trailhead in the parking lot near the Old Huffaker Schoolhouse
Distance: 1.5-mile loop
Hiking time: About 1 hour
Difficulty: Easy
Trail surface: Dirt, gravel, a short section of wooden flume
Best seasons: Spring, fall, and winter
Other trail users: None on the Quail Run and Flume Trails; equestrians and mountain bikers on the Ranch Loop Trail
Trailhead amenities: Parking, restrooms, water, picnic facilities; equestrian arena; an information center is located just down the trail from the parking area
Canine compatibility: Leashed dogs permitted
Fees and permits: None
Schedule: As a rule of thumb, Washoe County Parks are open from 8 a.m. to sunset. Formal hours are 8 a.m. to 9 p.m. from Memorial Day weekend to Labor Day weekend; 8 a.m. to 7 p.m. from Labor Day to the start of standard time; 8 a.m. to 5 p.m. from the start of standard time to the start of daylight savings time in spring; and 8 a.m. to 7 p.m. from the start of daylight savings time to Memorial Day weekend.
Maps: USGS Mount Rose NE NV; a map is posted on the exterior wall of the information center; www.nvtrailmaps.com
Trail contact: Bartley Ranch Regional Park, Washoe County Department of Regional Parks and Open Space, 2601 Plumas St., Reno, NV 89509; (775) 823-6500; www.washoecountyparks.com. The park's direct line is (775) 828-6612.

Finding the trailhead: From US 395/I-580 southbound, take the Kietzke Lane exit (exit 63). Stay left, following Kietzke Lane for 0.1 mile to South McCarran Boulevard. Turn right (west) on South McCarran Boulevard and continue for 0.7 mile to Lakeside Drive. Go left (south) on Lakeside Drive for 0.4 mile to Bartley Ranch Road on the left (east). Follow Bartley Ranch Road for about 0.1 mile to the park entrance at the covered bridge. Park in the first lot, near the Old Huffaker Schoolhouse. The trailhead is next to the restrooms. The park address is 6000 Bartley Ranch Rd. GPS: N39 28.125' / W119 48.424'

THE HIKE

In Bartley Ranch, a backyard park in Reno's southern suburbs, interlocking trails wind through native scrub, along irrigation ditches, and past preserved pieces of farm machinery. This loop, though never escaping the sight of private homes and the hum of highway noise, is able to evoke Reno's frontier days by showcasing remnants of the past, including a covered flume and the perfectly restored Old Huffaker Schoolhouse. Take a peek inside the schoolhouse if it's open. Clean and bright, with old-style desks and a glowing wooden floor, the building gives the impression of having absorbed the laughter of children into its sunshine-yellow walls.

Begin on the Quail Run Nature Trail, which passes through fragrant desert scrub and across several small wooden plank bridges to picnic sites fronting the Western Heritage Interpretive Center. The distant Virginia Range, brown and rolling in summer, fall, and much of winter, forms a backdrop to the park's equestrian facilities and the Hawkins Amphitheater, which are located near the trail beyond the interpretive center.

A short gentle climb leads to the Flume Trail; the neighboring Ranch Loop Trail rides the hillside above. Part of the Flume Trail is built on thick planks, silvered by weather, that cover the Last Chance Ditch. When the "boardwalk" ends, dirt singletrack parallels the now exposed ditch, which squirrels through a greenbelt of willows and piñon pines nurtured by the greenish-brown water.

The Flume Trail ends on the Ranch Loop Trail, where a bridge spans the ditch. Follow the Ranch Loop, which switchbacks downhill to the Anderson Trail (to Anderson Park) and past the end of the Quail Run Trail. The route then skims the fence lines of neighboring private pastures. Rusting farm implements—a wagon frame from Reno's Flindt Ranch, a hay loader, rakes, a Jackson fork with a Mormon hay derrick, a manure spreader—line the track, and interpretive signs provide information on their origins and uses.

Toward the end of the hike, the Ranch Loop arcs west, back toward the interpretive center and Old Huffaker Schoolhouse, skirting an adjacent neighborhood park (with a tot lot), and the modern Huffaker Elementary School. Views west climb over adjacent development to the high peaks of the Carson Range, snowcapped in winter and spring. The final stretch of trail leads through developed areas of the park—parking lots near the interpretive center and the like—before depositing you at the schoolhouse trailhead.

Green Tip:

Err toward safety In areas where dogs are permitted to run off-leash. Keep your dog restrained unless you are certain it will follow your voice and sight commands. Even then, keep the leash handy and your dog in sight. Do not let it approach other people and their pets unless invited to do so.

In addition to hiking trails, Bartley Ranch Regional Park also has an interpretive center.

MILES AND DIRECTIONS

0.0 Start at the signed trailhead for the Quail Run Nature Trail and the Ranch Loop Trail. Climb three steps and go immediately left (southeast) on the Quail Run Nature Trail.

0.1 Stay right (south) on the Quail Run Nature Trail where a side trail drops to the interpretive center. Cross the ditch to another trail crossing, again staying right (up and south) on the Quail Run Nature Trail.

0.3 Reach the junction with the Flume Trail. Go right (south) on the wooden planks.

0.5 Meet the Ranch Loop Trail at the end of the Flume Trail. Go left (east) over the bridge on the Ranch Loop Trail.

0.6 Arrive at the Anderson Trail intersection and stay left (north) on the Ranch Loop Trail.

0.7 Pass the end of the Quail Run Nature Trail, staying right (north) on the Ranch Loop Trail, toward a fenced pasture. At the next Ranch Loop Trail junction, about 50 yards beyond at the fence and wagon frame, stay right again, passing a hay loader alongside the Lake Ditch.

1.0 At an unmarked trail junction amid a collection of ranching machinery (including the Jackson fork), stay right (north) and circle through a picnic area. The left-hand trail leads toward the riding ring. About 100 yards farther, a trail sign points you right (north). Hike through a dry streambed to a T junction. Go left (west) on the trail; a wire fence runs alongside.

1.2 A paved path leads right (north) into an adjacent neighborhood park. Stay straight (west) on the Ranch Loop Trail.

1.3 A second trail breaks right (north) onto the fenced school property; the equestrian parking area is on the left (south). Bear left (southwest) across the lot, then across a bridge, to the Western Heritage Interpretive Center. Turn right (west), crossing another small parking lot at a covered picnic area to a gravel path that leads back toward the schoolhouse and trailhead.

1.5 Cross the main park road and follow the gravel path back to the trailhead.

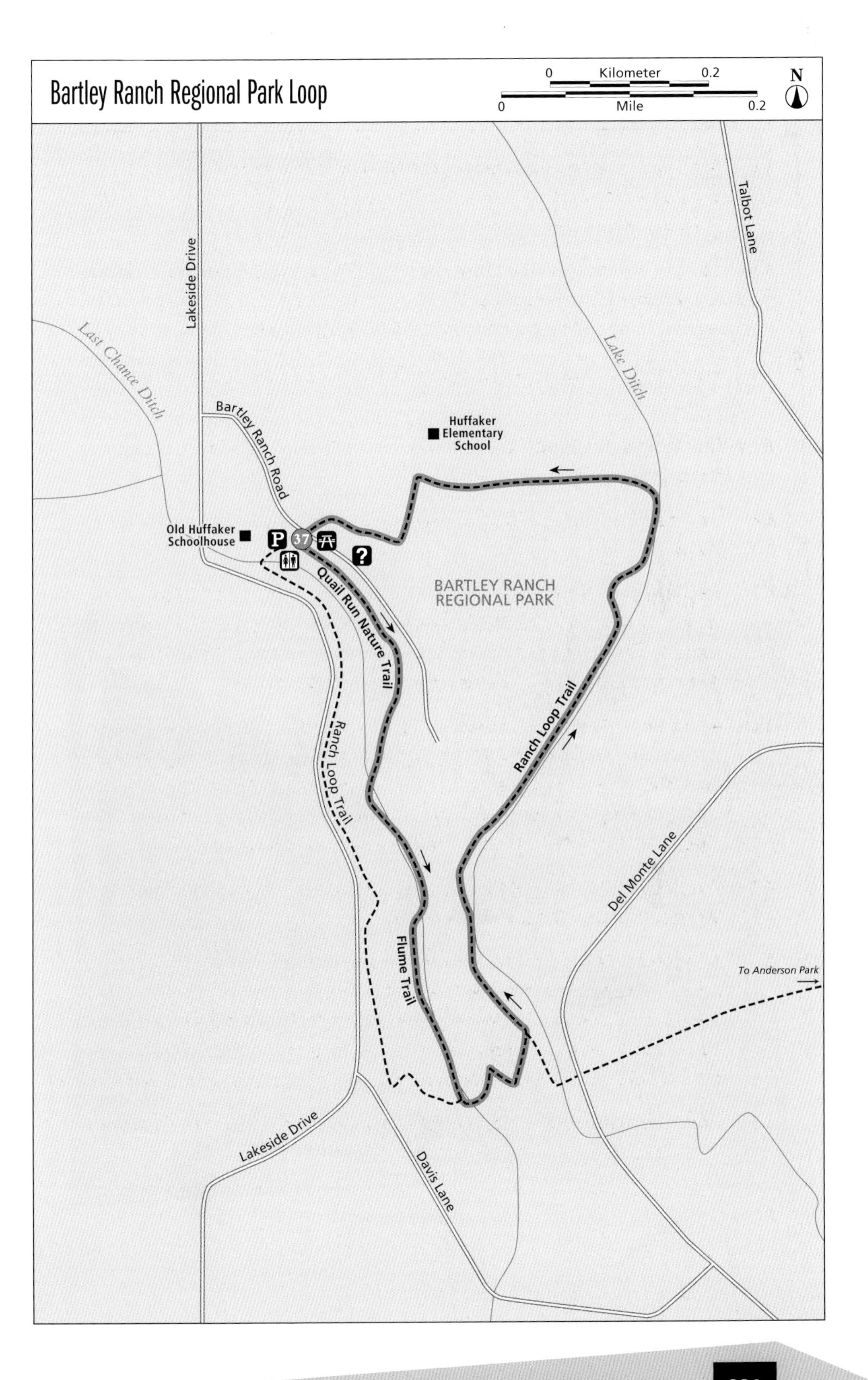
Bartley Ranch Regional Park Loop
0
Kilometer
0.2
0
Mile
0.2
N
Talbot Lane
Lakeside Drive
Last Chance Ditch
Lake Ditch
Bartley Ranch Road
Huffaker Elementary School
Old Huffaker Schoolhouse
P
37
?
BARTLEY RANCH REGIONAL PARK
Quail Run Nature Trail
Ranch Loop Trail
Ranch Loop Trail
Del Monte Lane
To Anderson Park
Flume Trail
Lakeside Drive
Davis Lane

HIKE INFORMATION

Local information: The Chamber, serving Reno, Sparks, and northern Nevada, offers information and links to community events, government, and businesses including restaurants and lodging. The Reno office is at 449 S. Virginia St. 2nd Floor, Reno, NV 89501; (775) 636-9550; www.thechambernv.org. For information about the city of Reno, call Reno Direct at (775) 334-INFO, or visit www.reno.gov/index.aspx?page=1.

Restaurants: Hiroba Sushi Restaurant, 3005 Skyline Blvd. #100, Reno, NV 89509; (775) 829-2788. The restaurant offers delicious, inexpensive sushi and creative rolls.

Local events/attractions: Park facilities, including the Old Huffaker Schoolhouse, the Western Heritage Interpretive Center, and the amphitheater, can be rented for private functions. Equestrian arenas are also available. Contact the park for more information.

A covered wooden flume forms the trail for a portion of the loop through Bartley Ranch Regional Park.

Lakeview Loop at Huffaker Hills

High and dry, the Huffaker Hills open on expansive views across the Truckee Meadows to the summits of Mount Rose and Slide Mountain. An easy trail rambles through these distinctive formations in the foothills of the Virginia Range.

Start: At the signed trailhead in the Huffaker Hills parking area
Distance: 0.9-mile loop
Hiking time: 45 minutes to 1 hour
Difficulty: Easy
Trail surface: Rocky dirt single-track
Best seasons: Winter, spring, and fall
Other trail users: Mountain bikers, equestrians
Canine compatibility: Leashed dogs permitted
Fees and permits: None
Schedule: As a rule of thumb, Washoe County Parks are open from 8 a.m. to sunset. Formal hours are 8 a.m. to 9 p.m. from Memorial Day weekend to Labor Day weekend; 8 a.m. to 7 p.m. from Labor Day to the start of standard time; 8 a.m. to 5 p.m. from the start of standard time to the start of daylight savings time in spring; and 8 a.m. to 7 p.m. from the start of daylight savings time to Memorial Day weekend.
Trailhead amenities: A paved parking lot, picnic tables, a restroom, an information signboard with trail map
Maps: USGS Steamboat NV; www.nvtrailmaps.com
Trail contact: Huffaker Hills Trailhead; Washoe County Department of Regional Parks and Open Space, 2601 Plumas St., Reno, NV 89509; (775) 823-6500; www.washoecountyparks.com
Special considerations: The trails are completely shadeless and oven hot on summer days.

Finding the trailhead: From US 395/I-580 southbound take the Kietzke Lane/South Virginia Street exit. Turn left (south) on Kietzke Lane for 0.1 mile to South McCarran Boulevard. Turn left (east) on South McCarran Boulevard and go 1.6 miles, past the signal at Longley Lane, to Alexander Lake Road (just behind the shopping center). Turn right (south) on Alexander Lake Road and go 1 mile up to the signed trailhead and parking area on the right (west). GPS: N39 27.995' / W119 45.228'

THE HIKE

Views from this rocky desert trail spread past the soft browns of the Twin Peaks onto the stony heights of Slide Mountain and Mount Rose, and across the Truckee Meadows, silver and green with development and pockets of open space. The towers of Reno's casino district rise to the northwest, with the rounded mass of Peavine Peak behind.

Huffaker Hills are part of a ranch established by Granville Huffaker in the nineteenth century. Huffaker homesteaded here in 1859 with 500 head of cattle, which he intended to sell to the men burning massive amounts of calories in the mines of the Comstock in nearby Virginia City. From a gritty start in a dugout cave at the base of the hills, Huffaker eventually built himself a mansion, a railroad and Pony Express station, a post office, and a store. The interpretive signboard at the trailhead details Huffaker's accomplishments and describes the cooperative effort that led to preservation of the land.

After you've read up on the park's namesake, set off on the merged Lakeview and Western Loops, which soon split at an interpretive sign. Head left (south) on the Lakeview Loop, traveling in a counterclockwise direction.

The stark landscape, with wide-open western and southern exposures, supports a minimalist desert scrub, which allows hikers to enjoy uninterrupted views of the Carson Range and Truckee Meadows. The park is also below the flight paths of jets taking off and landing at Reno International Airport; as much as this is a distraction from the natural world, it also adds a bit of spice to the hike, especially for kids.

As the trail continues south and the Twin Peaks impede vistas of the high Sierra, new views open into the dry Virginia Range to the east. These crusty peaks harbor the wealth of the Comstock Lode, so vital to the development of the region and still working today. Along this stretch you'll pass an interpretive marker that describes what you'll see when the Great Basin blooms in springtime, from mariposa lily to prickly pear. Several other interpretive signs line the trail loop as well.

The trail to Twin Peaks breaks off to the right (southwest), while the Lakeview Trail continues southeast past the sun-bleached trail sign. A fenced-off pea-soup green reservoir nudges into view as the trail starts a gentle descent. The junction with the short spur to the "lake" comes up quickly; go right to the

reservoir overlook, which boasts a bench installed by a local Eagle Scout. You can contemplate the reservoir, its concrete dam, and the parched Virginia Range behind from the bench. On a hot day the water might be tempting . . . if the chain-link fencing isn't enough of a deterrent, knowing that the reservoir holds treated effluent should keep you clear.

Back at the trail junction stay right (downhill and north), following the fence line away from the reservoir and back toward the trailhead. A short climb through broken rocks and scrub leads back to the starting point.

The Comstock Lode

California's Gold Rush made some men millionaires and busted others. In northern Nevada, the mogul maker and heartbreaker was silver.

Who exactly discovered the Comstock Lode is a matter of contention. Brothers Ethan and Hosea Grosch established gold mining claims at Gold Canyon in the Carson River valley and were stymied in their attempts to glean the precious metal from the rock. Instead, they recognized the blue mud oozing from their diggings as "silver lead," or silver ore. The brothers would die before they could realize any benefit from their discovery; that would fall to Henry Comstock, a Canadian miner with a sketchy reputation who set up residence in the Groschs' abandoned cabin and took over their claims. Other hopeful argonauts also unearthed silver ore from the holes they excavated in the mountainsides surrounding Virginia City; two of those miners, Peter O'Riley and Patrick McLaughlin, are credited with discovering a silver source at the head of Gold Canyon.

The yields of the Comstock are legendary. By 1882 almost $400 million in silver ore had been mined, worth about $9 billion in today's dollars. And the Comstock is still being mined: The primary company working in the region has the evocative stock ticker LODE.

Some of the biggest names in California and Nevada history have significant ties to the Comstock, including Adolph Sutro, whose impressive Sutro Tunnel drained off the water (some of it scalding) that flooded the mines; George Hearst, a US senator and father of media mogul William Randolph Hearst; William Ralston, founder of the Bank of California; Leland Stanford, who would later establish the prestigious Stanford University; and Collis Huntington, Charles Crocker, Theodore Judah, and Mark Hopkins, all colleagues of Stanford's on the Central Pacific Railroad, which was pivotal in moving the wealth of the Comstock to cities such as San Francisco.

MILES AND DIRECTIONS

0.0 Start on the combined Lakeview and Western Loop trails. The paths split about 25 yards beyond the trailhead at an interpretive signboard; stay left (south) on the Lakeview Loop.

0.3 Pass the junction with the Twin Peaks Trail on the right (southwest); remain left (southeast) on Lakeview Trail.

0.4 Arrive at the junction with the spur trail to the reservoir and go right (southeast).

0.5 Reach the reservoir overlook and bench.

0.6 Back at the spur trail junction stay right (north) on the continuation of the Lakeview Loop.

0.9 Descend along the fence line and climb past the park's picnic tables back to the trailhead.

Options: If you have the time and inclination, you can add the Western Loop and the out-and-back leg of the Twin Peaks Trail to your tour of Huffaker Hills.

Expansive views across the Truckee Meadows to Mount Rose and Slide Mountain open from the trails in Huffaker Hills Regional Park.

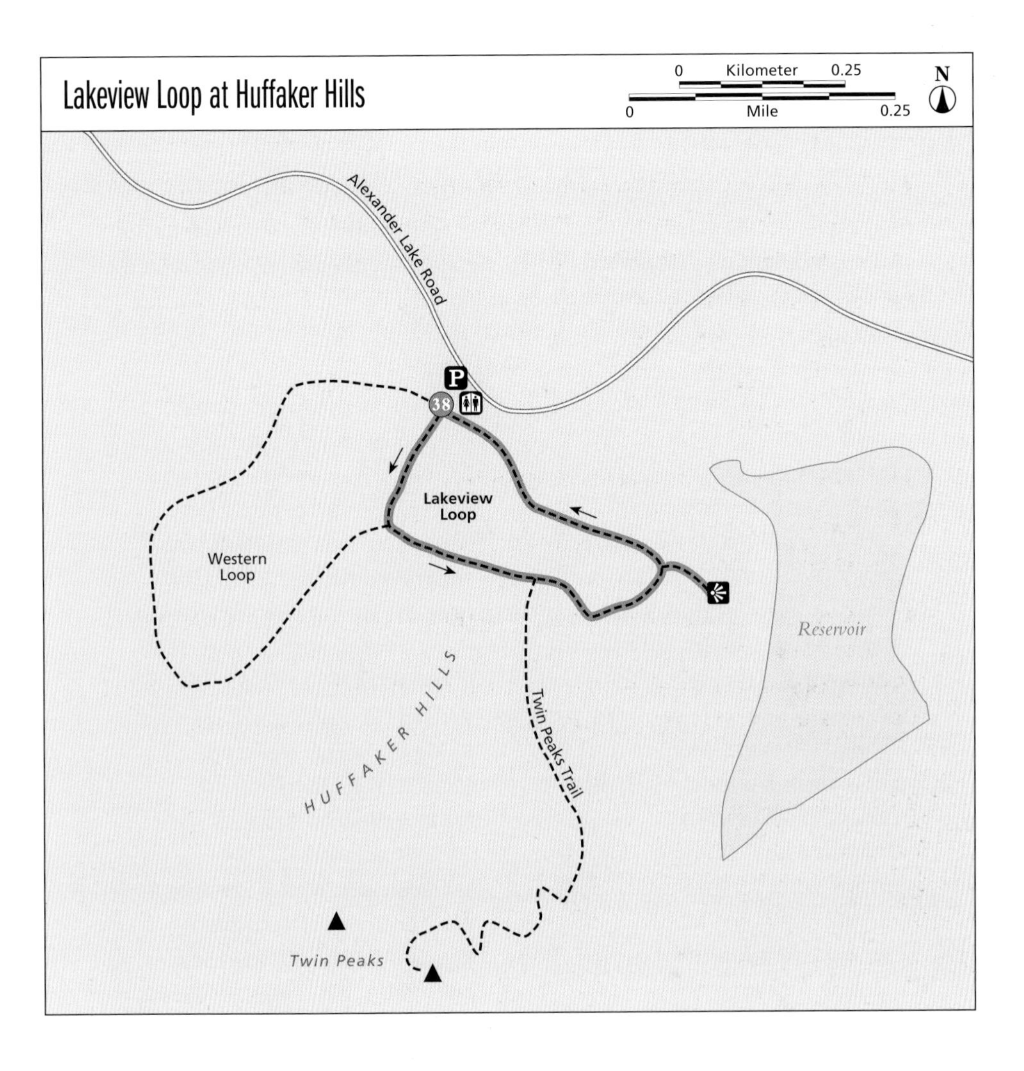

HIKE INFORMATION

Local information: The Chamber, serving Reno, Sparks, and northern Nevada, offers information and links to community events, government, and businesses including restaurants and lodging. The Reno office is at 449 S. Virginia St. 2nd Floor, Reno, NV 89501; (775) 636-9550; www.thechambernv.org. For information about the city of Reno, call Reno Direct at (775) 334-INFO, or visit www.reno.gov/index.aspx?page=1.

39

Lower Whites Creek Trail

This neighborhood treasure is tucked in a ravine surrounded by quiet residential subdivisions. Whites Creek supports a riparian habitat that envelops hikers in an unexpected, if narrowly defined, strip of desert wildland.

Start: At the trailhead in Whites Creek Park
Distance: 2.8 miles out and back
Hiking time: About 2 hours
Difficulty: Moderate due to steady incline
Trail surface: Dirt singletrack
Best seasons: Winter, spring, and late fall; avoid the heat of the day in summer
Other trail users: Mountain bikers, equestrians (no horse trailer parking), trail runners
Trailhead amenities: Parking, a tot lot, picnic facilities, a fenced playing field
Canine compatibility: Leashed dogs permitted
Fees and permits: None
Schedule: As a rule of thumb, Washoe County Parks are open from 8 a.m. to sunset. Formal hours are 8 a.m. to 9 p.m. from Memorial Day weekend to Labor Day weekend; 8 a.m. to 7 p.m. from Labor Day to the start of standard time; 8 a.m. to 5 p.m. from the start of standard time to the start of daylight savings time in spring; and 8 a.m. to 7 p.m. from the start of daylight savings time to Memorial Day weekend.
Maps: USGS Mount Rose NE NV; downloadable map at www.nvtrailmaps.com
Trail contact: Whites Creek Park, Washoe County Department of Regional Parks and Open Space, 2601 Plumas St., Reno, NV 89509; (775) 823-6500; www.washoecountyparks.com

Finding the trailhead: From US 395/I-580 southbound, take the NV 431 (Mount Rose Highway) exit. Follow Mount Rose Highway west for 2 miles to Telluride Drive (the second turnoff into Galena Country Estates). Turn right (north) on Telluride Drive and go 0.2 mile to Killington Drive. Turn left (west) on Killington Drive; the road ends in 0.2 mile at Whites Creek Park. Continue on the unpaved park road for 0.1 mile, past the fenced ball field, to the parking area at the trailhead. GPS: N39 23.786' / W119 47.980'

THE HIKE

The trail that follows Whites Creek is the perfect quick escape. Whether you've got an hour before work for a brisk workout, time after dinner for a leisurely wander, or want to spend a Saturday afternoon on the trail, a hike on the creekside trail, which winds through subdivisions at the base of Mount Rose, is both soothing and invigorating.

The trail begins in the dense riparian zone that thrives on the margins of the creek. Of all the foliage clogging the streamsides, perhaps most striking are the aspens, with leaves that are electric green in springtime and wedding-ring gold in autumn. Wildflowers (notably wild rose), stately cottonwoods, and tangles of willow clutter the banks as well, while the drier slopes of the gully walls are cloaked in desert scrub. Ringing the creek canyon on either side are neighborhood homes, their backyards sloping steeply to meet the creek.

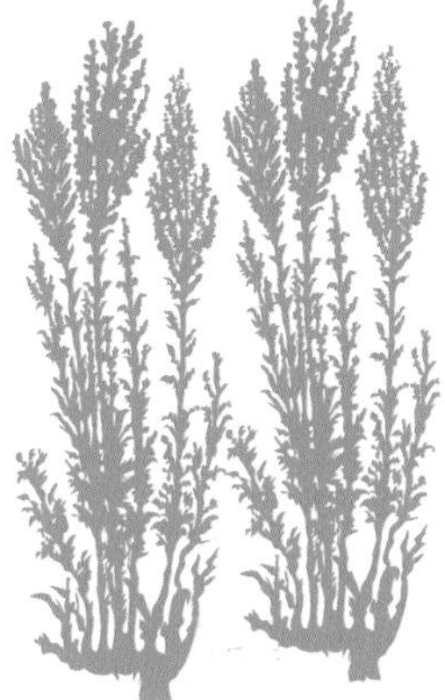

Cradled in a shallow canyon rimmed with neighborhood homes, the Lower Whites Creek Trail aspires to (and eventually reaches) the high country.

The route boasts views too—of Mount Rose and the lower peaks of the Carson Range as you head west, and of the southern reaches of the Truckee Meadows on the return trip.

The trail starts on the south side of the stream—boisterous in spring and early summer and dwindling to pools and trickles in summer and fall. Within the first 0.5-mile the route crosses the creek via a pair of small wooden bridges to the north side. A word of route-finding caution: Social trails on the south side may lead you past the turnoff to the bridges. If you end up climbing out of the canyon onto a neighborhood road, backtrack to the first bridge you reach.

Once on the north side of the stream, climb steadily toward the mountains. While occasionally the riparian veil hides the houses that frame the creek, there is no escaping suburbia when the trail crosses four-lane Thomas Creek Road (there is no crosswalk, so be careful). The trail drops streamside again on the other side of the roadway, tucking quickly back into the riparian zone.

Gentler climbing through willow and scrub, with short side trails dropping to creekside rest stops, leads to a fenced zone where waterside access is denied. A final climb takes you up and out of the drainage onto a dirt road at the entrance to private property: In 2010, a sign posted on the fence declared IF YOU CAN READ THIS YOU'RE IN RANGE. This is the turnaround point . . . unless you are prepared to take on a much longer trek, as the trail continues toward Mount Rose and links with the popular Jones-Whites Creek Loop.

Retrace your steps to the trailhead.

MILES AND DIRECTIONS

0.0 Start behind a large pine, following the trail best traveled into the creek canyon. Stay left (west) where a side trail breaks right (north) to diversion channels.

0.2 Arrive at the first bridge crossing on the right (north). Cross here or continue to the next bridge.

0.3 Reach the second bridge spanning the creek, this one made of less substantial boards. If you haven't already crossed, this is your last chance. Continue west on the trail on the north side of the stream.

0.8 Cross Thomas Creek Road and continue on the signed trail.

1.2 Reach the boundary of a fence that blocks access to the creek.

1.4 Arrive at the turnaround point on the unpaved neighborhood road. Then retrace your steps.

2.8 Arrive back at the trailhead.

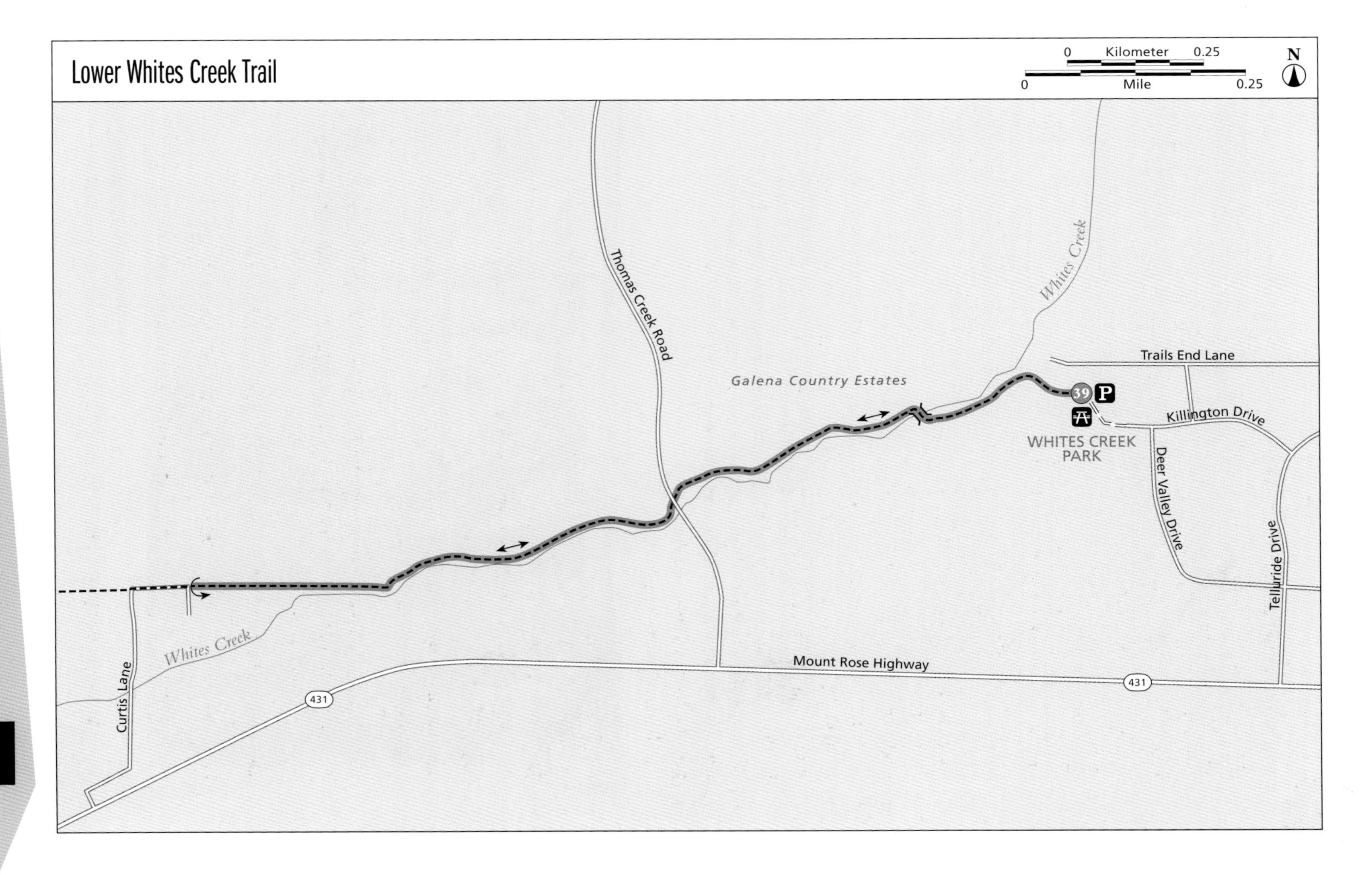
Lower Whites Creek Trail
0 Kilometer 0.25
0 Mile 0.25
N
Thomas Creek Road
Whites Creek
Galena Country Estates
Trails End Lane
39
P
Killington Drive
WHITES CREEK
PARK
Deer Valley Drive
Telluride Drive
Whites Creek
Curtis Lane
Mount Rose Highway
431
431

HIKE INFORMATION

Local information: The Chamber, serving Reno, Sparks, and northern Nevada, offers information and links to community events, government, and businesses including restaurants and lodging. The Reno office is at 449 S. Virginia St. 2nd Floor, Reno, NV 89501; (775) 636-9550; www.thechambernv.org. For information about the city of Reno, call Reno Direct at (775) 334-INFO, or visit www.reno.gov/index.aspx?page=1.

Restaurants: I've been in a few Whole Foods Markets across the West, but Reno's store stands out. It is enormous, colorful, and loaded. The trail mix bar is a highlight for hikers, where you can build your own mix of nuts, seeds, dried fruit, and chocolate chips for the trail. Not your ordinary GORP. The store is located at 6139 S. Virginia St. in Reno; (775) 852-8023; www.wholefoodsmarket.com/stores/reno/. Hours are from 8 a.m. to 10 p.m., seven days a week.

A variety of invasive and native species make up the flora of the riparian zones along creeks and streams throughout the Truckee Meadows. Among the plants once utilized by native peoples as medicine, food, or for ceremonial purposes are willow, wild rose, sage, mullein, chicory, and soaproot.

The riparian corridor watered by the lower reaches of Whites Creek provides shade for the trail.

Honorable Mentions

Verdi Nature Trail

Located just north of I-80 in the foothills west of Reno, the interpretive Verdi Nature Trail explores the Truckee River's bottomlands near the point where the river canyon opens into the high desert. The easy 0.5-mile loop explores the transition zone between the lower montane region of the Sierra Nevada, dominated by Jeffrey and ponderosa pine woodlands, and the high desert of the Great Basin, where desert peach, bitterbrush, and sagebrush vie for dominance. The path takes less than an hour to complete, though hiking the path with curious children may lengthen your exploration. An interpretive pamphlet is available at the trailhead. Couple the hike with a picnic in nearby Crystal Peak Regional Park (a Washoe County park) on the banks of the Truckee River for a great family outing.

The trailhead is located in the parking lot of the Verdi Community Library and Wildlife Education Center. From Reno, take I-80 west to the first Verdi exit (exit 5). Follow the frontage road to the traffic circle, then merge onto Old US 40. Follow US 40 west for about 2.3 miles to Bridge Street in "downtown" Verdi. Turn left (north) on Bridge Street and go 0.2 mile to the signed Verdi Community Library parking lot on the right (east). The address is 270 Bridge St. in Verdi.

Dorostkar Park Nature Trail

This pleasant nature trail provides an easy outing for river lovers, dog walkers, and families. An easy 1.4-mile lollipop loop, the trail cobbles granite pathway, dirt singletrack, and paved bike path along the banks of the cold, clear Truckee River on the western edge of the Reno metro area. Interpretive panels describe the riparian and high desert habitats traversed by the route, a rich and colorful ecotone that blooms with wild rose and desert peach in spring and early summer. The trail also highlights the juxtaposition of suburbia with wildland, as railroad tracks and tract homes buck up against the greenbelt.

To reach the trailhead from downtown Reno, travel west on I-80 to the West McCarran Boulevard exit. Go left (south) on West McCarran for 0.7 mile to West Fourth Street. Turn right (west) on West Fourth Street and travel 1.8 miles to Mayberry Drive. Turn left (south) on Mayberry Drive and go 0.4 mile to the signed park entrance on the left (north).

South Meadows Trail

Several suburban trail systems have been established as Reno's suburbs have expanded. Preservation of these dollops of wildland testifies to the city's recognition that parkland is integral to the well-being of its residents. A spread of wetland set aside amid South Valley subdivisions anchors the evolving South Meadows Trail, part of an urban trail system linking residents and visitors with parks, schools, shopping, and natural areas.

One section of the South Meadows Trail System skirts a wetland on the south side of Whites Creek. It's bounded on all sides by homes but still boasts views of Mount Rose, Slide Mountain, and the Virginia Range. The wetland supports habitat for a variety of urban wildlife, including rabbits and red-winged blackbirds. Cattails and reeds maintain a foothold in the center of the marsh, but the invasive weed commonly called whitetop clots the rim; the flowers are pretty but they've become a plague on Nevada's rangelands.

Incorporating stretches of sidewalk, a hike along the wetland stretch totals about 1.4 miles out and back. You will share the paved, wheelchair accessible, multiuse track with cyclists, trail runners, skaters, and dog walkers. When you reach the shopping center off of Lauren Court, return as you came, though there are options to link to other sections of the trail system. For more information contact the City of Reno Parks, Recreation, and Community Services Department by calling 775-334-2262 or visit www.reno.gov/index.aspx?page=194.

To reach the trailhead from US 395/I-580 southbound, take the South Meadows Parkway exit. Go left (east) on South Meadows Parkway for about 0.8 mile to Evergreen Street on the right (south), at Double Diamond Elementary School. Follow Evergreen Street to the parking lot behind the school for Evergreen Park.

Other Options

Another subdivision with an extensive urban trail system worth exploring is in **Somersett,** on the lower slopes of Peavine Peak in west Reno. For more information contact the City of Reno Parks, Recreation, and Community Services Department by calling 775-334-2262 or visit www.reno.gov/index.aspx?page=194.

Washoe County's **Hidden Valley Regional Park** explores the high desert on the east side of town. Route-finding can be a challenge, as some trails aren't signed and use trails are prolific. The park is located at 4740 Parkway Drive in Reno; contact Washoe County Department of Regional Parks and Open Space by calling (775) 823-6500 or visiting www.washoecountyparks.com.

Sun Valley Park, another in the Washoe County system, opened in 2009 and boasts great views across the North Valley area. Trails wind among unique rock formations, some of them tagged with graffiti that, while disappointing for the purist, does enliven the viewscape. The park is located at the north end of Sidehill Drive in Sun Valley north of Reno proper; contact Washoe County Department of Regional Parks and Open Space by calling (775) 823-6500 or visiting www.washoecountyparks.com.

Huffaker Park (not to be confused with Huffaker Hills) is a City of Reno property that offers a looping tour of the Huffaker Hills, with a gazebo offering a great place to take in the views. The park also has inviting trailhead amenities, including picnic areas and a tot lot. The park is located off Offenhauser Drive. Contact the City of Reno Parks, Recreation, and Community Services Department by calling 775-334-2262 or visit www.reno.gov/index.aspx?page=194.

In addition to its backcountry trails and open space parks, Reno has cultivated networks of urban trails, including this one in the South Meadows area.

CARSON CITY AND BEYOND

Looking out across the Washoe Valley from Davis Creek Regional Park

Nevada's capital city is located just about 30 miles south of Reno—little more than a half an hour via I-580—but in atmosphere and setting, it seems much farther afield. The Carson River valley, also called the Eagle Valley, is narrower than the Truckee Meadows, and the city itself is smaller and has a more historic feel.

Long inhabited by the Washoe Indians, the valley's modern origins date back to emigrant days, when a settlement was established along Carson River as a stopover for travelers on the last leg of the California Trail. The city's pioneering origins are reflected in its very name; mountain man Kit Carson is the namesake. Discovery of the Comstock Lode in the nearby Virginia Range, and the subsequent influx of miners and those who provided goods and services to them, resulted in a boom for Carson City. Even more prosperity flowed the city's way with the building of the Virginia & Truckee Railroad, also serving the mines, and with the building of flumes, which spilled timber down the eastern slope of the Sierra from Spooner Summit on the rim of the Lake Tahoe basin into the city. It has been the state capital since Nevada entered the Union in 1864.

At more than 4,600 feet above sea level, and located in the rain shadow of the Sierra, the climate of Carson City and the Eagle Valley is similar to that of Reno, with hot summers and freezing winters accompanied by minimal rain and snowfall. On the valley floor and the lower slopes of the Sierra, a high desert scrub flourishes; the higher you climb, the more wooded the terrain, until you reach the barren summits of the peaks that dominate the city's backdrop, including Jobs Peak, backed by Jobs Sister and Freel Peak, the highest summit on the rim of the Lake Tahoe basin, as well as Monument Peak, East Peak, and Genoa Peak closer to town.

Trails in the Carson River valley range from paved routes through city neighborhoods to explorations of the dry hills on the east side of the valley to the Fay-Luther trail system, which reaches into the wilderness surrounding Jobs Peak.

Yellow pines are an indicator species for the lower montane ecosystem, which sprawls along the mountain front up to about the 7,000-foot level.

40 Jones-Whites Creek Loop

This long trail loop links two steep creek drainages at the foot of Mount Rose. On both the long traverse along the lower slopes separating Jones and Whites Creeks and the top of the ridge between the two, hikers are greeted by sweeping views of Truckee Meadows and the Washoe Valley.

Start: At the Jones-Whites Creek trailhead in Galena Creek Regional Park
Distance: 9.4-mile lollipop
Hiking time: 5–6 hours
Difficulty: Strenuous
Trail surface: Dirt singletrack
Best seasons: Late spring, early summer, and fall
Other trail users: Mountain bikers on portions of the trail outside the Mount Rose Wilderness
Trailhead amenities: Parking, restrooms, information signboard. A visitor center, picnic facilities, additional parking, and more restrooms are located in Galena Creek Regional Park.
Canine compatibility: Dogs permitted; dogs must be leashed near the picnic grounds and parking areas
Fees and permits: None
Schedule: As a rule of thumb, Washoe County Parks are open from 8 a.m. to sunset. Formal hours are 8 a.m. to 9 p.m. from Memorial Day weekend to Labor Day weekend; 8 a.m. to 7 p.m. from Labor Day to the start of standard time; 8 a.m. to 5 p.m. from the start of standard time to the start of daylight savings time in spring; and 8 a.m. to 7 p.m. from the start of daylight savings time to Memorial Day weekend.
Maps: USGS Mount Rose NV, Mount Rose NW NV, Mount Rose NE NV, Washoe City NV
Trail contact: Washoe County Department of Regional Parks and Open Space, 2601 Plumas St., Reno, NV 89509; (775) 823-6500; www.washoecountyparks.com. The park's direct number is (775) 849-2511.

Finding the trailhead: From US 395/I-580 southbound, take the NV 431 (Mount Rose Highway) exit. Head west on the Mount Rose Highway for 7 miles to the north (first) entrance to Galena Creek Regional Park and visitor center. Follow the park road to the signed trailhead in the lower lot. The main trailhead is located at the visitor center in the upper parking lot. GPS (lower trailhead): N39 21.741' / W119 51.456'

THE HIKE

A steep divide separates the Jones Creek drainage from Whites Creek. No matter how you link the two, you've got a climb ahead and miles to travel. If you are tempted to turn around, remember that it will likely take just as much energy to go on as it will to go back. Make sure your water bottles are full, shift into a low steady gear, and enjoy some of the most spectacular landscapes the foothills outside Reno have to offer.

Described in a counterclockwise direction, the stick of this lollipop loop climbs gently away from the trailhead through the widely spaced yellow pines of Galena Creek Regional Park to the start of the loop. Go east on the signed trail to Whites Creek, climbing steadily and easily through the woods, and then through desert scrub. Where the trees part the views open up, looking across the Washoe Valley to the Virginia Range, south toward Washoe Lake, and north into the Truckee Meadows. An overlook atop a hill at 2.2 miles is followed by a shaded descent into the Whites Creek drainage.

The trail junction with the Whites Creek Trail and the connector to Dry Pond, located beside Whites Creek at the 2.5-mile mark, is a meeting place for hikers, mountain bikers, and dogs. Some of the hikers/bikers are embarked on out-and-back treks from the Whites Creek trailhead to the Mount Rose Wilderness. Others

A steady climb along Whites Creek is shaded by stands of aspen.

have chosen to hike the loop in the other direction, and are circling back toward Jones Creek. Regardless of the goal or destination, the creek, flowing year-round and supporting a shady riparian zone that includes aspen and willow, is a good rest stop.

To continue the loop, follow the Whites Creek Trail up alongside the stream. Beyond the connector trail to Dry Pond, the trail widens to doubletrack and, though the ascent is relentless and may leave you a bit breathless, is suitable for walking side-by-side.

Pass into the Mount Rose Wilderness at an information signboard, cross the creek on a log, and continue up the narrowing canyon on a rougher trail. The route has lost its social atmosphere at this point; the population of trail users dwindles as setting and distance evoke backcountry trekking. From here on up and over, even on summer days, the trail is not busy.

And "up" is the operative word. The trail climbs above the creek, which has cut a gorge with evergreens clinging to its edge, their exposed roots curling clawlike back into the embankment. Willows and aspen turn orange and yellow in fall, adding splashes of color to the hike. Cross the creek, again on a log, at the head of the loop, traverse an open north-facing slope, drop through another streambed, then begin the arduous climb over the ridge separating Whites Creek from Jones Creek.

Though mostly wooded, the trail does break into the open on occasion, offering views up and down the steep drainage, with the pinkish slopes of Mount Rose above. Arrive atop the divide, at more than 8,000 feet, and the views are even more impressive. As you look west, upcanyon toward Mount Rose, the wooded slopes of the Carson Range are steep, folded, and shadowy: an imposing barrier. Looking east, the dry, open Washoe Valley lies exposed, with the dun-colored Virginia Range in the distance and Washoe Lake a shimmer on the desert floor.

The Church Pond Trail meets the Jones Creek Trail on the divide; stay on the signed path to Jones Creek and begin the switchbacking descent. Though as relentless as the ascent, the drop into the Jones Creek drainage doesn't demand as much of a hiker's lungs. Instead, staying focused on the uneven terrain and pausing to take in views of the wooded canyon are the biggest challenges. The descent remains steep for about 2 miles before mellowing. The trail widens as it approaches the trail junction that closes the loop. From that point, retrace your steps to the trailhead.

MILES AND DIRECTIONS

0.0 Start at the signed trailhead on the left (north) side of the parking lot. If you begin at the trailhead kiosk at the visitor center, stay on the dirt pathway, cross the creek on the culvert "bridge," and continue to the junction of the Jones and Whites Creek Trails.

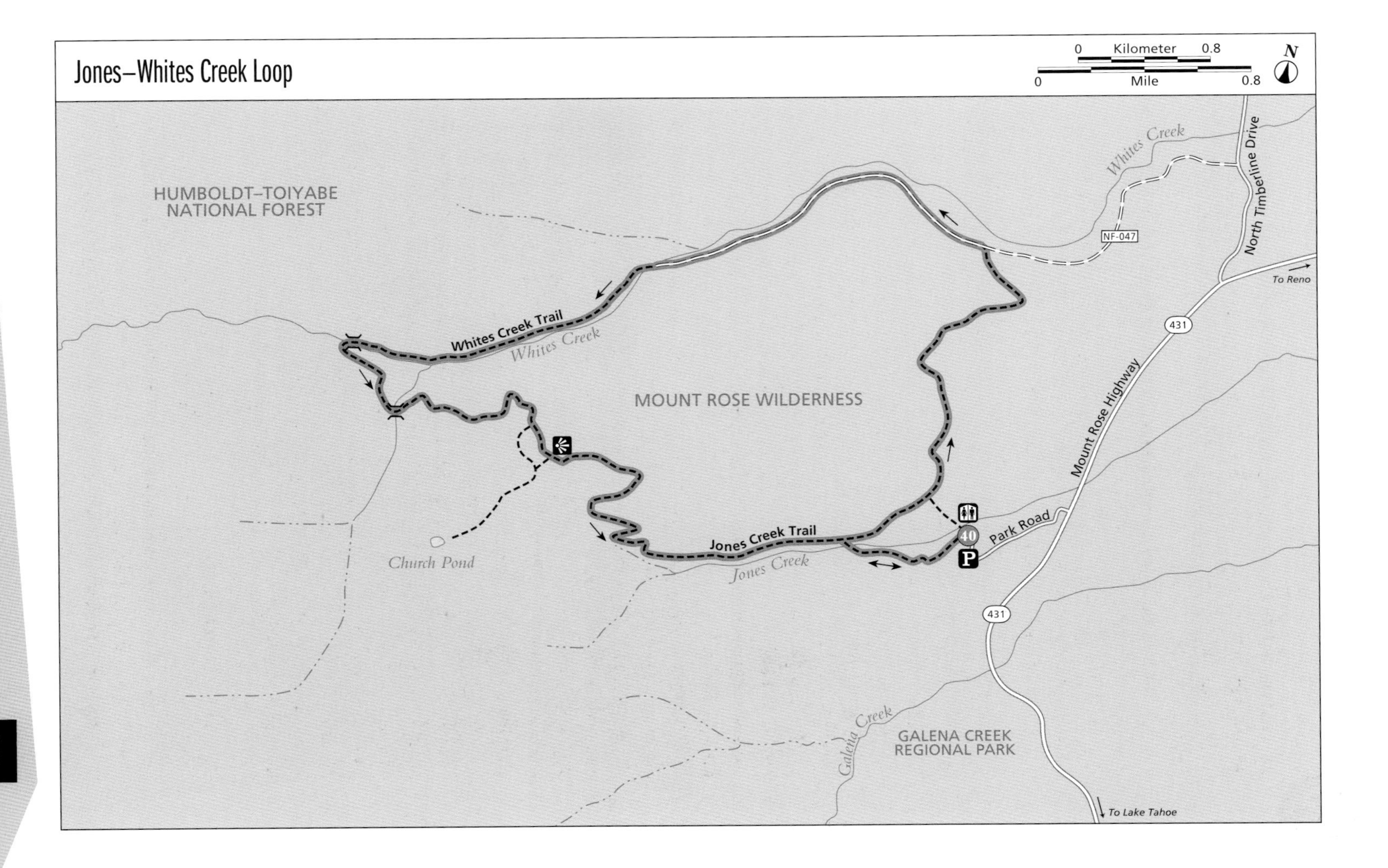
Jones–Whites Creek Loop
0 Kilometer 0.8
0 Mile 0.8
N
HUMBOLDT–TOIYABE
NATIONAL FOREST
Whites Creek
North Timberline Drive
NF-047
To Reno
431
Whites Creek Trail
Whites Creek
MOUNT ROSE WILDERNESS
Mount Rose Highway
Jones Creek Trail
40
Park Road
P
Church Pond
Jones Creek
431
Galena Creek
GALENA CREEK
REGIONAL PARK
To Lake Tahoe

0.3 At the trail junction, go right and uphill on the signed trail to Jones Creek.

0.6 At the signed intersection of trails to Church Pond and Whites Creek, go right on the Whites Creek Trail.

0.9 At the trail junction, stay straight on the Whites Creek Trail.

2.0 The path leaves the trees to traverse an open slope with great views.

2.2 Pass an overlook area. The trail descends from here into the Whites Creek drainage.

2.5 Reach the trail junction adjacent to Whites Creek. Follow the Whites Creek Trail uphill, adjacent to the waterway.

3.1 The horse trail meets the Whites Creek Trail. Continue on the Whites Creek Trail.

3.25 Arrive at the junction with the Dry Pond Trail; continue on the Whites Creek Trail.

3.9 Reach the Mount Rose Wilderness boundary (with a signboard). Go right, crossing the creek on a log, and continue upstream on the singletrack.

Views from the summit of the ridge between Jones Creek and Whites Creek open across the Washoe Valley to the Virginia Range.

4.2 Pass a second wilderness sign and cross a stream, likely dry in late season.

5.0 Reach the head of the loop. Cross the creek via logs, then traverse an open hillside.

5.7 Cross a stream via a little bridge. The trail begins to climb over the divide between the two creek drainages.

6.75 Arrive on top of the divide and savor the views. At the junction of the Church Pond Trail and the Jones Creek Trail, go left on the Jones Creek Trail. The descent begins.

8.4 Leave the Mount Rose Wilderness.

8.8 Close the loop at the junction with the White Creek Trail. From here, retrace your steps to the trailhead.

9.4 Arrive back at the trailhead.

HIKE INFORMATION

Local information: The Chamber, serving Reno, Sparks, and northern Nevada, offers information and links to community events, government, and businesses including restaurants and lodging. The Reno office is at 449 S. Virginia St. 2nd Floor, Reno, NV 89501; (775) 636-9550; www.thechambernv.org. For information about the city of Reno, call Reno Direct at (775) 334-INFO; the city website is at www.reno.gov/index.aspx?page=1.

Information about Carson City is available through the Carson City Chamber of Commerce, 1900 S. Carson St., Suite 200, Carson City, NV 89701; (775) 882-1565; www.carsoncitychamber.com. The city site is at carson.org; the address is 201 N. Carson St., Carson City, NV 89701. Phone numbers for the various city departments are on the site.

Local events/attractions: Galena Creek Regional Park is one of Washoe County's natural showplaces. In addition to long, challenging loops in the Galena Creek watershed, the park also boasts shorter nature trails, including the Visitor Center, Bitterbrush, and Galena Creek Nature Trails. The Galena Creek Visitor Center is the interpretive hub of the park, offering nature programs, interpretive hikes, and summer camps. For more information visit the visitor center at 18250 Mount Rose Highway, Reno, NV 89511; call (775) 849-4948; or visit www.galenacreekvisitorcenter.org. You can download guides to the nature trails from this site as well as get more information on park activities.

Restaurants: South Creek Pizza Co., 45 Foothill Road, Reno, NV 89511; (775) 622-1620; www.southcreekpizza.com. Wood-fired pizza at its finest, presented by a couple of the nicest people you'll ever meet.

41

Galena Creek Nature Trail

The lower reaches of Mount Rose and the steep canyons of the Galena Creek watershed offer long, arduous trail access to tantalizing altitudes. This gentle interpretive trail along lower Galena Creek offers a sampling of that alpine experience.

Start: At the trailhead in the second Galena Creek Regional Park parking area
Distance: 0.9-mile loop
Hiking time: 45 minutes to 1 hour
Difficulty: Easy
Trail surface: Dirt singletrack
Best seasons: Late spring, summer, and fall
Other trail users: None
Canine compatibility: Leashed dogs permitted
Fees and permits: None
Schedule: As a rule of thumb, Washoe County Parks are open from 8 a.m. to sunset. Formal hours are 8 a.m. to 9 p.m. from Memorial Day weekend to Labor Day weekend; 8 a.m. to 7 p.m. from Labor Day to the start of standard time; 8 a.m. to 5 p.m. from the start of standard time to the start of daylight savings time in spring; and 8 a.m. to 7 p.m. from the start of daylight savings time to Memorial Day weekend.
Trailhead amenities: Parking, restrooms, water, picnic tables, a dog waste station, trashcans
Maps: USGS Washoe City NV; no map is necessary, as the trail is well marked with interpretive posts
Trail contact: Galena Creek Regional Park, Washoe County Department of Regional Parks and Open Space, 2601 Plumas St., Reno, NV 89509; (775) 823-6500; www.washoecountyparks.com.

Finding the trailhead: From US 395 southbound, take the NV 431 (Mount Rose Highway) exit. Head west on the Mount Rose Highway for 7.2 miles to the south entrance to Galena Creek Regional Park (the second park entrance). Go past the garage and park sign, then down into the lower parking lot. The trailhead is at the west end of the parking lot. The main park address is 18350 Mount Rose Highway in Reno. GPS: N39 21.245' / W119 51.458'

THE HIKE

Galena Creek begins, as most mountain streams do, as a trickle in the snow-packed heights. But by the time it reaches the lowland park that shares its name, it's a rumbling, tumbling, defining watercourse. Kid-friendly and popular, the Galena Creek Nature Trail explores the ecotone that surrounds the creek.

The stream is particularly raucous in spring and early summer, when engorged with meltwater generated in the heights of the Mount Rose Wilderness. Later in the season it mellows, inviting foot-soaking or, if the flow is slow enough, water play. But regardless of the season and its vigor, Galena Creek supports a riparian strip lively with aspen and willow. On the slopes farther from the water, a lovely lower montane yellow pine forest, dominated by Jeffrey and ponderosa pines, thrives. Check the cones to identify which tree is which: ponderosa pine cones have sharp points (prickly ponderosas), the Jeffrey cones don't (gentle Jeffreys).

The nature trail consists of two stacked loops, one about 0.5 mile in length—easy for younger schoolchildren to negotiate—and the second closer to 1 mile in length. Eighteen signposts keyed to an interpretive brochure, available in a kiosk at the trailhead, help hikers identify and learn more about the forest they wander through.

Galena Creek rushes under the bridge near the beginning of the nature trail.

Begin your exploration by crossing Galena Creek on a sturdy wooden bridge. On the far side a trail sign directs you left (west). Pass the junction of the Bitterbrush Trail, then the path narrows to singletrack and gently climbs to the intersection of the two legs of the loop. Stay straight (west), traveling the trail in a clockwise direction, with the creek on the left (south) and the forest on the right (north).

The path climbs gently alongside the wall of the steep, narrowing canyon. Pause along the way to ponder the purpose of a circular concrete structure on the far side of the creek (a flood containment pond? a livestock watering hole? a bear bathtub?). The nature trail curves right (north) up a short flight of steps, earning views of the Truckee Meadows as it climbs.

Once out of the creek drainage, the route meanders through woodlands scattered with boulders (glacial erratics) and low-growing mountain manzanita. Stone and log steps break up the steepest section of a slow descent that skirts a striking split rock. On flat terrain again, the rock-lined trail swings south, back toward the creek. Close the loop back alongside the creek, and unless you want to do laps, retrace your steps to the trailhead.

The Galena Creek Nature Trail offers a peaceful, educational romp through the woods.

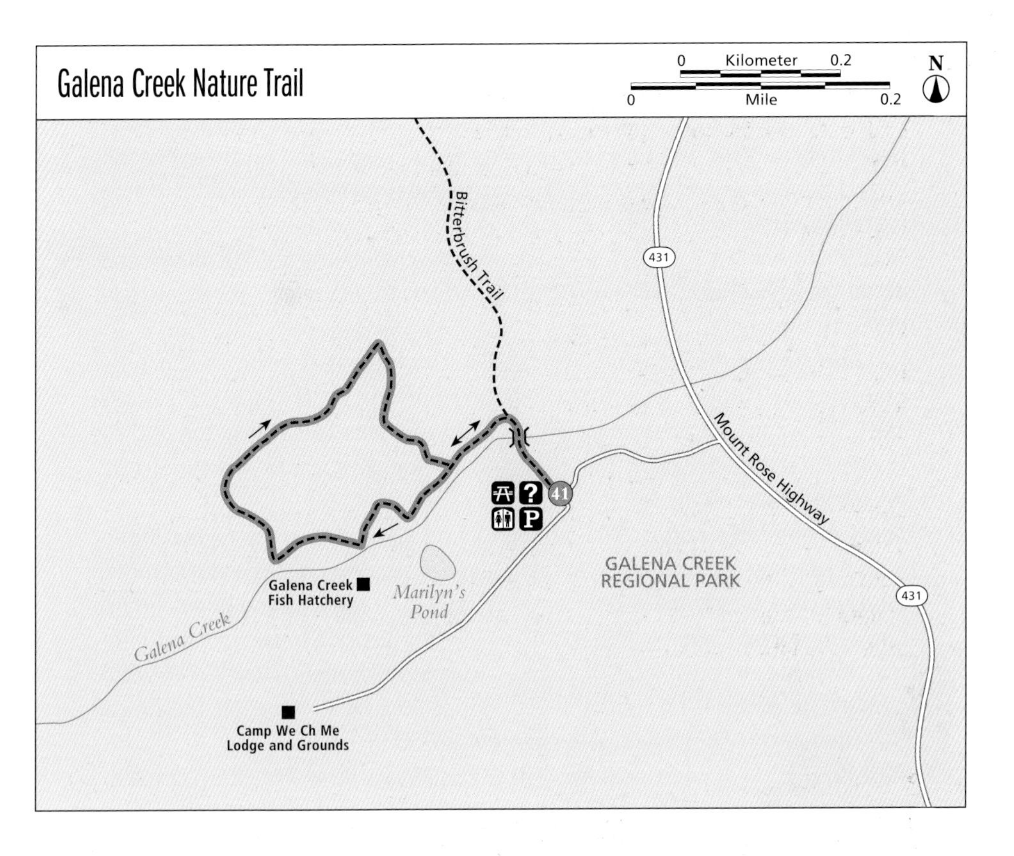

MILES AND DIRECTIONS

0.0 Start by heading right (northeast) down the gravel road at the south end of the lower parking lot. Once across the bridge turn left (west), following Galena Creek upstream.

0.1 At the junction of the Bitterbrush Trail, stay left (west) on the signed nature trail. The junction of the two legs of the loop is less than 0.1 mile farther; stay straight (streamside) to complete the route in a clockwise direction.

0.4 As a concrete structure appears on the opposite side of the canyon, the route bears right (north).

0.8 Close the loop where the two legs meet. Turn left (east) and retrace your steps toward the trailhead.

0.9 Arrive at the parking area.

HIKE INFORMATION

Local information: The Chamber, serving Reno, Sparks, and northern Nevada, offers information and links to community events, government, and businesses including restaurants and lodging. The Reno office is at 449 S. Virginia St. 2nd Floor, Reno, NV 89501; (775) 636-9550; www.thechambernv.org. For information about the city of Reno, call Reno Direct at (775) 334-INFO, or visit www.reno.gov/index.aspx?page=1.

Information about Carson City is available through the Carson City Chamber of Commerce, 1900 S. Carson St., Suite 200, Carson City, NV 89701; (775) 882-1565; www.carsoncitychamber.com/. The city site is at carson.org; the address is 201 N. Carson St., Carson City, NV 89701. Phone numbers for the various city departments are on the site.

Local events/attractions: With shaded picnic grounds, access to the Mount Rose Wilderness, an overnight camping lodge (Camp We Ch Me), a visitor center, outdoor campfire programs, winter sports activities, and a fishing pond and fish hatchery, Galena Creek Regional Park is a wonderful place to spend a day. Information about all activities in the park is available from the Galena Creek Visitor Center. The center is located at 18250 Mount Rose Hwy., Reno, NV 89511; call (775) 849-4948; or visit www.galenacreekvisitorcenter.org.

Restaurants: Midtown Eats Reno, 719 S. Virginia St., Reno, NV; (775) 324-3287; midtowneatsreno.com. The lunch menu is simple and the selections are delicious, whether you want a quinoa salad or a burger with habanero. The dinner menu is more refined (even if pork belly and veal cheeks don't sound elegant). The restaurant is also open for Sunday brunch.

Bowers Mansion

Sandy Bowers, an immigrant from Missouri, struck it rich in the wake of the California Gold Rush. He and his wife, Eilley, mined silver claims near the Carson River that turned out to be bonanzas; they were Comstock Lode tycoons by the mid-1850s. To celebrate, the couple built the Bowers Mansion and hosted lavish parties for fellow millionaire miners. The glory was short-lived, however; within twenty years, Sandy was dead and Eilley had lost the mansion to foreclosure.

Bowers Mansion is now the centerpiece of a Washoe County regional park, located on Old US 395 between Reno and Carson City. In addition to touring the mansion and the historic artifacts contained therein, visitors can also enjoy picnic facilities and the hot springs pool. For more information call (775) 849-1825 or visit www.co.washoe.nv.us/parks/parkdetails~pkid=1.

Little Washoe Lake Trail

A narrow footpath skims the east shore of Little Washoe Lake, with the domineering heights of Slide Mountain looming in the distance. The trail ends in a small nature area, a pleasure for both bird-watchers and lake lovers.

Start: At the trailhead just off East Lake Boulevard near the junction with Old US 395
Distance: 1 mile out and back
Hiking time: 1 hour
Difficulty: Easy
Trail surface: Dirt and sand single-track; overgrown in places
Best seasons: Year-round; avoid the exposed route at midday in summer
Other trail users: None
Trailhead amenities: Restrooms, picnic facilities, an information signboard
Canine compatibility: Leashed dogs permitted
Fees and permits: A day-use fee is levied
Schedule: Sunrise to sunset daily
Maps: USGS Washoe City NV; www.nvtrailmaps.com
Trail contact: Washoe Lake State Park, 4855 East Lake Blvd., Carson City, NV 89704; (775) 687-4319; parks.nv.gov/parks/washoe-lake-state-park
Special considerations: Intersecting paths and a lack of trail signs may give you the feeling of having been led astray. Remain close to the shoreline to stay on track. As the path is between the lakeshore and East Lake Boulevard, you won't get lost.
Other: Bring binoculars and a birding guide—the lake and surrounding wetlands harbor a host of shorebirds, songbirds, and birds of prey.

Finding the trailhead: The Little Washoe Lake trailhead is in the northernmost part of the state park, which occupies much of the Washoe Valley between Reno and Carson City. From US 395/I-580 southbound from Reno, take the East Lake Boulevard exit (near the summit with the pass into the Carson Valley). Follow East Lake Boulevard back north for 10.6 miles to the signed trailhead, which is on the left (west). If you head south on Old US 395 from Reno, the turnoff for East Lake Boulevard is at the signed summit of Washoe Hill, and the turnoff is 0.2 mile south of the summit. Follow the park road for 0.1 mile, past the fee station, to the parking area. The trailhead, marked with a little, easily missed TRAIL sign, is at the southern end of the lot near a picnic table. GPS: N39 19.574' / W119 47.540'

THE HIKE

If you venture onto the Little Washoe Lake Trail in the morning or evening, the light is soft, the lake surface glitters, and the birds—ducks plying the quiet waters, herons stalking the margins, songbirds flitting from bush to bush, and maybe even a hawk cruising low over the scrubland—demonstrate their abundance in song and flight. Slide Mountain and Mount Rose form an impressive skyline above the lake's western shoreline. The setting is postcard-perfect.

The trail is short and easy, weaving through the scrub above the narrow rocky beach that forms when the lake's water level is low. The beach lures sunbathers, kids, and swimming dogs; the birdlife and setting draw nature lovers to the neighboring Scripps Wildlife Management Area. The route proper sits on the high ground above the beach, linking lake to nature area and ringing with birdsong. When it's wet, the croaking of frogs and toads joins the cacophony and helps drown out any noise that drifts off the neighboring highway.

Route-finding can be a bit challenging at the outset, since paths and overgrown dirt tracks intersect in the scrub and there are few trail markers. But you can't get lost: This is open country, and it's easy to see where you're going and where you've come from. Begin by hiking down a narrow path; the trail widens

The combination of water and fruitful scrub makes Little Washoe Lake a haven for birds and hikers alike.

within 100 yards and views open across the lake. Where paths cross stay right (southbound and parallel to the shoreline), picking through the well-spaced brush should the path become indistinct. If you venture left (eastward), you will eventually intercept the dirt road leading into the Scripps Wildlife Management Area, which is your ultimate destination anyway. No worries if you wander.

As you approach the Scripps wildlife area, the narrow singletrack crosses a patch of white hardpan and passes through marsh grasses that resonate with birdsong and the hum of crickets. The track ends on the Scripps road about 200 yards from the restrooms, which have been visible for most of the route and can be used as a homing beacon. Cross the road and take a short trail down to the north shore of big Washoe Lake to check out boaters and birds. When ready, return as you came.

Vehicle noise is a constant here: Nearby I-580/US 395 is busy and East Lake Boulevard can be busy as well. Don't let that dissuade you—the views and the birds make up for it.

Washoe City

With the opening of I-580 in 2012, historic Washoe City eased a little closer to irrelevance. It's been a long time coming. The burg at the foot of Slide Mountain is long past its heyday, which came during the late nineteenth century as part of the mining legacy of the Comstock Lode. Virginia City, to the east, is still a thriving tourist attraction. Washoe City, by comparison, is now a drive-by on US 395, which itself has been relegated to drive-by status as those seeking swift passage between Reno and Carson City whiz south on the new freeway.

But it wasn't always that way. Washoe City was once the county seat of Washoe County and a hub of supplies for the boomtown of Virginia City. It had thousands of residents, its own newspaper, and all the trappings of a thriving city, including schoolhouses, warehouses, homes, and businesses, as well as mills in the nearby Ophir Creek drainage and on Little Washoe Lake. According to Nevada author and poet John Evanoff, the city also boasted a "superbly built courthouse and jail . . . constructed of brick created and fired in ovens near what is now the middle of Washoe Lake. Stone was carried off Slide Mountain for the steps and the entire two buildings were constructed for a little more than $40,000, a stately sum at that time."

MILES AND DIRECTIONS

0.0 Start behind the picnic table at the south end of the parking lot; there is a small TRAIL sign here.

0.2 At the unmarked junction with a social trail stay right (southwest/toward the shoreline).

0.3 Follow the path parallel to the beach to another worn trail sign at a pole hung with orange and white flags.

0.5 The trail ends on the Scripps Wildlife Management Area road. Cross the road to check out bigger Washoe Lake, then return as you came.

0.9 Trail signs direct you to the right (beachside), then left (toward East Lake Boulevard) to put you on the right trail back to the picnic area.

1.0 Arrive back at the trailhead.

HIKE INFORMATION

Local information: The Carson City Chamber of Commerce provides information for both residents and visitors about amenities in the city and environs, including places to stay and places to eat. For more information contact the chamber at 1900 S. Carson St., Suite 200, Carson City, NV 89701; (775) 882-1565; www.carson citychamber.com.

The Carson Valley Chamber also provides information for residents and visitors to Carson City, Mindon, Gardnerville, and other valley cities and towns. Contact the chamber at 1477 US 395, Suite A, Gardnerville, NV 89410; (775) 782-8144 or toll free (800) 727-7677; www.carsonvalleynv.org.

Camping: Washoe Lake State Park offers forty-nine sites in the Main Area Campground. It is open year-round and sites are available on a first-come, first-served basis. There are no hookups, but several sites are RV friendly. A fee is charged. Contact the park at (775) 687-4319 or visit parks.nv.gov/parks/washoe-lake-state-park for more information.

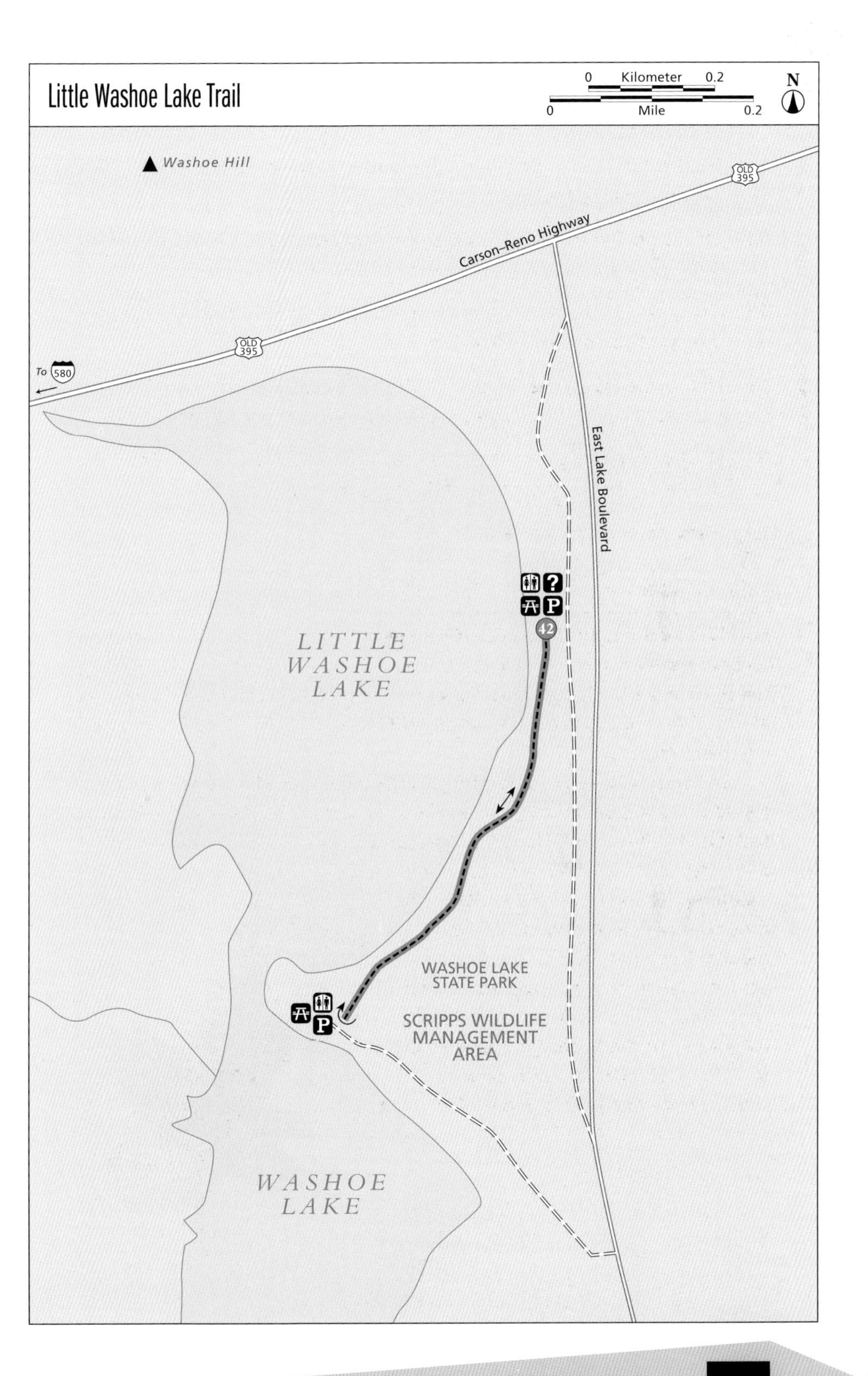
Little Washoe Lake Trail
0 Kilometer 0.2
0 Mile 0.2
N
Washoe Hill
OLD 395
Carson–Reno Highway
OLD 395
To 580
East Lake Boulevard
42
LITTLE WASHOE LAKE
WASHOE LAKE STATE PARK
SCRIPPS WILDLIFE MANAGEMENT AREA
WASHOE LAKE

43

Deadman's Overlook Trail

If dead men could enjoy great views, they'd love the overlook at the apex of this loop. Fortunately this hike isn't hard enough to suck the life out of anyone, and from the gazebo at the high point, survivors will be treated to vistas of Washoe Lake, the Washoe Valley, and Slide Mountain.

Start: At the roadside trailhead off East Lake Boulevard
Distance: 1.2-mile lollipop
Hiking time: 1 hour
Difficulty: Moderate due to steep inclines
Trail surface: Dirt singletrack
Best seasons: Spring and fall
Other trail users: Mountain bikers, equestrians
Trailhead amenities: Parking for four or five cars, an information signboard with a trail map. More parking is available along the shoulder of East Lake Road. Restrooms, information, and the fee station are located at the main park entrance.
Canine compatibility: Leashed dogs permitted
Fees and permits: A day-use fee is levied; pay at the park entrance station about 0.3 mile north of the trailhead
Schedule: Sunrise to sunset
Maps: USGS Carson City NV; a trail map is posted on an information board at the trailhead; www.nvtrailmaps.com
Trail contact: Washoe Lake State Park, 4855 East Lake Blvd., Carson City, NV 89704; (775) 687-4319; parks.nv.gov/parks/washoe-lake-state-park
Special considerations: A complete dearth of shade makes this route a scorcher in the heat of a summer day.

Finding the trailhead: Washoe Lake State Park is located in the scenic Washoe Valley between Reno and Carson City. From US 395/I-580 southbound from Reno, take the East Lake Boulevard exit. From Carson City northbound, you'll also take the East Lake Boulevard exit. Follow East Lake Boulevard north for 2.8 miles to the trailhead parking area on the right (east) side of the road. GPS: N39 14.161' / W119 45.481'

THE HIKE

The gazebo at the top of the Deadman's Overlook Trail boasts panoramic views across Washoe Lake and Little Washoe Lake onto the steep, scarred east face of Slide Mountain. Washed white with snow in winter and spring, streaked gray and dark green during the long dry summer, this distinctive peak dominates nearly every vista along the stretch of the mountain front between Reno and Carson City.

Slide Mountain's name is derived from its unstable geology. Reaching a height of 9,632 feet, the scars on its south- and east-facing slopes have been caused by repeated landslides. The most recent was catastrophic: In May 1983 the southeast face, made more unstable by snowmelt, gave way and cascaded down the Ophir Creek drainage into the Washoe Valley, taking out two small reservoirs and damaging or destroying everything in its path.

A partially interpreted loop leads to the wooden gazebo that opens onto the mountain. The structure is perched on a high point on the east side of Washoe Lake and is visible from the trailhead. The route begins in a riparian corridor fed by a seasonal stream, passing a memorial cross and the first of several metal interpretive markers. These signs identify the desert and riparian plants along

The gazebo at the top of the Deadman's Overlook Trail offers stunning views of Slide Mountain.

the trail, including watercress, monkeyflower, Mormon tea, desert peach (sporting delicate pink blooms in spring), bitterbrush, stinging nettle (watch out for this one!), and the ubiquitous sagebrush.

After a brief walk through the stream-fed greenbelt, ignoring side trails that wander into the brush creekside, you'll reach a trail junction. Cross the streambed, which runs dry in late season, and begin a moderate climb up timber stairs across the scrub-covered slope. Several switchbacks offer views of Slide Mountain and Washoe Lake before curling to the east.

Pass another trail intersection on the left (east); stay right (west), cross a dry drainage, then make a rocky uphill traverse to the gazebo. Jumbles of red rock surround the wooden structure; in springtime, wildflowers sprinkle the inhospitable landscape with patches of purple, white, and yellow.

After enjoying the views from the gazebo, you have the option to return the way you came. To complete the loop, stay on the obvious main trail (the middle route) that traverses the hillside as it drops into the drainage. The route is crisscrossed with social paths, but the main track is well used and obvious. Small gardens colonize the rocky landscape in spring—pillows of white and pink blossoms spilling from crevices in the hillsides. Pass another interpretive sign (for serviceberry) as you descend.

Back in the drainage, turn left (west) and hike back down toward the trailhead. Slide Mountain and other peaks in the Carson Range are spread across the western horizon. Pass additional interpretive signs as you close the loop, then retrace your steps back to the trailhead.

MILES AND DIRECTIONS

0.0 Start on the signed interpretive trail.

0.2 At the trail junction go right (south) on the path with wooden timbers that leads up toward the overlook.

0.4 Pass a trail that breaks off to the left (east).

0.5 Arrive at the gazebo and enjoy the views. To complete the loop, stay straight on the obvious trail leading northeast into the creek drainage, ignoring the road to the right (south) and several side trails that intersect the descending traverse.

0.8 At the trail junction in the drainage, turn left (west), back toward Slide Mountain and the trailhead.

0.9 Reach the trail junction at the beginning of the loop. Stay straight (west) toward the lake and mountains.

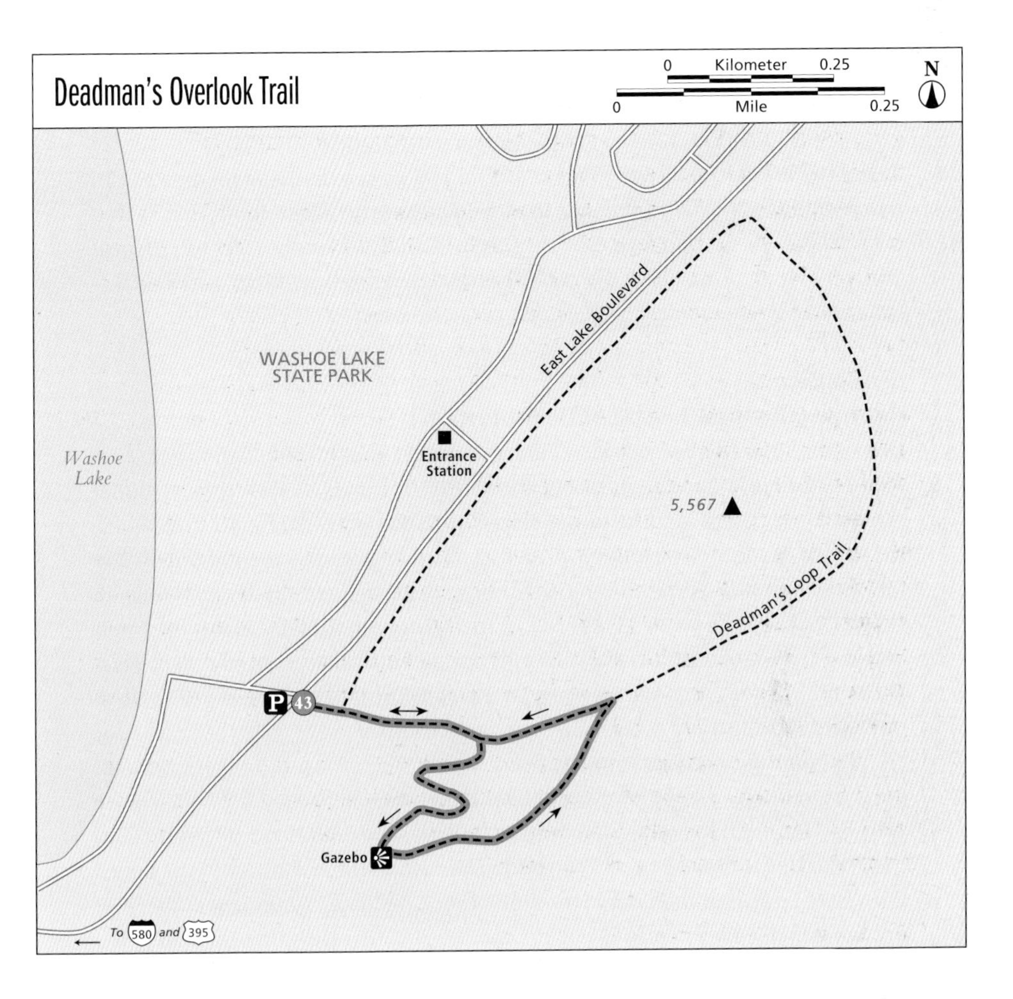

1.2 Arrive back at the trailhead and parking area.

Options: Washoe Lake State Park offers a variety of trail options, the most obvious being an extension of the Deadman's Overlook Trail known as Deadman's Loop.

HIKE INFORMATION

Local information: The Carson City Chamber of Commerce provides information for both residents and visitors about amenities in the city and environs, including places to stay and places to eat. For more information contact the chamber at 1900 S. Carson St., Suite 200, Carson City, NV 89701; (775) 882-1565; www.carsoncitychamber.com.

The Carson Valley Chamber also provides information for residents and visitors to Carson City, Minden, Gardnerville, and other valley cities and towns.

Contact the chamber at 1477 US 395, Suite A, Gardnerville, NV 89410; (775) 782-8144 or toll free (800) 727-7677; www.carsonvalleynv.org.

Camping: Washoe Lake State Park offers forty-nine sites in the Main Area campground. It is open year-round and sites are available on a first-come, first-served basis. There are no hookups, but several sites are RV friendly. A fee is charged. Contact the park at (775) 687-4319 or visit parks.nv.gov/parks/washoe-lake-state-park/ for more information.

In Addition

Rearranging Ranches on Slide Mountain

One of the signature peaks on the Sierra mountain front overlooking the Washoe Valley, Slide Mountain seems placid enough. It sits across NV 431 from its higher sibling, Mount Rose, and its upper slopes are chiseled with the ski runs of the misnamed Mount Rose Ski Area. A trail climbs to its radio tower–crowned summit, and its southwest face slopes gently into the grasslands of Tahoe Meadows. When cloaked in snowpack it looks like many other mountains along the front. Yes, you can see the slide paths, but they appear more integral to the mountain. In summer, devoid of snow, the scars on the peak's southeast face are more obvious and ominous. Slide Mountain has a dangerous side.

The most recent earth-moving event was in 1983. The mountain's southeast face, saturated by the melting snowpack of an unusually heavy snow year, gave way. The resulting rockslide slammed into Upper Price Lake and forced most of the water out of the reservoir. The rockfall and water poured through the Lower Price Lake basin and then down the Ophir Creek drainage, settling near the floor of the Washoe Valley in an alluvial fan near US 395. One person was killed in the event.

But the mountain's proclivity to landslides reaches back hundred of years. Preeminent satirical journalist Mark Twain described both the terror of slides and the arcane enforcement of property rights in his 1880 book entitled *Roughing It*. In the book Twain describes the lawsuit that ensues when a landslide on a Washoe County mountain (he doesn't name the peak, but one can assume its identity) deposits one mountain ranch atop another. Says the judge in deciding the case: "If Heaven, dissatisfied with the position of [a] ranch upon the mountain side, has chosen to remove it to a position more eligible and more advantageous for its owner, it ill becomes us, insects as we are, to question the legality of the act or inquire into the reasons that prompted it. No—Heaven created the ranches and it is Heaven's prerogative to rearrange them, to experiment with them around at its pleasure. It is for us to submit, without repining."

Pasture River–Mexican Ditch Trail

This meditative hike in the heart of the Carson Valley links the pastures of a working ranch to an historic diversion dam on the Carson River.

Start: At the signed trailhead near the Silver Saddle Ranch buildings
Distance: 3.6-mile lollipop
Hiking time: 2.5 to 3 hours
Difficulty: Moderate
Trail surface: Mostly dirt ranch road; some dirt singletrack
Best seasons: Winter, spring, and late fall. You'll find shade along the river and the ditch, but the hike may be uncomfortably hot in summer at midday.
Other trail users: Mountain bikers, equestrians, trail runners, birders
Trailhead amenities: Parking, restrooms, and an information signboard at the trailhead. A handicapped-accessible restroom is located farther along the park's loop road.
Canine compatibility: Leashed dogs permitted
Fees and permits: None
Schedule: 7 a.m. to 5 p.m. daily, year-round
Maps: USGS New Empire NV; trail maps are in the red mailbox at the trailhead
Trail contact: Silver Saddle Ranch operates under a cooperative agreement between the Bureau of Land Management and the Carson City Parks and Recreation Department. Bureau of Land Management, Carson City District Office, 5665 Morgan Mill Rd., Carson City, NV 89701; (775) 885-6000; www.blm.gov/nv/st/en/fo/carson_city_field.html. Carson City Parks and Recreation Department, 201 N. Carson St., Carson City, NV 89701; (775) 887-2262; www.carson-city.nv.us or www.carson.org/Index.aspx?page=1203
Special considerations: Several signs warn of frequent rattlesnake sightings. If you don't bother them, they're not likely to bother you. Keep your pet on a leash. Do not swim in the ditch; the water moves deceptively fast. So does the Carson River when swollen with runoff in spring.
Other: This is a working ranch, so be sure to close gates behind you or leave them open as instructed by signs or the ranch manager.

Finding the trailhead: From US 395/I-580 in Carson City, take the Fairview Drive exit (the end of the freeway in 2012). Go left (east) on Fairview Drive for 1.2 miles to the roundabout. Bear right on East Fifth Street. Follow East Fifth Street for 0.2 mile to Carson River Road (NV 513). Turn right (south) on Carson River Road and drive 1.3 miles to the signed park entrance on the right (south). Follow the park road (which becomes one way) around to the ranch complex and trailhead. GPS: N39 08.320' / W119 42.699'

THE HIKE

This pleasant ramble through Silver Saddle Ranch and along the Carson River begins amid hay fields that are irrigated with water from the Mexican Ditch. If the fields have gotten water, they grow lush and green. If they haven't, native sages, bitterbrush, and desert peach reclaim the fallow space.

Transforming high desert into cultivated farmland seems simple enough on the Silver Saddle Ranch: Open a gate on the ditch and let the water flow. But water in the West is treasured, measured, and fought over, and winning the battle for water rights can make or break any project, whether spearheaded by a city or by a family farm. The water in the Mexican Ditch comes from the Carson River; from the ditch the water is divided between private and public lands in the agricultural bottomlands of the Eagle Valley, with flows gauged as carefully now as they were a century ago.

Built in the early 1860s, the Mexican Dam and Ditch initially supplied water to power the ore-crushing wheels of the Mexican Mill, part of a complex of mills that processed the output of Nevada's fabled Comstock Lode. But even before the lode played out, water from the ditch was being diverted for agriculture, according to the Friends of Silver Saddle Ranch. That conflict drove one of the aforementioned water rights battles: Miners and ranchers duked it out in court over the precious resource. The demise of the Comstock ultimately decided the winner, with agriculture and development taking shares of Mexican Ditch water in the wake of mining's decline.

These days the ditch carries water to valley ranchers even when the hot summer whittles down flows in the Carson River. On Silver Saddle Ranch the Mexican Ditch also leaches enough moisture into the dry desert soils to support a riparian strip ringing with birdcall. The trail that runs alongside the ditch attracts birdwatchers as well as mountain bikers, trail runners, and day hikers.

The route begins amid Silver Saddle Ranch's red-painted buildings; if you are lucky, the ranch manager will be on hand to give you advice about the route.

Interpretive signs around the ranch give information about the Mexican Ditch and the ranch property itself.

From the ranch you will pick up the Pasture River Trail, a straight shot that leads along the north side of one of the fenced hayfields to the banks of the Carson River. A small picnic area shaded by cottonwood sits riverside, possibly occupied by picnickers and anglers. Head south along the ranch road that runs between the river and the pastures, passing through a couple of gates. An avenue of cottonwoods provides shade as you proceed.

After 1 mile pass a gate and an interpretive sign that describes the "ribbon of green" that is the Carson River in all seasons, whether full and swift with winter runoff or dried to fish-clumped puddles in fall. Drop to riverside, staying left on a sandy road through the bottomlands (which can be wet in spring), then climb to the junction with the Mexican Ditch Trail.

Head south on the flat dirt road, which is wedged between river and ditch. Quail scurry from bush to bush on the riverside, lizards scamper from rock to rock on the ditch side, and songbirds flit from branch to branch in the cottonwoods and willows. You may spot anglers scattered along the far shore, but unless the birders are out, you may have the trail to yourself.

Ranch roads serve as trails that follow the Carson River downstream to the Mexican Dam.

The muffled thunder of water spilling over the diversion dam wafts up the route long before you arrive. The dam marks trail's end; in spring it overflows in a 10-foot whitewater fall that spans the Carson River from bank to bank but diminishes as the summer progresses. The Carson pools behind the structure, widening between shallow slopes covered in desert scrub. The gate that funnels water into the ditch is on the right (west); when the Carson begins to dry, sandbags are used to divert the flow into the ditch.

The dam is the turnaround point; retrace your steps to the junction of the Mexican Ditch Trail and the Pasture River Trail. To complete the loop portion of the hike, stay left (northwest) on the ditch trail, following the green strip alongside pastures as you hike back to the ranch complex and trailhead. Enjoy views of the Carson Range and Slide Mountain as you return.

MILES AND DIRECTIONS

0.0 Start by walking through the ranch property to the fence line of the first hayfield. Go left (north) along the fence to the signed Pasture River Trail, then head east toward the river.

0.4 Reach the gate and picnic site on the bank of the Carson River. Turn right (south) on the wide track.

0.6 The trail narrows and passes through a gate. Remain on the obvious path along the fence line.

0.7 Pass another gate and into a second pasture. Stay left (riverside) on the main ranch road/trail, ignoring side roads.

1.0 Reach a gate and an interpretive sign. Pass through the gate (if open) or the stile (if closed) and follow the sandy road that drops left (riverside) then climbs to the junction with the Mexican Ditch Trail.

1.2 Go left (south) on the broad dirt Mexican Ditch Trail. The river is on the left (east) and the ditch is on the right (west).

2.0 The trail swings around a curve in the river and ends at the Mexican Dam. Turn around and retrace your steps to the last trail junction.

2.8 Back at the junction of the Mexican Ditch Trail and the Pasture River Trail, stay left (north/on the high road) on the Mexican Ditch Trail.

3.0 Carefully cross the ditch overflow and continue on the dirt road to the gate/stile at the interpretive sign. Stay left (northwest), following the pasture's fence as it curves along the ditch.

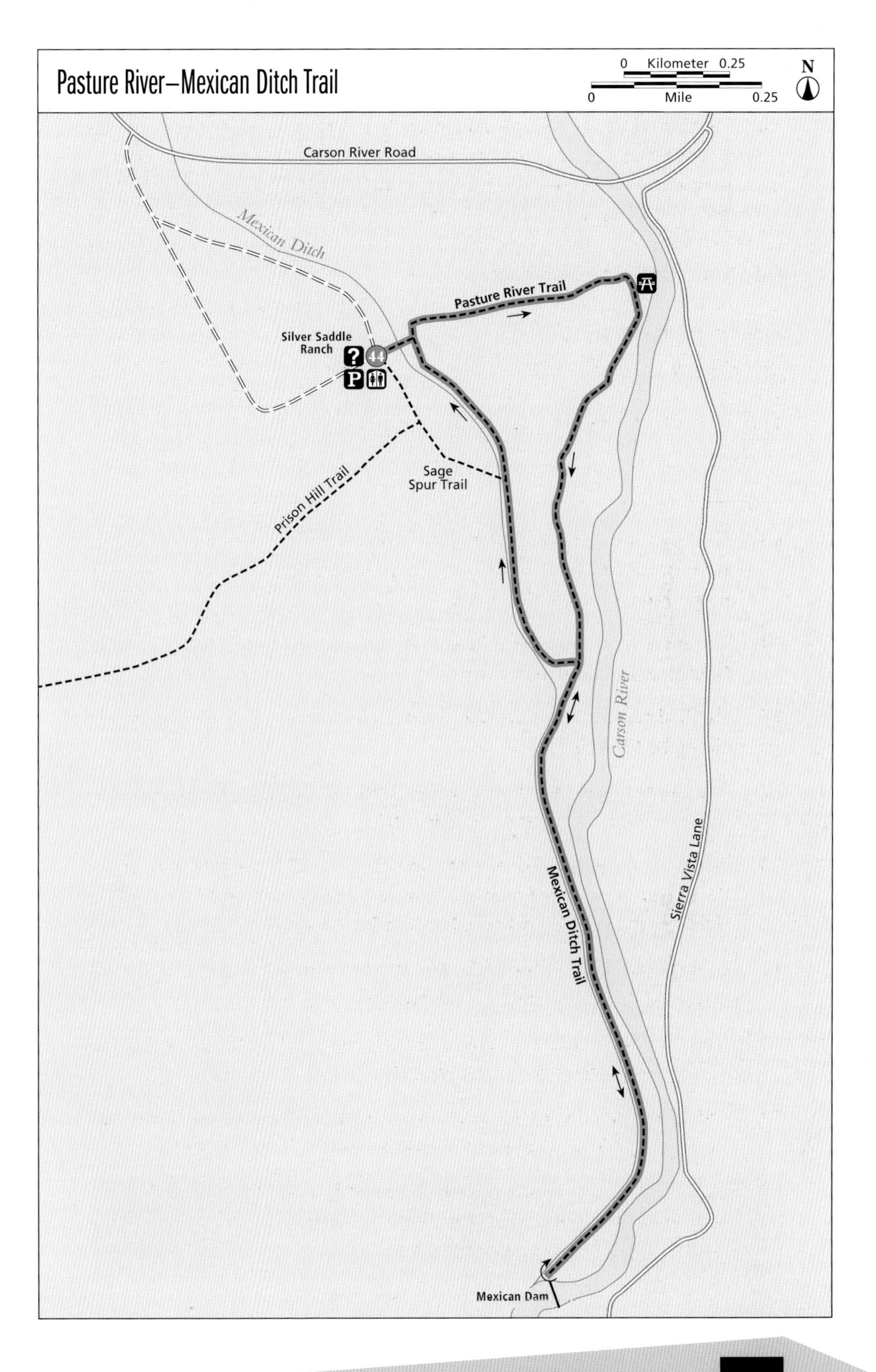
Pasture River–Mexican Ditch Trail
0 Kilometer 0.25
0 Mile 0.25
N
Carson River Road
Mexican Ditch
Pasture River Trail
Silver Saddle Ranch
44
Sage Spur Trail
Prison Hill Trail
Carson River
Sierra Vista Lane
Mexican Ditch Trail
Mexican Dam

3.3 Pass the gate and bridge of the Silver Sage Trail on the left (west). Stay right (northwest) on the Mexican Ditch Trail.

3.4 Pass a gate into another hayfield; at the intersection of the ranch roads stay left (straight/north) on the ditch trail. Cross an irrigation ditch and go through another gate as you approach the ranch complex.

3.6 Arrive back at the trailhead.

HIKE INFORMATION

Local information: The Carson City Chamber of Commerce provides information for both residents and visitors about amenities in the city and environs, including places to stay and places to eat. For more information contact the chamber at 1900 S. Carson St., Suite 200, Carson City, NV 89701; (775) 882-1565; www.carson citychamber.com.

The Carson Valley Chamber also provides information for residents and visitors to Carson City, Minden, Gardnerville, and other valley cities and towns. Contact the chamber at 1477 US 395, Suite A, Gardnerville, NV 89410; (775) 782-8144 or toll free (800) 727-7677; www.carsonvalleynv.org.

Organizations: Members of the nonprofit Friends of Silver Saddle Ranch provide interpretive programs and perform maintenance projects and other support services at the ranch. For more information visit fossr.org.

A quote from Mark Twain posted on an interpretive sign along the Mexican Ditch in Silver Saddle Ranch: "Whiskey is for drinking, water is for fighting."

Green Tip:
Never let your dog chase wildlife.

Fay-Luther Interpretive Loop

This superlative loop meanders along the lower slopes of Jobs Peak in the Carson River valley, passing from pristine highland desert scrub into shady montane forest and back again.

Start: At the Fay-Luther trailhead off Foothill Road
Distance: 2.8-mile lollipop
Hiking time: 2 hours
Difficulty: More difficult due to steep inclines and trail length
Trail surface: Sand, decomposed granite, dirt singletrack
Best seasons: Spring and fall; avoid heat of the day in summer
Other trail users: Mountain bikers, equestrians
Trailhead amenities: Parking, an information signboard. A trail map and dog waste disposal station are about 50 yards beyond the gate on the Sandy/Jobs Peak Ranch Trails. No restroom is available. Equestrians are asked to clean up after their horses.
Canine compatibility: Dogs permitted year-round, but must be leashed from Oct 15 to Mar 30 to protect mule deer habitat. Also, please pick up after your pet.
Fees and permits: None
Schedule: Sunrise to sunset
Maps: USGS Woodfords CA-NV; an excellent trail map is posted 50 yards from the trailhead and is available online via links at the BLM and Carson Valley Trails Association websites.
Trail contact: Bureau of Land Management, Carson City District/ Sierra Front Field Office, 5665 Morgan Mill Rd., Carson City, NV 89701; (775) 885-6000; www.blm.gov/nv/st/en/fo/carson_city_field.html

Finding the trailhead: Heading south on US 395 from Carson City, go right (southwest) on NV 88. Follow NV 88 for 2.1 miles to NV 207 (Waterloo Lane). Turn right (west) on NV 207 and go 3.2 miles to Foothill Road (NV 206). Go left (south) on Foothill Road for 4.4 miles to the signed trailhead parking area on the right (west). GPS: N38 52.216' / W119 48.637'

THE HIKE

Massive Jobs Peak dominates the mountain front south of Carson City and provides the backdrop for this wonderful trek through high desert and lower montane forest. Views from the trail stretch east across a patchwork of green and brown ranchland to the dry slopes of the Pine Nut Mountains and climb west up the wooded draws of the foothills of the Sierra Nevada.

The Fay-Luther trail system, more than 8 miles of interlocking paths surrounding Luther Creek and rugged Fay Canyon, is a justifiable source of pride for its developers, which include the BLM, the Humboldt-Toiyabe National Forest, the American Land Conservancy, and the Carson Valley Trails Association. The interpretive loop described here is just one of several options showcasing the relatively untouched natural beauty of the area.

The route begins on the high desert, among fragrant big sage, bitterbrush, and desert peach, with unimpeded views in all directions. The Sandy Trail is aptly named, with a surface that melts beneath your boots, but the incline is gentle so the hiking is easy. Keep in mind, however, that this section of desert track is

The forested peaks of the high Sierra form a backdrop to the high desert portion of the Fay-Luther Interpretive Loop.

exposed and potentially dehydrating in summer. Pass the doggie waste station, the California National Historic Trail marker (commemorating the route used by emigrants to California's fabled gold country), and the California/Nevada state border as you climb, staying left (southwest) at junctions with the Jobs Peak Ranch Trail.

A bench in the shade of a massive Jeffrey pine, positioned on the line of transition from the high desert to the montane environment, offers incredible views across the Carson River valley to the Pine Nuts and north up the mountain front. The views continue as the trail traverses a pine-shaded, scrub-scented slope to the junction with the Interpretive Loop; stay left (south) to complete a clockwise circuit. The setting is especially lovely in spring, when the desert blooms yellow and pink, the pastures in the valley are verdant, and the Pine Nut Mountains are painted in shades of green and brown.

Pass the first junction with the Bitter Cherry Trail to Luther Creek. The willow-lined stream accompanies the trail west and uphill toward the mouth of Fay Canyon: Say goodbye to valley views and hello to the steep, gray and evergreen slopes of the Sierra.

Climb more steeply as the trail passes the second junction with the Bitter Cherry Trail, then curves away from the creek. A switchback and traverse lead up a steep slope and past the intersection with the Grand View Loop. Now on the back of a small ridge and heading north on the return leg of the loop, the vistas open again, stretching across the river valley below and up the steely mountain front.

The descent includes switchbacking traverses of forested gullies and several opportunities to contemplate the layered greens and browns of the valley on perfectly placed dedicated benches. Pass two junctions with the Jeffrey Pine Trail before a final drop closes the Interpretive Loop. Retrace your route through the transition zone and the high desert to the trailhead.

MILES AND DIRECTIONS

0.0 Start up the Sandy Trail behind the information sign.

0.1 Pass junctions with the California National Historic Trail and the Jobs Peak Ranch Trail, then cross the California/Nevada state border, staying straight (southwest) on the obvious Sandy Trail.

0.3 At the second junction with the Jobs Peak Trail stay left (southwest) on the Sandy Trail.

0.5 Pass the Red Barn Ranch bench in the shade of a giant Jeffrey pine.

0.6 Reach the Lonesome Trail junction; stay left (southwest) on the Sandy Trail.

0.7 The Sandy Trail ends at the beginning of the Interpretive Loop. Go left (southeast) to complete the route in a clockwise direction.

0.9 At the intersection with the Bitter Cherry Trail stay left (southeast). The trail comes parallel with Luther Creek.

1.1 At the unsigned junction with a social trail stay right (south) on the Interpretive Loop.

1.2 Reach the second Bitter Cherry Trail junction and stay left (south) on the Interpretive Loop.

1.3 Stay right (up) and north around the switchback at the unsigned junction.

1.4 Arrive at the signed Grand View Loop intersection. Stay left (north) on the Interpretive Loop, passing the Charles Phillips bench and heading down the ridgeback.

1.6 Switchback in and out of a gully to the first junction with the Jeffrey Pine Trail. Stay right (northeast) on the Interpretive Loop.

2.0 Switchback through a steeper gully to the second Jeffrey Pine Trail intersection. Again, stay right (northeast) on the Interpretive Loop.

2.1 Drop to the junction and close the Interpretive Loop. Retrace your steps down the Sandy Trail.

2.8 Arrive back at the trailhead.

Options: You can extend your tour of the Fay-Luther area by venturing out on either the Jeffrey Pine Trail or the Grand View Loop. The trail also links to the Jobs Peak Ranch route and trailhead to the north.

HIKE INFORMATION

Local information: The Carson City Chamber of Commerce provides information for both residents and visitors about amenities in the city and environs, including places to stay and places to eat. For more information contact the chamber at 1900 S. Carson St., Suite 200, Carson City, NV 89701; (775) 882-1565; www.carsoncitychamber.com.

The Carson Valley Chamber also provides information for residents and visitors to Carson City, Minden, Gardnerville, and other valley cities and towns. Contact the chamber at 1477 US 395, Suite A, Gardnerville, NV 89410; (775) 782-8144 or toll free (800) 727-7677; www.carsonvalleynv.org.

Local events/attractions: The historic towns of Minden, Genoa, and Gardnerville lie along the mountain front in the Carson River valley south of Carson City.

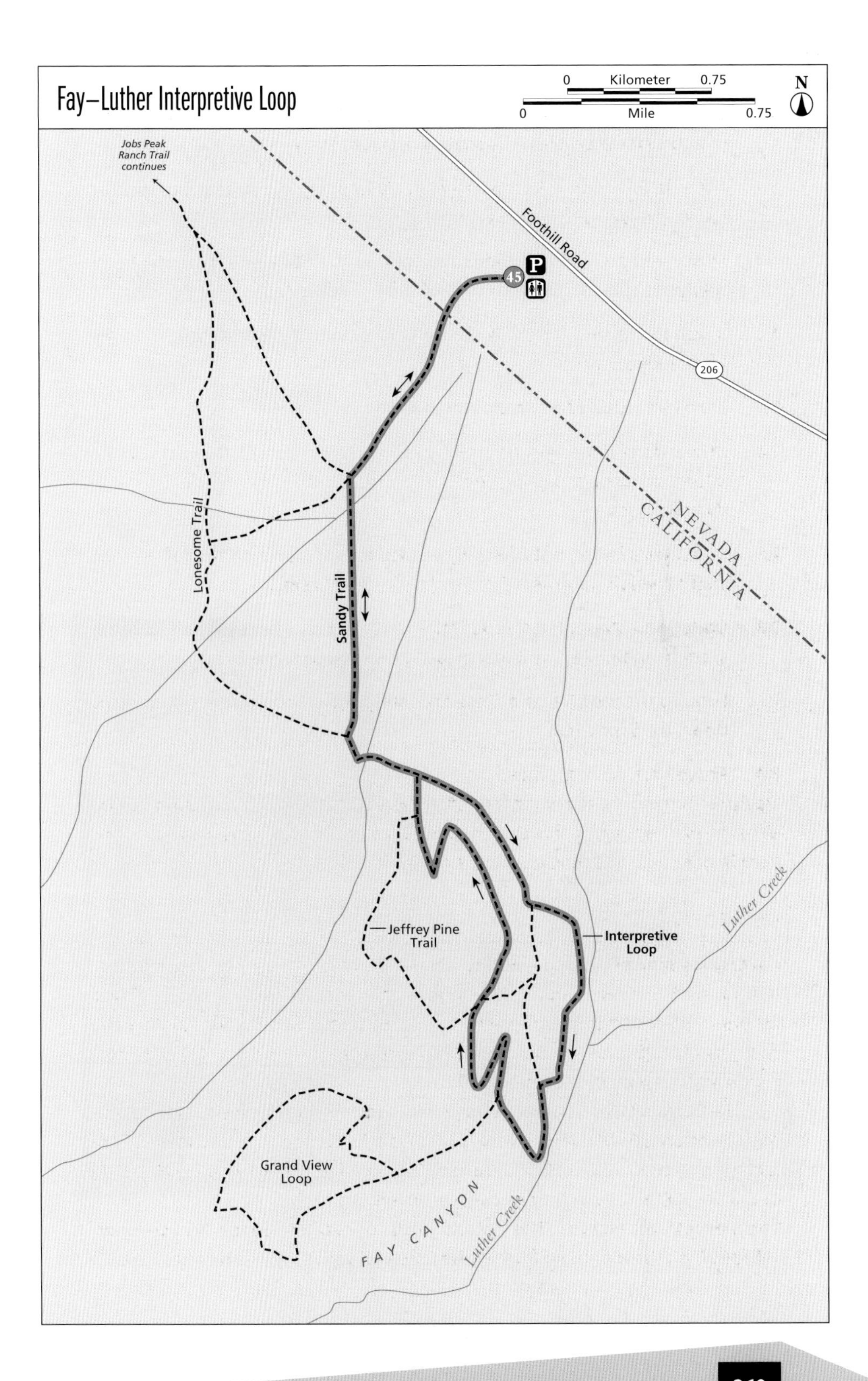
Fay–Luther Interpretive Loop
0 Kilometer 0.75
0 Mile 0.75
N
Jobs Peak Ranch Trail continues
Foothill Road
45
P
206
NEVADA
CALIFORNIA
Lonesome Trail
Sandy Trail
Jeffrey Pine Trail
Interpretive Loop
Luther Creek
Grand View Loop
FAY CANYON
Luther Creek

Each small town offers historic sites, restaurants, lodging, and access to recreational opportunities in the Sierra, including Lake Tahoe. For more information on Minden, contact the Town of Minden, 1604 Esmeralda Ave. Suite 101, Minden, NV 89423; (775) 782-5976; www.townofminden.com. For more information on Genoa, home of the annual Candy Dance Arts and Crafts Faire, an event dating back more than ninety years, contact the Town of Genoa, PO Box 14, Genoa, NV 89411-0014; (775) 782-8696; www.genoanevada.org. For more information on Gardnerville, call the Town of Gardnerville, 1407 US 395 N, Gardnerville, NV 98410; (775) 782-7134; www.gardnerville-nv.gov.

The dry slopes of the Virginia Range are visible from the Fay-Luther Interpretive Trail.

Honorable Mentions

Prison Hill

The Prison Hill Recreation Area, located adjacent to Silver Saddle Ranch in Carson City, offers hiking trails on the scrub-covered hill bordering the ranch on the west. Dry and exposed, these trails are best traveled in cool weather, either at the beginning or end of a summer's day, or in colder seasons. The northern end of the recreation area is open to motorized vehicles. Foot access to the Prison Hill trail system from Silver Saddle Ranch is via the Silver Sage and Prison Hill Trails.

To reach the trailhead from US 395/I-580 in Carson City, take the Fairview Drive exit (the end of the freeway in 2012). Go left (east) on Fairview Drive toward Fallon for 1.2 miles to the roundabout. Bear right on East Fifth Street. Follow East Fifth Street for 0.2 mile to Carson River Road (NV 513). Turn right (south) on Carson River Road and drive 1.3 miles to the signed park entrance on the right (south). Follow the park road (which becomes one way) around to the ranch complex and trailhead.

Davis Creek Regional Park

Perfect for a family outing, the pretty little **Davis Creek Nature Trail** offers a quick and easy tour of the ecological transition zone between the lower montane forest and the high desert, where the yellow pine forests of the Sierra's lower slopes give way to the sages and scrubs of the Great Basin. The 1-mile loop takes less than an hour to walk. A naturalist guide, keyed to numbered posts, is available at the trailhead and describes the geology and habitats that you'll encounter along the lovely footpath. Views are of Slide Mountain and the Washoe Valley; you'll also skirt the park's little pond and a junction with the much more challenging Ophir Creek Trail.

The **Ophir Creek Trail** begins or ends in Davis Creek Regional Park, depending on whether you want to hike uphill or down. Leading from the woodlands at the base of the Carson Range into the alpine heights below the summit of Mount Rose, the Ophir Creek route is a suitable one-way goal for the ambitious, experienced hiker. Heading up from Davis Creek Park, you'll travel the length of the Ophir Creek drainage, passing Upper Price Lake and the site of Lower Price Lake, which was obliterated in a landslide that cascaded down aptly named Slide Mountain in the 1980s. The route terminates in the sprawling Tahoe Meadows, above Lake Tahoe and below the summits of Mount Rose and Slide Mountain. At about 8 miles one way, the route is best traveled as a shuttle, with a car left at either the Tahoe Meadows or the Davis Creek trailhead.

To reach the trailhead from US 395/I-580 in the Washoe Valley (between Reno and Carson City), take the NV 429 (Old US 395) exit (signed for Davis Creek and Bowers Mansion). Follow NV 429 to Davis Creek Park Road (also signed for the park) and turn right (west). Follow the park road past the entry station and campground, staying left (south) into the day-use area. The parking lot is approximately 0.1 mile from the park gate on the left (east); it's the lot just before the last group picnic area at the Ophir Creek trailhead. The park's address is 25 Davis Creek Park Rd.

Who says the desert isn't full of color? Desert peach blooms along the Deadman's Overlook Trail in spring.

Organizations, Hiking Clubs, and Other Associations

Lake Tahoe

The Tahoe Rim Trail organization hosts events in the Tahoe region. Contact information is: 948 Incline Way, Incline Village, NV 89451; (775) 298-0233; www.tahoerimtrail.org.

Tahoe Trail Trekkers, part of the American Volksport Association, sponsors hiking, cycling, and winter sports events in the Lake Tahoe region. The website is www.tahoetrailtrekkers.org.

Tahoe Donner Hiking Club organizes both long and short hikes. Visit the website at https://sites.google.com/site/tahoedonnerhikingclub for more information.

Reno

Nevada Trail Maps.com, an online trails clearinghouse created and maintained by the University of Nevada–Reno's Great Basin Institute, provides basic information and detailed maps for routes throughout the state. Visit www.nvtrailmaps.com to research trails and download maps. Contact information is Great Basin Institute, University of Nevada–Reno, Mailstop 0099, Reno, NV 89557; (775) 784-1192.

The Truckee Meadows Trails Association maintains trail descriptions of area routes on its website, www.truckeemeadowstrails.org.

The Carson Valley Trails Association website includes information about trails in the Carson River valley. Visit www.carsonvalleytrails.org.

Land Management

The following government agencies manage public lands described in this guide and can provide further information on these hikes and other trails in their service areas.

- US Forest Service–Lake Tahoe Basin Management Unit, Forest Supervisor's Office, 35 College Dr., South Lake Tahoe, CA 96150; (530) 543-2600; www.fs.fed.us/r5/ltbmu
- US Forest Service–Lake Tahoe Basin Management Unit, North Tahoe Forest Service Office, 3080 North Lake Blvd., Tahoe City, CA 96145; (530) 583-3593; www.fs.fed.us/r5/ltbmu
- Nevada Division of State Parks, Lake Tahoe–Nevada State Park, PO Box 8867, Incline Village, NV 89452; (775) 831-0494; www.parks.nv.gov/lt.htm
- Humboldt-Toiyabe National Forest, Carson Ranger District, 1536 South Carson St., Carson City, NV 89701; (775) 882-2766; www.fs.fed.us/r4/htnf

- City of Reno Parks, Recreation and Community Services Department, 1 East First St. (PO Box 1900), Reno, NV 89505; (775) 334-2262; www.cityofreno.com
- Washoe County Department of Regional Parks and Open Space, 2601 Plumas St., Reno, NV 89509; (775) 823-6500; www.washoecountyparks.com. A downloadable guide to the county parks is available on the website.
- Nevada Division of State Parks, Washoe Lake State Park, 4855 East Lake Blvd., Carson City, NV 89704; (775) 687-4319; parks.nv.gov/parks/washoe-lake-state-park
- Bureau of Land Management, Carson City District, 5665 Morgan Mill Rd., Carson City, NV 89701; (775) 885-6000; www.blm.gov

Further Reading

Alden, Peter. *National Audubon Society Field Guide to California.* New York: Knopf, 1998.

Hauserman, Tim. *Tahoe Rim Trail.* Birmingham, AL: Wilderness Press, 2012.

"New Truckee Meadows Trail Guide." *About.com Reno/Tahoe.* Nov. 4, 2012. http://renotahoe.about.com/b/2009/11/07/new-truckee-meadows-trail-guide.htm.

Salcedo-Chourré, Tracy. *Best Easy Day Hikes Lake Tahoe* (1st ed.). Helena, MT: Falcon, 1999.

Salcedo-Chourré, Tracy. *Best Easy Day Hikes Lake Tahoe* (2nd ed.). Guilford, CT: FalconGuides, 2010.

Salcedo-Chourré, Tracy. *Best Easy Day Hikes Reno.* Guilford, CT: FalconGuides, 2010.

Schaffer, Jeffrey, and Ben Schifrin. *The Pacific Crest Trail: Northern California, from Tuolumne Meadows to the Oregon Border.* Berkeley, CA: Wilderness, 2003.

White, Michael C. *Afoot & Afield Reno-Tahoe: A Comprehensive Hiking Guide.* Berkeley, CA: Wilderness, 2006.

Hike Index

About the Author

Tracy Salcedo-Chourré has written guidebooks to a number of destinations in California and Colorado, including *Hiking Lassen Volcanic National Park, Exploring California's Missions and Presidios, Exploring Point Reyes National Seashore and the Golden Gate National Recreation Area, Best Rail-Trails California, Best Hikes Near Sacramento,* and Best Easy Day Hikes guides to San Francisco's Peninsula, San Francisco's North Bay, San Francisco's East Bay, San Jose, Lake Tahoe, Reno, Sacramento, Fresno, Boulder, Denver, and Aspen. She is also an editor, teacher, and gardener. She lives with her family in California's Wine Country. You can learn more by visiting her website at www.laughingwaterink.com.

American Hiking Society
Because you
hike.
We're with you
every step of the way